Euripides and the Gods

Onassis Series in Hellenic Culture

The Age of Titans: The Rise and Fall of the Great Hellenistic Navies
William M. Murray

Sophocles and the Language of Tragedy
Simon Goldhill

Nectar and Illusion: Nature in Byzantine Art and Literature
Henry Maguire

Adventures with Iphigenia at Tauris: A Cultural History of Euripides' Black Sea Tragedy
Edith Hall

Beauty: The Fortunes of an Ancient Greek Idea
David Konstan

Euripides and the Gods
Mary Lefkowitz

Brother-Making in Late Antiquity and Byzantium: Monks, Laymen and Christian Ritual
Claudia Rapp

Onassis
Foundation (USA)

EURIPIDES AND THE GODS

Mary Lefkowitz

OXFORD
UNIVERSITY PRESS

OXFORD
UNIVERSITY PRESS

Oxford University Press is a department of the University of Oxford.
It furthers the University's objective of excellence in research,
scholarship, and education by publishing worldwide.
Oxford is a registered trade mark of Oxford University Press
in the UK and in certain other countries

Published in the United States of America by
Oxford University Press
198 Madison Avenue, New York, NY 10016, United States of America

Library of Congress Cataloging-in-Publication Data
Names: Lefkowitz, Mary R., 1935– author.
Title: Euripides and the gods / Mary R. Lefkowitz.
Description: Oxford : Oxford University Press, 2016. | Includes
bibliographical references and index.
Identifiers: LCCN 2015023268 | ISBN 9780199752058 (hardcover : alk. paper) |
ISBN 9780190939618 (paperback : alk. paper)
Subjects: LCSH: Euripides—Religion. | Greece—Religion.
Classification: LCC PA3978 .L44 2016 | DDC 882/.01—dc23 LC record
available at http://lccn.loc.gov/2015023268

ἦ μέγα μοι τὰ θεῶν μεληδήμαθ᾽, ὅταν φρένας ἔλθηι,
λύπας παραιρεῖ· ξύνεσιν δέ τιν᾽ ἐλπίδι κεύθων
λείπομαι ἔν τε τύχαις θνατῶν καὶ ἐν ἔργμασι λεύσσων·
ἄλλα γὰρ ἄλλοθεν ἀμείβεται, μετὰ δ᾽ ἵσταται ἀνδράσιν αἰὼν
πολυπλάνητος αἰεί.

When thoughts about the gods' concerns come to my mind, they greatly
relieve my sorrow. I hold some hope within me, but I am lost when I look at
what happens to mortals and their accomplishments. One thing comes after
another; the life of men changes and is always drifting. (Euripides, *Hippolytus*
1102–10)

Οὐκ ἔστιν οὐδὲν δεινὸν ὧδ᾽ εἰπεῖν ἔπος
οὐδὲ πάθος οὐδὲ ξυμφορὰ θεήλατος,
ἧς οὐκ ἂν ἄραιτ᾽ ἄχθος ἀνθρώπου φύσις.

There is nothing so dreadful to speak of, no suffering or disaster sent by the
gods of which human existence might not take up the burden (Euripides,
Orestes 1–3)

CONTENTS

Conclusion 193

FIGURES

PREFACE

Why do the gods play more prominent roles in Euripides' dramas
than those of Aeschylus or Sophocles? Was it in order to put
before his audiences new and revolutionary ideas about the gods,
calling traditional religion into question? Should we even care, if
as modern readers, we instinctively concentrate on the behavior
of the human characters in the dramas, and regard the gods as
irrelevant, foreign to our modern sensibilities? In modern stage
or film productions, the gods who appear *ex machina* are usually
altogether omitted or satirized. I know that I had thought of
the gods in Euripides' dramas as a kind of literary convention,
and believed that Euripides was skeptical of traditional religion.
But when I began to work on the biographies of Greek poets
(Lefkowitz 1979, 1981 [second ed. 2012], 1984), I discovered
that most of the material about Euripides' life was derived from
his dramas or from caricatures in Attic comedy, not from the
kinds of materials that modern biographers rely on, such as

correspondence and historical records—information that no ancient biographer appears to have had access to. If Euripides' biography was based primarily on his dramas and on comedy, could we continue to suppose that he had been a close friend or disciple of Socrates and other philosophers? Did he go to Macedonia at the end of his life because he was unpopular in Athens? Did he believe in new-fangled gods (as Aristophanes suggests), or in no gods at all? If in reality he did none of those things (Lefkowitz 1987, 2003b [1989]), we could consider the role of the gods in his dramas without presuming that he was undermining or pointing out the flaws in traditional theology. Instead of regarding appearances by the gods as perfunctory or absurd, we might instead begin to understand them as accurate descriptions of the powers of the gods, and descriptions of their relationship to mortals. The purpose of this book is to suggest that we should take the action of the gods in Euripides' dramas literally and seriously.

Like most people who have been raised in one of the monotheistic traditions, I have found it hard to imagine how anyone could revere and honor deities so diverse and different in nature from the ones with whom we are familiar. How could gods worthy of our respect kill people or let them die for what seem to us to be trivial reasons? Why don't the Greek gods consistently punish evildoers and rescue the virtuous? Why do the gods sometimes do what seems right, but at other times appear not to punish horrendous crimes, as when Medea murders her own children? Couldn't the answer be that what seems right (or wrong) to us is irrelevant? In Greek literature it is the gods who are in charge and set the rules. The ancient Greek gods did not exist for the benefit of humankind, they did not create humankind, but merely inherited them from an earlier generation of divinities. So by definition the involvement of these gods with

humans is intermittent and exceptional. Humans usually will not
see justice done in their lifetimes, because the gods work on a
different timetable from mortals, who are by nature ephemeral,
literally "creatures of a day." If for some reason a god decides to
do something on behalf of a particular mortal, it is unusual, and a
great blessing, but not at all something that the mortal had reason
to believe that he or she was entitled to, or had any reason to
count on or expect.

In the works of Aeschylus and Sophocles the gods can be cruel
and vindictive, like Athena in Sophocles' *Ajax*. Or they can rescue
their mortal allies, like Apollo and Athena in Aeschylus' *Eumenides*,
or Heracles in Sophocles' *Philoctetes*. But even when gods are
prepared to help particular mortals, they can also seem remote
from or indifferent to the suffering of human beings. They can
be reluctant to communicate with mortals directly, preferring
instead to relay information to them through oracles, dreams, or
omens, which are ambiguously or obscurely phrased and easy for
mortals to misinterpret. Usually the mortal characters are unable
to understand exactly what the gods are telling them, whether
through prophets, or oracles, or dreams. They often fail to realize
that the gods have intervened in their lives, until sometime after
the gods have done so. Then it suddenly dawns on them that
what happened was timed too precisely not to have been the
consequence of an action of a power higher than themselves.

In this book I hope to show that the gods in Euripides' dramas
do not behave all that differently from the gods portrayed by
Aeschylus and Sophocles. But because Euripides was characterized
as a philosophical poet and an atheist in the ancient biographical
tradition, we are predisposed to believe that he meant his
audiences to view divine action in his dramas as troubling and
ambiguous, or that he intended his original audience to begin
to question the gods' very existence. If the poet was reputed to

be an unconventional thinker, wasn't he was trying to get his audiences to become more aware of the gods' shortcomings, and (although without saying so directly) attempting to make the more intelligent members of his audience consciously aware of the deficiencies of their religion?—all this on the basis of Aristophanes' caricatures of Euripides and anecdotes derived from them. Yet Euripides' dramas were written and performed for audiences in a city-state whose citizens were otherwise particularly suspicious of impiety and atheism, among them the men who in 415 BC sought to have Alcibiades tried for impiety on the grounds that he had desecrated the herms located throughout the city, and who in 399 put Socrates on trial for alleged impiety and atheism. Unquestionably Euripides does put sophistic and even radical ideas into the mouths of his characters, and gives his audience an opportunity to contemplate these character's untraditional explanations of cause and effect in the natural world. Yet by putting more gods on the stage than any other extant ancient Athenian dramatist, Euripides makes his audience aware of the discrepancies between sophistic theories and the unpredictable and often brutal reality of divine motivations and actions.

In this book I ask my readers to question their assumptions about the "proper" nature of divinity, and make an effort to understand the ancient Greeks' ways of envisioning the role of divine action in a world where the notion of a loving, caring, and all-powerful divinity would seem as foreign as the notion of many anthropomorphic gods seems to us. In my view, the best way to remove oneself from the modern world is to immerse oneself, so far as possible, in the ancient sources, and to rely on them to help us understand the ancient customs and beliefs that have long since fallen out of use. In seeking to understand the role of the gods, I have not, as least so far as I know, tried to make use of modern theoretical approaches adapted from anthropology or linguistics, helpful as they sometimes are for understanding the meaning of human behavior. Rather, I try to focus on ancient Greek theology, as opposed to the religious practices of mortals, on the motivations and actions of gods and how mortals understand them. My aim has been to try to represent what it is that the gods do in Greek drama, and to show why Euripides presents a portrait of divine action that is dramatically distinctive, but not conceptually different from that of the other surviving dramatists. In the process, I shall also try to give an account of what Euripides and the other dramatists emphasize in their works, but without trying to speculate about the particular social or practical purposes that the dramatic performances may have served. We have no evidence that suggests that the vast majority of ancient Greeks questioned the existence of the traditional Olympian gods, even if many of them had a closer relationship with other local and familiar deities. Certainly the gods of tragedy are concerned with issues of justice that ordinary people were rarely or never involved in (Parker 1997, 158–9), and the action in drama is always set in past time, rather than in the present. But we know from the works of the poet Pindar (a contemporary of Aeschylus) that people continued to worship the gods of epic alongside of the heroes of their communities and the nymphs of the countryside. Athenian audiences knew enough about ecstatic religion to be able to appreciate the descriptions of Dionysiac cult in Aeschylus' *Edonians* and Euripides' *Bacchae* (Allan 2004, 139–40). They could also understand how Ion, although only a slave at the temple of Apollo at Delphi, nonetheless could be deeply devoted to that particular god (Versnel 2011, 128–9).

My understanding and description of divine action in Euripides' dramas owes a profound debt to the work of other scholars. In his book *The Justice of Zeus* Hugh Lloyd-Jones explained that the idea of a Greek Enlightenment was a product of "unconscious identification" by scholars in the last quarter of the nineteenth century (1971 [1983], 148). To him, "the gods of the *Hippolytus* and the *Trojan Women* seem scarcely less vivid and awe-inspiring than the Athene of Sophocles' *Ajax*" (1983, 150). He understood that the appearance of a god at the end of a drama was not "a mere device for finishing a plot that has reached an impasse"; "literally descended as they are from the divine epiphanies in epic and early tragedy, these descents from the machine continue the Greek tradition of a divine participation in the affairs of men" (1983, 155).

As David Kovacs has pointed out in several different books, it is misleading to think of Euripides as a sophist critical of traditional religion. Instead he has observed that in some of his plays Euripides' stance is "precisely anti-Sophistic," and that scholars have been too eager to accept uncritically a portrait of the poet that was based almost exclusively on Aristophanes (1980, 83, 109)—a point I shall return to in Chapter 1 of this book. Kovacs (1987, 118–22) understood clearly how the assumption that Euripides must have been a sophist could lead to critics to suppose that the poet naturally would have shared some of their negative views about the traditional anthropomorphic gods, and like some of them had become a proponent of a new and more egalitarian morality. Here was a Euripides with whom modern people could feel comfortable—*Euripides Our Contemporary*, as the theater historian J. Michael Walton calls him in a recent book, suggesting that we treat the gods in his plays as "a dramatic device" (2009, 86).

In his book about Euripides' *Andromache*, William Allan offered a historically grounded discussion of the role of the gods in Euripides' dramas, suggesting that the characterization of divine action is disturbing because of its uncertainty and unpredictability, and observing that his plays explore more explicitly than those of the other poets the differences in mortal behavior among the gods (2000, 264–6). Donald Mastronarde advanced the discussion in many specific ways by providing an overview of divine action in Euripides' dramas (2005, 321–32; with more detailed analysis in 2010, 153–206). He showed how the presence of the gods serves an important dramatic purpose; for example, by speaking the prologue of the drama, a god gives the audience a greater awareness of divine action than either the characters or the chorus (2010, 176). Greater awareness brought by divine action helps to raise the question of inevitability: Could disasters and deaths have been avoided (2010, 188)? In particular, Mastronarde saw that the power of divine action in the dramas derives from its inscrutability: ". . . the gods of traditional Greek religion (and tragedy) would be much less interesting, and much less worthy of awe, if they acted in ways that are fully and perfectly understandable" (2010, 206).

Many recent commentaries on individual dramas reflect this more sophisticated understanding of the role of the gods in Euripides' dramas, but unfortunately most are accessible only to people who know at least some ancient Greek. This book was inspired by their work and depends upon it, and while it cannot claim always to have broken new ground, it does at least to try to present their understanding of Euripides' theology to a wider audience. The discussion is intended to be accessible to readers who do not know ancient Greek: all quotations from the original texts are translated (by me, unless otherwise noted), Greek words are transliterated, and some general background is provided. But at the same time I have also tried to make the book useful for more advanced students and for professional scholars, by including fuller discussions and additional references in the notes.

The book provides an examination of Euripides' relations with the sophists and individual philosophers, and considers his place in what is often called the Greek "Enlightenment." It considers all of Euripides' surviving dramas and the fragments of his work in which the gods appear. But it differs in several respects from other studies of Euripides' treatment of the gods. I do not attempt to offer a comprehensive account of Euripidean criticism, but instead try to examine the assumptions that have caused particular critics to be disappointed in or resentful of the gods' behavior in Euripides' dramas. In surveying divine action in the dramas, I have chosen to treat the gods not as an undifferentiated collective, but as individual beings with distinctive and recognizable characteristics and powers, as an ancient audience would have perceived them. I also try to show how it is that an ancient audience would have been able to understand that the gods were at work even when they do not appear in the drama and their action is not noticed, much less understood, by the mortal characters on the stage.

ACKNOWLEDGMENTS

I was able to get started on this project thanks to a Mellon
Emeritus Fellowship and faculty research grants from Wellesley
College, which enabled Daphne François and Megan Wilson
to provide useful assistance in the early stages of my work. The
encouragement and support of the Alexander S. Onassis Public
Benefit Foundation helped me to bring it to completion as a
volume in the Onassis Series in Hellenic Culture. I owe a special
debt of thanks to Professor Jean-Fabrice Nardelli, for many helpful
suggestions and corrections, and to Professor Martin Cropp
for many specific improvements and corrections. My husband,
Professor Sir Hugh Lloyd-Jones, insisted that I finish this project,
even though he knew that he would not live to read it; I wish I had
been able to take fuller advantage of his keen eye for error and his
vast knowledge of the history of scholarship. I have also benefited
greatly from many conversations with Professor Barbara S. Held,
whose work on the intersection of psychology and philosophy has
helped me better to understand the premises on which arguments
are based, and to identify fallacies in logic.

ABBREVIATIONS

In general I have followed the conventions of spelling of ancient names and the abbreviations of modern reference works used in the *Oxford Classical Dictionary* (Fourth Edition).

INTRODUCTION
Greek Drama without the Gods?

Before we can even begin to think we can understand Greek
tragedy, we need to start with our own modern religions,
and remind ourselves of our basic assumptions about the
nature of divinity. Whatever we believe, or do not believe,
given the distance between us and the ancient Greeks in
both time and geography, in the Western world, at least, our
ideas about the nature of divinity are bound to be different.
To begin with a simple example: When you first enter
the chapel at Wellesley College, your eyes are drawn to a
prominent inscription: "GOD IS LOVE." This text comes
from a verse in a pastoral letter in the New Testament,
written in Greek around the end of the first century AD: "he
who does not love has not known God, because God is
Love" (1 John 4:8). The author of the letter is encouraging
his readers to love one another, in the special sense that love
had come to mean for Christians. The author of the letter
uses the word *agapē*, a word that had come to mean a love
that followed the example of Jesus, who was believed to
have died in order that others might live, or the example
of God himself, who was willing to allow his own son to
die so that humankind could be absolved from their sins.[1]
The text "God is Love" was given its prominent place in the

Wellesley College chapel because it expressed the ideals of the founders, who had established the college in order to train young women as Christian missionaries. Their vision was exemplified also in the college's motto: *non ministrari sed minstrare*, the Latin version of a verse from the gospel of Matthew in which Jesus describes his mission on earth as "not to be served but to serve (*diakonēsai*), and to give his life as a ransom for many" (Mt. 20:28).[2]

A god who cares for men so much that he allows his son to die to save mortals from their sins; the son of a god who gives his life on behalf of mortals unrelated to himself and unknown to him—such a concept would have seemed completely foreign to Athenians in the last half of the fifth century BC, when Sophocles and Euripides were presenting their plays. To begin to understand what the original audiences of Greek drama would have expected from their gods, modern readers need to work hard to set aside their assumptions about the nature of divinity, which surround and affect them even if they do not literally believe in the existence of the divinities described in the Bible. Though to us monotheism appears to be the norm, it was anomalous in the ancient world, particularly in the form in which the ancient Hebrews practiced it. Their religion probably had the same origin as that practiced by the people known to the Hebrews as Canaanites and the Greeks as Phoenicians, who inhabited the area now occupied by Lebanon, Israel, and adjacent parts of Syria and Jordan. The Canaanites believed that there were many gods who behaved in most respects like human beings, eating and drinking, having sexual relations with each other. In the earlier books of the Hebrew Bible, God also seems somewhat anthropomorphic, at least in his interactions with the human beings whom he created in his own image (Gen. 1:26–31). He created man from the dust of the earth and breathed life into him, gave him animals, and later created woman from one of the man's ribs (Gen. 2.5–21). God communicates with the man and the woman, and punishes them when they disobey him. God seems to eat, and sleep and walk. But in the later books of the Old Testament, God seems not to need anything; he does not eat or drink, or sleep. He has no need for any kind of physical pleasure, such as that derived from sex. He has no fixed or identifiable residence or physical appearance.[3] The God of the Old Testament repeatedly claims that he is unique, the only divinity, who is the creator and ruler of the world that humans inhabit. God sees everything that happens on earth and is all-powerful.

By contrast, the ancient Greeks, like the ancient Canaanites, believed that there were many gods. Like the God of the Old Testament, they were immortal, ageless, and powerful. But none were as powerful and omniscient as the God of the Old Testament, and none could be in more than one place at one time. So even the most powerful god among all the gods, Zeus, could never keep complete control over all the others. Also, unlike the God of the Old Testament, the Greek gods are not self-sufficient; they need to eat and drink, though they have their own special food and drink, and they need to receive honor from humankind, in the form of gifts left in their temples, or of the smoke from the meat of the animals which mortals killed and cooked in their honor. The relationship between the Greek gods and humankind is complicated and certainly less protective than that between God and the humans in the Old Testament. The Greek gods tolerate the presence of human beings, but without making any promises to them, or giving them dominion over any other creatures.

According to the earliest known ancient Greek account of the creation of the world, the *Theogony* by the eighth-century BC poet Hesiod, there was a time when gods and mortal men ate meals together (535–7).[4] But men lost that privilege, apparently because of their connection with Prometheus, one of Zeus' uncles.

Prometheus served Zeus an inferior portion of meat at a feast. Zeus then took fire away from mortals, but Prometheus gave fire back to them. So Zeus punished Prometheus, and also punished mankind by having gods loyal to him create a woman who was sent to the mortals with a jar full of evils. After that, human life became hard. Hesiod does not explain why Prometheus in particular should have wanted to help mortal beings. But according to a myth that was known in the fifth century, and which may well date to earlier times, it was Prometheus who created humans and animals out of earth and water, possibly as allies for himself.[5] The story helps to explain why Prometheus was eager to help humans, and why Zeus' attitude towards mortal men was distant and at times even hostile.

Hesiod offers another account of why mortal life is now hard, in which he attributes the tension between gods and mortals to a failure on the part of humans to behave peacefully and treat one another with justice (*Works and Days* 106–201). While Zeus' father Cronus was chief god, a golden race (*genos*) of humans led happy and easy lives. But after Zeus took over, he and the other gods who live on Olympus created successive generations of humans of increasingly inferior character, silver, bronze, and the warlike heroes. Hesiod said that he himself belonged to the next race of iron, and he believed that Zeus would destroy it when mortals became totally unjust and immoral. Yet another account, attributed to Hesiod but almost certainly not written by him, also blames humans for the separation between themselves and the gods. According to the author of this epic, the *Catalogue of Women*, the Olympian gods came to earth to mate with mortal men and women during the age of heroes. But after Helen went to Troy with Paris, and her sister Clytemnestra killed her husband Agamemnon, Zeus wanted to destroy humankind through war and natural disasters (*Cat.* fr. 204.96–100 M-W). This story has a counterpart in the Hebrew tradition and may possibly have been influenced by it. The immortal giants known as Nephilim had come to earth to mate with mortal women, but God saw that humans were evil and destroyed them by sending a flood. God allowed Noah and his family to survive and made a covenant with him never to send another flood (Gen. 9:8–11). But Zeus makes no such covenant with humankind. After the Trojan War, the gods stopped mating with mortals and spent little time with human beings.

These accounts of Zeus' treatment of humankind help to explain why the gods that appear as characters in Greek drama seem to us to be distant and supercilious, even when they are in the presence of mortals who are their relatives or former spouses or close friends. The gods do not hesitate to treat mortals cruelly, if they believe the mortals have dishonored or wronged them. The stories also show why the action of most extant Greek tragedies takes place during the age of the heroes, after the gods stopped sharing meals with mortals, but before the gods had ceased to intervene directly in the lives of men and women. But even when mortals do not see the gods in action, they do not doubt that the gods are aware of what is happening, and control the outcome of events. No gods appear as characters in Aeschylus' *Persians*, the one surviving drama that portrays a recent historical event, the return of the Persian king Xerxes to his homeland after his army was defeated by the Greeks at Salamis in 480 BC. But nonetheless the human characters in that drama believe that gods have intervened, either to help or to punish them.

Before we even begin to consider the role of the gods in Euripides' dramas, it is essential to keep in mind that the gods exist to please themselves, not human beings. Zeus and his family of gods are not the kind of gods that humankind might have chosen, if anyone had offered them the choice; rather, the dramatists are saying that these are the kinds of gods that there *are*, the gods who were described by the first poets, Homer and Hesiod, and that were worshiped throughout the Greek-speaking world for centuries, even after 313 AD, when the Roman Emperor Constantine stopped the persecutions of Christians. Like the epic poets, the writers of tragedies in fifth-century BC Athens explore and describe the relationship between gods and mortals, both to demonstrate the relative powerlessness and ignorance of human beings and to celebrate the ways in which humans can help each other to live in an unwelcoming universe that was not created for their benefit. That is not to say that the dramatic poets portray the gods exactly as they were portrayed in Homer, or that they necessarily approve of the gods' behavior. But (as I shall try to show in this book) the dramatists' notion of the nature of divinity does not differ in any significant ways from that of Homer and Hesiod, and there is no reason to suppose that through their dramas the playwrights were trying to offer a theology that people raised in a monotheistic tradition might find more acceptable than that described by their predecessors. The dramatists portray a world in which gods can become involved in human life, either in concert or at cross-purposes with one another. Ultimately, however, as in Homer, all gods are subject to the will of Zeus, and what he determines to be just. All humans who hope that justice will be done appeal to Zeus. But it is hard for mortals to know if and when Zeus' justice will be done, since he and the other immortals work on a different timetable from that of short-lived mortals. While mortals are waiting for wrongs to be righted, other gods may intervene in ways that suit their own interests, or appear to ignore human problems altogether.

Among extant tragedies, gods appear in just one of Aeschylus' surviving tragedies. In the *Eumenides*, Apollo and then Athena intervene to stop the avenger goddesses known as the Erinyes

from persecuting Orestes for murdering his mother.[6] In the
Prometheus Bound (which probably was written by another poet),
all but one of the characters are gods. Gods appear in two of
Sophocles' seven dramas. In the prologue of the *Ajax*, Athena
tells Odysseus that she has made Ajax slaughter a herd of sheep
and cattle, supposing that he was killing the leaders of the Greek
army. Odysseus pities Ajax, but Athena is merciless; she tells
Odysseus to remember never to speak an arrogant word against
the gods or suppose that he is great because he is superior to other
mortals (118–33). Heracles plays a more positive role at the end
of Sophocles' drama *Philoctetes*, appearing *ex machina* to ensure
that his old friend Philoctetes will go to Troy with his bow and
poisoned arrows, so he can kill Paris and help the Greeks defeat
the Trojans, thus carrying out Zeus' plans for the destruction of
Troy. Gods appear much more frequently in the eighteen surviving
dramas of Euripides. They speak in the prologues of four plays, and
in the epilogues of nine, and they appear surprisingly in the middle
of his drama *Heracles*. Gods also appear in the middle and at the
end of the *Rhesus*, a drama attributed to Euripides but probably
written by another author sometime after Euripides' death. Even
in those dramas where gods do not appear as characters, their
presence is felt, either through oracles, or portents, or reports by
human witnesses of their intervention offstage.

If this is how the ancient Greeks portrayed their gods, it is
understandable that modern readers seem reluctant to suppose
that the sophisticated ancient Greeks actually could have believed
in or worshiped their own gods. We want to think that the ancient
Greeks were more like ourselves than other ancient peoples,
because we regard them as our intellectual ancestors. The ancient
Greeks are still celebrated in popular culture as the founders of
democracy, and as the inventors of philosophy and science. But
in emphasizing these legacies, however indirectly they may have

come down to us, we tend to ignore the important differences between ancient Greek culture and our own, especially in the case of religion. Religion in ancient Greece required continual public demonstrations of respect, such as animal sacrifice, for many different deities. In essence the staging of dramas in Athens was an elaborate and costly demonstration of such respect for the gods, especially for the god Dionysus, at whose festival the performances were held.

Our modern tendency to downplay, ignore, or even dismiss the roles played by gods in Greek tragedy is a problem of reception, that is, the cultural filter that keeps modern eyes from being able to visualize the theology of an ancient and foreign civilization.[7] Much recent scholarship describes the particular ways in which scholars and critics in the past have tried to understand the art and literature of ancient Greece. But it is easier to recognize the strengths and weaknesses of our predecessors' interpretations than to understand and take into account our own preconceptions. We continue to talk about Greek mythology but avoid using the term "myth" in connection with the theological narratives of modern religions, such as those collected in the Bible. Modern scholarship on Greek religion has also tended to be concerned with practice rather than questions of belief. We turn to Greek drama as a source of sociological and political information about fifth-century Athens, but not as a possible means of investigating and understanding the theology of their religion. For example, when we now read Euripides' drama the *Trojan Women*, we understand it, first of all, as a protest against the horrors of war, and as a record of the brutality with which even innocent survivors are treated. Modern producers often adapt Euripides' original script so audiences can connect it to current events. At Wellesley College several years ago, the women of Troy were portrayed as the women of Iraq; Menelaus was dressed like a Texas oilman.

There is no reason to suppose that changing the women's nationality does violence to the intention of Euripides' portrayal of the suffering inflicted on the innocent victims of war. Athenian audiences were accustomed to seeing the problems of the present reflected in the myths of past actions. To them Troy could stand for any city that had been destroyed by a conquering army. Euripides' younger contemporary Thucydides in his history of the Peloponnesian War describes how in 421 BC the Athenians killed the men and enslaved the women of the city of Scione in Chalcidice in northern Greece (near the modern city of Thessaloniki, 5.32.1). A few months before the *Trojan Women* was performed in Athens in the spring of 415 BC, the Athenians with great ruthlessness had killed the men and enslaved the women and children on the island of Melos because the Melians had refused to pay tribute to them and join their alliance against the Spartans (5.84–116).[8] So even though it is unlikely that Euripides could have known about the way in which the Athenians treated the Melians before he wrote the *Trojan Women*, there were plenty of other similar events that he could have known about or even witnessed to use as models for his description of the fall of Troy.[9] Although we like to think of the ancient Athenians as humane and enlightened, in war they followed the standard Greek practice of killing the men and selling the women and children into slavery.[10] But unlike other ancient peoples, the Greeks, starting with Homer, did not celebrate the defeat and suffering of their enemies; their religion encouraged them to be aware that human success, like life itself, would never last for very long.

Modern directors almost always treat the *Trojan Women* as if it were primarily a war protest play, but in so doing almost always alter or leave out one of its most important original features: its prologue. The prologue is a dialogue between two gods, Poseidon and Athena. In ancient theaters the actors who portrayed the gods were placed by a crane on top of the stage building, above where the human action took place; hence the Latin term *deus ex machina*, "god from the machine."[11] In modern theaters scenes with such gods are difficult to stage, and even more difficult to make credible. Where do you put the gods? How can you make them look god-like? To avoid putting on stage strange deities in whose existence no one believes, modern producers and directors usually replace the gods in the prologue with a narrator who offers a rundown on the story of the Trojan War, delivered by someone in modern dress or, as the lights go down, an amplified voice from somewhere offstage.

The gods were nowhere to be seen in the most influential modern adaptation of *The Trojan Women*, Michael Cacoyannis' 1971 film, starring Katharine Hepburn.[12] Cacoyannis made a deliberate decision to leave out the gods, on the grounds that they were "hard to film and make realistic." So his movie begins not with Poseidon and Athena but with a scene showing the women and children of Troy being escorted from the city at night. Suddenly armed men rush up and snatch the children from their mothers' arms. The children are put into a cart and driven off, then the women are led away; a voice-over explains that Troy's wealth had been legendary, and the Greeks had been waiting for an opportunity to come to get Troy's gold. "Fools," says the disembodied male voice, "to lay a city waste, so soon to die themselves." Then the voice speaks about the women who are being led off, first Helen; then we see the queen of Troy, Hecuba (Katharine Hepburn), lying on the ground: her husband Priam and her sons are dead. We see Troy from a distance, burning; we see smoke and desolation. Then it is morning, and Hecuba begins to speak: "the ways of fate are

the ways of the wind," a line not in the original text. There is no
reference to the gods.

But in the original text of the *Trojan Women* the gods appear
in the prologue and then leave the rest of the action to the
human characters, with whom they never directly engage. In
the fifth century BC, the actors playing the roles of the gods
would have appeared on the roof of the stage building (or *skēnē*)
in front of which the human action of the drama took place.
The god Poseidon speaks first. He says that he has come from
the sea to say farewell to Troy, the city he and Apollo helped to
build. He is leaving because the temples, altars, and sanctuaries
of the gods are now deserted, and the Greeks are taking back
to their country all the wealth of Troy. Captured treasure
would include the wealth stored in sanctuaries and the
many rich dedications to the gods. Poseidon says that there
is no longer any reason for him to care about the city and
its people, because "when evil desolation seizes a city, the
sanctuaries of the gods decay and do not receive their honors"
(25–7). However much he says that he loved the city of
Troy and regrets leaving it, Poseidon's reasoning will seem
materialistic and uncaring to anyone brought up in one of the
great monotheistic traditions. What about its people and their
suffering? Why doesn't Poseidon try to stop and help them if
(as he says) he loves the city so much? The Athenian audience
would not have needed to be told the answer to those
questions. Poseidon is Zeus' brother; Zeus and his generation
of gods feel no particular responsibility for humankind. They
did not create them; with very few exceptions Zeus and his
divine family pay attention to mortals only when they are
honored by them, or find one of them sexually appealing.
Such divine indifference to the suffering of mortals is one

of the principal reasons why we find the Greek gods hard to understand and to respect.

So in the original texts humans cannot expect much sympathy or support from the gods; in modern terms, they would be like the kind of landlords who throw their tenants out on the street when the tenants can't pay the rent. But the prologue also conveys other significant theological information, which modern audiences almost never hear, because the gods have been edited away, not just by translators and producers, but by their own imaginations. The most important of these facts is that it is not mortals but the gods who determine the ultimate outcome of all human action, whether or not the mortals are aware of it. In his opening speech in the *Trojan Women*, the god Poseidon speaks of the Trojan War as a contest among *gods*, rather than as we would see it, a war between the Trojans and Greeks, Hector and Achilles, Sarpedon and Patroclus, and all the other heroes described in the *Iliad* who fought and died at Troy. But as Poseidon describes it in the *Trojan Women, he* lost the war and the goddesses Hera and Athena won it. He says: "Because I have been defeated by Hera and Athena, who have destroyed the Trojans, I am leaving famous Troy and my altars" (23–4). Poseidon does not explain why Hera and Athena were particularly hostile to the Trojans, because an ancient audience would not have needed to be told that Hera and Athena had been defeated in a beauty contest by Aphrodite, the goddess whose particular sphere of influence was sexual passion. The judge of the beauty contest was Paris, the son of Priam and Hecuba, the king and queen of Troy. Paris picked Aphrodite over Hera and Athena because she offered him the most beautiful woman in the world as a reward for choosing her. At that time the most beautiful woman in the world was Helen, the daughter of Zeus. But Helen was already married to Menelaus of Sparta, who was bound to be angry when Paris came and carried her off to Troy. An even bigger problem with Paris' judgment in favor of Aphrodite was that he made enemies of the two other contestants, the powerful goddesses Hera and Athena, the wife and daughter of Zeus. Because Paris had offended them, Hera and Athena took the side of the Greeks against the Trojans.[13] As Poseidon says in the *Trojan Women*, when he prepares to leave Troy: "And now farewell from me, once prosperous city and your tower of polished stone; if Pallas [Athena] the daughter of Zeus had not destroyed you, you would still be firm on your foundations" (45–7).

As Poseidon prepares to leave Troy, Athena appears and asks for his help in attacking the same Greeks whom she has consistently supported throughout the ten years of the Trojan War. Poseidon wonders why she has had such a sudden change of heart: has Zeus or another god issued a new command (55–6): "why do you leap thus from one attitude to another, and hate and love whomever you chance to?"(67–8). Athena explains that she has been treated insolently (that is, with *hybris*) by the Greeks. While the Greek army was sacking Troy, Ajax the son of Oïleus raped Cassandra in Athena's temple, and the Greeks did not punish him for violating the goddess' sanctuary. In refusing to do so, not only did the Greeks fail to give due honor to Athena, they also did not express sufficient gratitude for her support for their army during the course of the war. So Athena now says that Zeus will send a storm on them as they return home, and she herself will attack their ships with her father Zeus' lightning bolt. She asks Poseidon (who has dominion over the seas) to stir up huge waves and whirlpools in the Aegean: "Fill the deep bay of Euboea with corpses, so that in future they [the Greeks] will behave piously in my temples and behave piously towards the other gods" (77–86). Poseidon promises Athena that he will send the storm.

There is an implicit message in these lines, not just about divine power, but about the nature of divine justice. The gods' justice

is violent, unforgiving, and administered disproportionately.
Many will die because of the wrongs of a few individuals. There
is another message as well. In the final words of the prologue,
Poseidon also insists on the importance of piety. No mortal should
forget that the gods require due honor and devotion: "The mortal
is a fool who sacks cities, temples, and tombs, the sanctuaries
of the dead. He gives them over to destruction, but he himself
perishes later" (95–7). In most modern productions this emphasis
on piety also tends to be lost. For example, the voice-over in
Cacoyannis' film retains a version of these lines: "Fools, to lay a
city waste, so soon to die themselves." But Euripides' original lines
referred not just to the city, but also to its temples and tombs,
sacred places that should be regarded with respect because of
their connection to the gods. Without the presence of gods, that
important message cannot be forcefully conveyed. Of course
the original prologue underscores the importance of religious
observance. The sanctuaries of the gods must be treated with
respect, and due honors must be given to the gods, in the form
of tangible gifts or public action. Poseidon deserts Troy when it
no longer has anything to offer him; Athena deserts the Greeks
when they do not punish the man who has dishonored her and
desecrated her temple. Humans neglect the gods at their peril,
and that whether or not the humans are aware of it, it is the gods,
not themselves, who are in control. Euripides' original prologue
informs the audience that the gods will soon punish the Greeks
for their greed and excessive cruelty, and that their losses will be
comparable in scale to those that they have inflicted on the Trojans.

The introductory section of Cacoyannis' film does not refer
specifically to what will happen after the action of the drama or
to the gods' plans to destroy the Greeks after they set sail for
their homes. If the characters in the film mention the gods, it is
only to call attention to their cruelty or to claim that particular

individuals, such as Helen, have been manipulated by them. The screenplay emphasizes the suffering of the innocent women and children of Troy, who will live the rest of their lives as slaves. But as the ancient Greeks saw it, the gods do care for some particular mortals and try to help them, but at the same time the gods do not try to stop people from doing things that will harm themselves. The gods send accurate information to mortals, such as omens, dreams, or prophecies, but in ways that mortals find difficult to interpret and almost always get wrong.

In Euripides' original text Helen blames Hecuba and Priam for making it possible for her to be abducted by their son Paris. As she explains, soon after Paris was born, they should have destroyed the infant, because he was "the cruel representation of the firebrand" (918–22). Euripides' ancient audience would have known the story, that when Hecuba was pregnant with Paris, she was warned in a dream that she would give birth to a firebrand that would destroy the city of Troy.[14] In order to prevent the prophecy from happening, Hecuba gave the infant Paris to a herdsman to "expose," that is, leave out to die in the wilderness, which in the fifth century BC was an acceptable way to dispose of unwanted children. But the herdsman took pity on the child and took it home and raised it as his own son. So Paris lived and was able to make his disastrous choice among the goddesses.

Ignoring or failing to carry out instructions from the gods, even for what seemed like humane reasons, always results in disaster for mortals. The same pattern of humanitarian disobedience occurs in the story of Oedipus. His father Laius had been told by Apollo's oracle that he would be killed by his son (OT 711–3). So when a son was born to them, Laius and his wife Jocasta gave the baby to a slave to abandon in the wilderness of Mt. Cithaeron. But the slave took pity on the infant and gave it to a shepherd, who in turn gave it to the childless king and queen of Corinth to bring up, and so

Oedipus lived to fulfill the prophecy.[15] In the script of *The Trojan Women* film Cacoyannis does not mention the firebrand dream that brought an obscure warning from the gods about the destruction that would be caused by Paris' birth. Instead Helen argues that Hecuba, along with her husband Priam, was responsible for Paris' actions simply because she gave birth to him, and Priam knew "the stuff that Paris was made of." The women of Troy and Hecuba reject these arguments, but the ancient audience would have known that Helen was not being deceitful or unreasoning in making the argument that Hecuba was responsible for what happened. If Hecuba and Priam had seen to it that the baby was put to death, Paris would not have lived to be able to make his disastrous judgment in favor of Aphrodite, who offered him Helen as a reward if he chose her (*Tro.* 929–31). Aphrodite, because she had prevailed, was obliged to help him take Helen away from Menelaus, an act that set in motion the events that led up to the destruction of Troy.

In his film version Cacoyannis concentrates on human action. With its desolate landscape and images of armed men threatening women and children, his version of the *Trojan Women* presents human brutality more vividly than would have been possible on the ancient stage. The film is dedicated to "all those who have opposed the oppression of man by man." That is certainly one of the central messages of the original drama, as it is also of Homer's *Iliad.* But another message, which really cannot come across without the original references to the gods, has to do with human willfulness and ignorance. Tragedy describes how human beings consistently fail to recognize the limitations of their knowledge. They suppose that they can ignore or circumvent dreams, omens, and prophecies, because they do not want them to be true. Most humans cannot bring themselves to kill their own children, even when it would be in their best interests to do so. They believe that they can take control over the outcome of events, and fail to realize that it is not they, but the gods who will determine what will happen in the future.

Aristotle understood that the contrast between human ignorance and divine omniscience was a central feature of Athenian drama. He discusses the issue in the *Poetics*, which he wrote sometime between 335 and 323 BC, seventy-plus years after Sophocles and Euripides had died. The theater of Dionysus was extensively rebuilt around 350, while Aristotle was teaching in Athens.[16] Aristotle first came to Athens from Macedonia in 367 BC, when he was seventeen, to study with Plato, and stayed until 348/7. During that time he would have been able to see tragedies written by the great dramatists of the fifth century, especially Euripides, because starting in 386 Euripides' works were regularly performed along with dramas by living authors.[17] Aristotle left Athens for five years, but returned in 343 and stayed there until 323. So he had an extended opportunity to watch performances that we can know about only in our imaginations or in modern interpretations.

Aristotle says that the tragic hero tends gets into trouble because of some *hamartia* (1453a6). In English the Greek word *hamartia* is often translated as "tragic flaw," but in fact the basic meaning of *hamartia* is "missing the mark." It does not denote a deficiency in character but rather an unlucky conjecture that has the potential to lead to terrible consequences.[18] As an example Aristotle cites the case of Oedipus. When I was an undergraduate I remember being told that Oedipus' "tragic flaw" was his temper, which led him to kill Laius. Certainly striking the old Laius with his stick was not Christian behavior (which would have required both Laius and Oedipus to have turned the other cheek). In Sophocles' drama, Oedipus' *hamartia* was not his temper; it was that he thought that he could somehow avoid the oracle, an error in judgment that in fact ensured that everything would happen as the god had predicted. By taking action that he supposed would prevent the oracle from coming true, he was able not only to bring about the deaths of his mother and father, and also cause his own blindness and exile, and the deaths of his sons and his daughter Antigone. Aristotle called the tragic hero's recognition of the truth *anagnōrisis*, which he defines as "a change from ignorance to knowledge" (1452a30–1)—the root *gnō-* in *anagnōrisis* is cognate with English *know*. Aristotle considered *anagnōrisis* to be an essential feature of tragedy, and specifically mentions Sophocles' *Oedipus Tyrannus* as a play where the process of recognition or discovery has been successfully portrayed (1455a18).

Human error (*hamartia*) was also responsible for the fall of Troy. The Trojans are not random victims of events, or fate, or human savagery. They are at least to some degree responsible for the destruction of their own city. Hecuba and Priam did not ensure that the infant Paris was put to death. Paris made a selfish decision when he judged in favor of the goddess who offered him the most beautiful woman in the world, rather than choosing the gifts offered to him by the goddesses Hera and Athena. In the *Iliad* Homer speaks of Paris' famous judgment as *atē* ("delusion"): "he quarreled with the goddesses when they came to his courtyard, and favored the one who gave him painful lust" (24.28–30).

But Euripides' drama is not just a morality play about the errors of judgment made by the Trojans. Through his prologue the poet makes it clear that Agamemnon and the Greek army will also become victims because they too have behaved ignorantly, by desecrating the sanctuaries of the gods, and failing to punish Ajax, son of Oïleus, for defiling Athena's temple. Indirectly also, the play is a warning for everyone in the audience, at the time when the Athenians seemed to be winning their war against the Spartans, advising them to behave with restraint, to honor the gods, and to

remember the limitations of their knowledge. It was a warning
that appears to have been unheeded, at least by the majority of
propertied Athenian men. In his *History of the Peloponnesian War*
Thucydides describes how the Athenians also became victims of
atē and ultimately lost the war against Sparta. His description of
the Athenians' brutal treatment of the population of Melos in 415
BC precedes his account of Athens' biggest strategic mistake, their
invasion of Sicily later that same year, which ended in their total
defeat, after many casualties as well as loss of vital resources.

Cacoyannis' two other film adaptations of Greek drama are
also based on plays by Euripides, *Electra* and *Iphigenia at Aulis*. It
is certainly easier to present Euripides' dramas on the modern
stage or screen than those of the other dramatists, because
Euripides portrays his characters realistically; they are flawed,
short-sighted, immoral, angry, passionate. Aristophanes in his
comedy the *Frogs* has Euripides say that he "put what was familiar
on the stage, things we use, things we're familiar with" (959–60),
and has the poet Aeschylus allege that the characters in Euripides'
dramas were low and immoral (1077–82). Aristotle records
that Sophocles remarked that "he himself made his characters
as they ought to be, Euripides [made them] the way people are"
(*Poet.* 1460b32–5).[19] For that reason, characters in Euripides'
dramas seem less remote from us than those of the other
Athenian dramatists. The British historian of the theater Michael
Walton calls his 2009 book *Euripides Our Contemporary*. Certainly
the realistic way in which Euripides portrays human emotions
can make his dramas seem immediately relevant. Removing
appearances by the gods helps make the dramas seem even more
accessible. Certainly it could be argued that modern audiences do
not need to know (and do not care about) the action of the gods in
Euripides' dramas. But in this book I would like to explain why we
will not obtain full value from modern performances of Euripides

if we treat the gods merely as projections of human desires or as a quaint literary convention.[20]

What if the original religious content of the dramas still had something to tell modern readers and audiences about the nature of human life and the forces beyond their control? Like Homer before him, Euripides depicts a world where at times gods take a close interest in human life, but at other times appear to ignore it. Justice is done, but often so slowly that those who have been wronged will see it accomplished only when it is too late for them get any benefit from it. The gods favor certain mortals but are hostile to others, and they often disagree about which mortals to favor. Whether or not the mortals are aware of it, the gods control what happens in human life, but human beings are almost always unable to accept the fact that they do so, and this failure on the part of mortals to recognize their own shortcomings again and again leads them to disaster. This view of human life, although bleak, is intended to represent the world in the manner most mortals, then and now, will experience it. Through his characterization of the gods and their relations with humankind, Euripides is making "a statement about the nature of the world and human life, terrible and dispassionate," as Homer did in the *Iliad*, and Aeschylus and Sophocles in their dramas.[21]

In this book I argue that ancient Greek theology still has value for modern readers. I describe the ways in which Euripides characterizes divine behavior, and then demonstrate why his characterization does not deviate significantly from that portrayed by Homer or the other dramatists, even though many critics have understood his intentions quite differently. These critics have assumed that it is reasonable to suppose that Euripides did not literally believe in the traditional gods on the grounds that in antiquity some comic poets and critics characterized Euripides' dramas as heretical or atheistic in intention. Even scholars who are prepared to disregard the ancient biographical traditions continue to believe that Euripides sought in his dramas to call attention to its limitations by bringing the gods onstage with greater frequency than the other poets, and having them behave with the greatest cruelty towards those mortals who refuse to give them the honor that they think they deserve. But if we look closely at what Euripides himself said, and not at what the comic poets represented him as saying, we will not find any compelling reason to suppose that Euripides was particularly sympathetic towards the radical ideas about divinity expressed by philosophers like Anaxagoras or Socrates. When Euripides puts the words and ideas of contemporary philosophers and thinkers into the mouths of his characters, I would argue that he does not do so in order to promote or espouse those ideas, but because as a dramatist he wants his characters to express themselves in a contemporary manner, and to discuss the kinds of theorizing that members of his audience had heard about, whether from the sophists themselves, or from references to them in comedy.

In the next chapter I would like to describe how the caricatures of Socrates and other philosophers in Athenian comedy led ancient critics to think that Euripides shared their nontraditional views of the nature of the gods, even to the point of believing that the gods did not exist. Then in Chapter 2 I shall discuss how ancient and modern critics have sought to interpret some statements about the gods made by the characters in the *Heracles*, a terrifying drama in which the great hero first rescues and is then compelled by the goddess Hera to kill his wife and his children. Was Euripides being blasphemous? Or ironic? Or did he wish to portray in the most arresting way possible some of the differences between divine cruelty and mortal compassion?

On the basis of that discussion, in the next chapters I shall try to offer an open-minded look at what the gods actually do in Euripides' other dramas. There are many ways in which such a discussion could be presented. One could talk about the role of gods in the structure of the plot, and the different functions of divine appearances at the beginnings or at the end of plays. But since this is a book about the characterization as well as the behavior of the gods, I would like to discuss the roles played by individual gods, and to show why the dramatist has chosen to bring some gods rather than others into the action of his dramas, and why some gods seem more sympathetic to humans than others. Often the poet's choice is dictated by the myths on which the dramas are based, for example, the role of Apollo in the story of Ion, or Athena in plays involving her city, such as the *Suppliants* or *Erechtheus*. I shall begin with chapters on the dramas in which Athena and Apollo play important roles, because they are the two most powerful children of Zeus, and the two gods who most often communicate directly with mortals. Then I shall consider how Euripides characterizes the other gods who appear *ex machina* in his dramas, and why he has chosen them, rather than Athena or Apollo, to appear. Finally, I want to look at the several dramas in which gods do not appear as characters, in the hope of being able to show that even when no god comes on stage, the gods nonetheless determine what mortals are able to do, and bring about the final outcomes of the dramatic action. In those dramas the characters onstage and the audience may not be satisfied with what has happened. Justice may not appear to have been done, and not all issues will have been resolved to everyone's or even to anyone's satisfaction. But that sense of incompleteness does not imply that the gods do not exist, or that Euripides sought to have his original audiences cease to honor them. On the contrary, if the endings of the dramas are disturbing, it reminds us that the gods exist to please themselves, not in order to make humans happy.

Whatever Euripides' personal beliefs may have been, in his dramas Euripides did not seek to get his audiences to abandon their theology or religious practices. He does not try to glorify the gods, but presents them as what they were. The dramas do not set out to undermine traditional theology, so much as use it to portray and affirm the virtues conferred on humans by the fact of their mortality: human compassion, endurance, and courage.

1

EURIPIDES, SOCRATES, AND OTHER SOPHISTS

Surprising as it may seem, little historical information about Euripides' life has come down to us, other than the approximate dates of his birth and death, and the names of his parents, wife, and children. We have no way of knowing how he learned how to compose his dramas, or why he wrote what he did, or, in many cases, precisely when his dramas were performed. None of his biographers appears to have been a contemporary of his, and none seems to have had any information about him other than what was recorded on a public inscription, or what the comic poets said about him, or lines that might be thought to be autobiographical in his own dramas.[1] No contemporary portrait of him has survived. In the "portrait" sculptures that date from the Roman era, he is represented as a bearded man with a serious expression, like other intellectuals. We also have no way of knowing why none of his contemporaries sought to write an account of his life, or indeed the lives of Sophocles or any other of the poets whose dramas were performed at the same festivals as Euripides' plays. Was it because people at the time thought that what a person *did* was more important than who that person *was*? Or that in the second half of the fifth century it seemed more important to write about the past than to describe what was happening in the present?

Writers as well as artists, it seems, preferred to make their subjects conform to archetypes, rather than emphasize those qualities that made them different from other people. In the fourth century BC, when writers began to compose "lives" of the famous poets, they chose to model their narratives on traditional mythological patterns.[2] They appear to have agreed with Aristotle that poetry is more philosophical and serious than history, because poetry deals with the universal (*ta katholou*), but history with particulars (*ta kath' hekaston, Poet.* 1451b7). Biographers represented the poets as quasi-heroes, figures who possessed significant flaws along with their greatness. As they saw it, even though poets may have achieved fame in their lifetimes, most of them died ignominiously, often away from their homelands, like the great heroes of legend, Heracles, Theseus, or Oedipus. The narrative patterns of the traditional myths, as preserved in epic poetry, gave a lasting meaning to the new stories that the biographers were creating, making them more worthy of record, or memorable, and at least in an abstract sense, true—the root meaning of the Greek word *alētheia*, which we translate as "truth," is "that which is not hidden or unknown" and hence real or genuine.[3] Some biographers, certainly, intended the narratives which they created to serve an ethical or instructional purpose, like the works of the famous historians. The fourth-century orator Alcidamas said that he wrote his biography of Homer as a means of thanking the poet for his work (fr. 7 Avezzù = fr. 27 Muir). He portrayed Homer as a poor man who, though honored in his lifetime for his wisdom, had been told by an oracle that he must die when he was asked to solve a riddle, but could not do so. Then, according to Alcidamas, Homer composed his own epitaph and was honored as a hero by the inhabitants of the island of Ios, where he died. It seems that Alcidamas meant to honor Homer by representing him as a poor man; one of Alcidamas' other works was a treatise "In Praise of Poverty" (*POxy* 5130).[4]

Alcidamas' and Homer's other biographers may have based some parts of their narratives on local legends, but essentially the model for their portrait of Homer was Demodocus, the blind bard who in the *Odyssey* sings for his living in the service of a king. Euripides' biographers also looked for passages in his dramas that might be thought to represent the poet's own thoughts. But in practice they drew most of their material from comedies by Aristophanes and his contemporaries. Biographers appear to have regarded Aristophanes as a reliable source, because he lived and wrote during the lifetimes of both Sophocles and Euripides and clearly knew their work well, along with that of their predecessor Aeschylus. But even though Aristophanes was Euripides' contemporary, he certainly did not set out to be his biographer, at least in the sense that we use that term today. He was not interested in writing a history of Euripides' life, nor did he seek to consult historical records about him, or (as far as we know) conduct systematic interviews of his acquaintances. Aristophanes' goal was first of all to make his audiences laugh. Unfortunately for those of us who would like to have had more information about Euripides' education or intentions, it is Aristophanes' comic portraits of Euripides, however exaggerated and however far from reality, which have formed the basis of all subsequent attempts to write an account of Euripides' life.[5]

Anyone inclined to doubt the power of comic characterization needs only to consider what happened to Socrates. According to Plato, when Socrates was put on trial for impiety in 399 BC, he listed as his first and more dangerous accusers the many people who told lies about him and slandered him, portraying him as "a kind of wise man, who contemplated what was in the air (*meteōra*) and scrutinized everything under the earth and who made worse arguments appear to be better." That characterization marked him as someone whose teaching was dangerous: "People who hear such claims suppose that anyone who is interested in such matters does not believe in the gods" (Pl., *Apol.* 18b–c). The charge of being an unbeliever (*atheos*) did not mean being an atheist in the modern sense of the word, that is, someone who does not believe in the existence of god(s) or in the notion of divinity or divine causation.[6] As the ancient Athenians appear to have understood it, being *atheos* meant that one believed in nontraditional or different gods that did not have established cults.[7] These are the kind of charges that Plato has Socrates address in his *Apology*. In that work Plato represents Socrates as saying that if his first accusers, including the comic poets, had actually brought formal charges against him, they would have alleged: "Socrates does wrong because he goes around looking for *what is underneath the earth and what is in the sky* and making worse arguments appear to be better, and teaches these same methods to others" (Pl., *Apol.* 19b).

In particular Plato has Socrates mention a scene in Aristophanes' comedy the *Clouds*. There, says Plato's Socrates, Aristophanes put on the stage "someone called Socrates being carried around and saying that he was walking on air and uttering a lot of other nonsense, matters about which I don't know anything at all" (Pl., *Apol.* 19c). These were, in effect, the same charges that Aristophanes brought against Socrates in the *Clouds*, which was produced in 423 BC. In that play Aristophanes' Socrates prays to new gods that have no established cult: Air, Ether, and Clouds (264–5). This comic Socrates has a school where he teaches his pupils to produce a Worse Argument, in order to "plead an unjust cause and overturn the better argument" (884–5). His religion, like his rhetoric, lacks a moral element, and at the end of the comedy his would-be pupil Strepsiades sets fire to Socrates' school because he realizes that he must have been crazy "when he tossed out the gods on account of Socrates" (1476–7).[8] The three men who prosecuted Socrates for impiety in real life made it clear that holding such unconventional views about the gods was a threat to the citizens of Athens: "Socrates does wrong because he corrupts the youth and does not believe in the gods in whom the city believes, but in other new-fangled divinities" (Pl., *Apol.* 24b).

In his comedies Aristophanes makes the same charges against *Euripides* that he made against Socrates, associating him with the philosopher in any way he can. In the first version of the *Clouds* (now lost) a character claimed that Socrates was "that man who wrote the hyper-talky tragedies, the clever ones, for Euripides" (fr. 392 K-A, *PCG* IIIb 216–7). In the surviving version of the *Clouds* Aristophanes showed Socrates trying to travel in the air and contemplate the sky, presumably to be closer to the special gods he worshiped. In the *Women at the Thesmophoria* (411 BC), Aristophanes has Euripides tell a story of creation in which he claims that the Upper Air (*Aithēr*) is the source of all living things (9), rather than Earth (*Gaia*), as in the traditional narrative in Hesiod's *Theogony*. The comic Euripides in Aristophanes' *Frogs* (405 BC) prays to "other, private gods": "*Aithēr*, my sustenance; Pivot of my tongue, Comprehension, and Nostrils keen to scent" (891–3). In the same comedy a woman complains that Euripides has spoiled her livelihood (selling wreaths for statues of the gods) because he does not believe in the traditional gods: "by working in tragedies he has persuaded men that the gods do not exist" (*ouk einai theous*, 450–1). Aristophanes may be alluding here to some striking lines from Euripides' *Bellerophon*, in which a character says: "Does anyone say that there are gods in heaven? No, they do not exist (*ouk eisin*); they don't exist, unless someone is a fool and wants to rely on the old story" (*TrGF* 5.1, F 286.1–3).[9] In the

Frogs (405 BC) Aristophanes has his comic Aeschylus call Euripides an "enemy of the gods" (836).

Socrates' accusers claimed that he corrupted the youth and that he was "clever at making arguments" (*deinos legein*, Pl., *Apol.* 17a). That is also how Aristophanes represented Euripides in his comedies. Several of his comic characters allude to a line from Euripides' *Hippolytus* (612) whenever they want to break a promise: "my tongue swore it, but my mind did not take the oath" (*Thesm.* 275–6 and *Frogs* 102, 1471). The charge is manifestly unfair, since Hippolytus dies rather than break his oath (schol. *Hipp.* 612, II p. 78 Schwartz).[10]

In the *Frogs* Aeschylus accuses Euripides of corrupting the Athenians' morals, by writing about incest (850) and putting whores like Phaedra and Stheneboea on the stage (1043), when he ought instead "to hide what is shameful, not to bring it on the stage or to write about it. Little boys have a teacher to tell them [what is right]; grown men have poets" (1053–5). Euripides, claims this comic Aeschylus, has caused a general moral decline in Athens: "For what evils is he *not* responsible? Hasn't he exhibited procuresses, and women who bear children in temples, and have intercourse with their brothers, and state that life is not life?" (1078–2). At the end of the *Frogs* Aristophanes has Dionysus quote Euripides' line "who knows if life is death," so he can break a promise, on the grounds that his words were meaningless (1478). That was certainly not the way the lines were used in their original context, where a speaker in Euripides' (lost) drama *Phrixus* wonders if death is not a better form of life.[11]

In Aristophanes' comedy *Acharnians* Euripides' slave states that his master "is home, but not at home, if you see what I mean" (396), the idea being that while the poet's body is in the house his mind is elsewhere. In every case Aristophanes ignores the context in which Euripides had his characters express "Socratic" or philosophical ideas, and instead pretends that whatever his tragic characters say represents the poet's own personal opinion. Socrates and Euripides probably knew each other, and certainly Socrates would have been present at the performances of Euripides' dramas. Both men appeared as characters in the (now lost) dialogue *Miltiades* by Socrates' pupil Aeschines of Sphettos (*POxy* 2889 + 2890 = *TrGF* 5.1, T 43). But biographers seem to have relied primarily on comedy and Euripides' own works when they sought to construct narratives of the poet's life. Practically the first thing that the third-century AD biographer Diogenes Laertius says about Socrates in his *Lives and Opinions of Eminent Philosophers* is that "he appears to have collaborated with Euripides" (2.18).[12] The evidence for this claim is four quotations from Athenian comedy (*TrGF* 5.1, T 51). Diogenes begins with Teleclides, a contemporary of Aristophanes, who described Euripides' father-in-law Mnesilochus "cooking up the *Phrygians*, a new play for Euripides," and Socrates supplying him with firewood (*phrygana*) (fr. 41 K-A, *PCG* VII, 683). Diogenes adds the line "Euripideses nailed together by Socrates" (fr. 42 K-A, *PCG* VII, 684).[13] Then he quotes a couple of lines from a dialogue in a play by Callias, in which someone asks a woman why she is so pompous and has such profound thoughts, and she replies, "I can do it; Socrates is responsible" (fr. 15 K-A, *PCG* IV, 46).[14] Diogenes' last example is the pair of lines from the first version of Aristophanes' *Clouds*, in which someone says that Socrates "wrote the hyper-talky tragedies, the clever ones, for Euripides" (fr. 392 K-A, *PCG* III.2, 316–7).

Diogenes relied on the work of earlier biographers, who had mined the dramas for further "evidence" of collaboration between Euripides and Socrates. These biographers followed Aristophanes' practice of quoting lines out of context, and assuming that Euripides believed anything that he made his characters say.

We can catch a glimpse of how the biographers worked from the fragments of a dialogue about the life of Euripides composed by the third/second-century BC biographer Satyrus of Callatis, a town in what is now Rumania. The interlocutors in Satyrus' dialogue discuss lines in Euripides' works with thoughts or phrases that might possibly be construed to have biographical significance. When a character in Euripides' (now lost) *Danae* says "no man is stronger than money, unless there is someone (who does)— but who that is I don't see" (*TrGF* 5.1, F 325), an interlocutor in Satyrus' dialogue claims that Euripides was referring specifically to Socrates. The same interlocutor says that Euripides "came into disgrace" among the Athenians because he admired Socrates so much that "when speaking about avarice in the *Danae*, he made Socrates alone exempt from it" (F 6 fr. 38.iv–39.i).[15] When an interlocutor claims that Euripides says that the gods see everything that mortals do (*TrGF* 5.2, F 1007c), another interlocutor suggests "that sort of opinion might be 'Socratic' " (F 6 fr. 39.ii). A more fanciful version of this kind of biographical inference is preserved by Diogenes Laertius in his biography of Socrates (2.33). Diogenes includes an anecdote in which Euripides criticizes the Athenians for executing Socrates: "Greeks, you have killed, you have killed the wisest man, who did no harm, the Muses' nightingale" (from the *Palamedes, TrGF* 5.2, F 588), even though (as Diogenes notes) Euripides died in 406, seven years before Socrates was executed![16]

As Diogenes' anecdote about Euripides and Socrates indicates, most Greeks came to believe that Socrates should never have been put to death. But Euripides' reputation only became worse as time went on. Later writers portrayed Socrates as an innocent, while Euripides went on being represented as a corrupting influence, as he had been for Aristophanes. Diogenes relates an anecdote (2.33) that tells how Socrates left the theater because one of the lines in Euripides' *Electra* appeared to be encouraging immorality: "it's

best to leave such matters in disorder" (379). Even though
Euripides had put those words into the mouth of Orestes, who
was discussing how hard it is to determine who is virtuous, in
the anecdote Socrates blames *Euripides* on the grounds that he
was willing "to let virtue (*aretē*) be lost like that."[17] Euripides also
gets the worst of a verbal exchange in another anecdote, this
time to bring out the contrast between his ethics and those of
Socrates' followers. In the original drama the line was spoken by
Macareus, the son of Aeolus, god of the winds, as a justification
for committing incest: "What is shameful, if it doesn't seem so
to those who practice it?" (*Aeolus, TrGF* 5.1, F 19).[18] In the *Frogs*
Aristophanes took the line out of context and gave it to Dionysus
so he can break his promise to bring the dead Euripides back to
life, but with a slight amendment: "What is shameful (*aischron*) if
it doesn't seem so *to the audience?*" (1475).[19] The second-century
AD Roman author Serenus relates that Euripides was applauded
for having said the line in the theater, but when Plato happened
to see him, he said: "Euripides, 'shameful is shameful, whether
or not it seems so'" (Stob., *Anthol.* 3.5.36.1–5 = SSR V, A 195).
In Plutarch's version of the same story (*Mor.* 33c), it is Socrates'
friend Antisthenes rather than Plato who states that "shameful is
shameful," when he sees that the audience became agitated when
they heard the line from the *Aeolus*—Plutarch must have known
that Plato could not have been more than eight years old when the
Aeolus was produced. The anecdote about the exchange probably
originated in a comedy or mime, because the response to the line
from the *Aeolus* is also in iambic trimeter, the standard meter used
for verse dialogue. In another anecdote Euripides appears to be
even more radical and clever than Socrates: according to Diogenes
Laertius, Euripides gave Socrates a book by the philosopher
Heraclitus, who was known for his criticism of the traditional
gods. When Euripides asked Socrates what he thought of it,

Socrates claimed that he couldn't understand it: "it's fine so far as I understand it, and I think also the part that I don't understand, but it needs a Delian diver [to get to the bottom of it]" (2.22).

The comic poets' negative characterization of Euripides as a would-be philosopher stuck, even though we have no reason to believe that they meant their jokes and exaggerations to be taken literally or even seriously. Biographers followed the lead of Aristophanes' and Socrates' accusers in depicting Euripides as a disciple of the sophist Anaxagoras (500–428 BC). Anaxagoras was famous (or notorious) for his theories about the power of mind (*nous*), which he said was the origin of motion (D.L. 2.8), and considered it to be the ordering power in the universe.[20] Traditionalists considered his theory to be a challenge to the conventional theology, which held that the universe was under the control of Zeus and the gods who were loyal to him. Anaxagoras also was said to have claimed that the sun was a fiery coal (*mydros*) larger than the Peloponnesus and that there were houses, hills, and ravines on the moon (Diog. Laert. 2.8). In the mid-fifth century BC stating that the sun was a stone and the moon was earth would have been considered to be a *blasphemia*, a remark that was at the very least disrespectful to Helios, the Sun-god, and Selene, the goddess of the moon. Presumably it was for that reason that Socrates' prosecutor Meletus accused him saying that the "sun is a stone and the moon is earth." Socrates replied that Meletus was accusing Anaxagoras, not himself (Pl., *Apol.* 26d).

The question of Anaxagoras' influence on Euripides was an important topic in Satyrus' dialogue *The Life of Euripides*. An interlocutor says that Euripides honored Anaxagoras to an exceptional degree (*etima daimoniōs*, F 6 fr. 37i). The interlocutor then cites a passage from a lost play where the speaker brings an offering to "Zeus, or, if you prefer to be called Hades" (*TrGF* 5.2, F 912), observing that Euripides "has caught with complete accuracy Anaxagoras' world-view in three verses" (F 6 fr. 37 iii). The interlocutor then adds, "and in another place Euripides is at a loss to say what is the power that presides over the heavenly gods: 'Zeus, whether you are the necessity of nature or the mind (*nous*) of men (*Tro.* 886).'" The interlocutor appears to suppose that the lines he quotes represent Euripides' personal views, although of course in their original contexts they were spoken by characters in the dramas.

If the whole of Satyrus' dialogue had survived, we might have seen that one of the other interlocutors might have had some objections to the notion that these lines were "Anaxagorean." Someone could have pointed out that the speaker of the "Anaxagorean" first line quoted by Satyrus' interlocutor is addressing Zeus Chthonios, the ruler of the Underworld, the brother of Zeus on Mt. Olympus and equivalent of Hades. In the second passage cited by Satyrus' interlocutor, the speaker is Hecuba in the *Trojan Women* (884–8). She has just learned that she and the other women of Troy have been assigned as slaves to Greek masters, and wonders if the gods have abandoned her (469–71). Her grandson Astyanax has been led away to be hurled to his death from the walls of Troy, an act that moves even the Greek herald Talthybius to pity (787). The chorus echoes her lament about the gods: "the gods' love for Troy has vanished" (858–9). Just before Hecuba addresses her prayer to Zeus, Menelaus comes to get Helen. The Greeks have given him permission to kill her, but he wants to wait until after he returns to Sparta. It is at this point Hecuba utters her "Anaxagorean" prayer to Zeus: "Conveyance of the earth and you who have a base on earth, whoever you are, most difficult to estimate, Zeus, whether you are necessity of nature or the mind (*nous*) for mortals, I address you in prayer. For as you go along your noiseless path, you direct all mortal affairs according to justice" (*Tro.* 884–8). When Hecuba finishes her prayer, Menelaus seems confused by what she has said: "What is this?You've invented new prayers to the gods" (889). His response seems to support the idea that there is something radical about Hecuba's prayer.

But in fact it is not the content of Hecuba's prayer that is new-fangled, but the way in which it is expressed.[21] To ask a god by what name he or she prefers to be addressed is an act of piety, and the purpose of the inquiry is to make the prayer effective by pleasing the god. Asking the question does not mean that Hecuba doubts that Zeus exists, but rather indicates that she is not sure what name would please him, since he is "most difficult to estimate."[22] Addressing Zeus as "the conveyance of the earth" is an abstract and impersonal way of associating him with the *aithēr*, the bright upper air. The identification of *aithēr* and Zeus goes back to Aeschylus ("Zeus is *aithēr*"; *TrGF* 3, F 70). A connection between Zeus and the *aithēr* is inherent in the epic phrase *aitheros ek diēs* (*Il.* 16.365, *Od.* 19.540); the adjective *dios* comes from the same root **diw-*, "bright sky, Zeus."[23] Euripides speaks of Zeus as *aithēr* in other plays, using anthropomorphic language, for example, "do you see the boundless *aithēr* who embraces the earth in his moist arms; think of him as Zeus, think of him as a god" (*TrGF* 5.2, F 941).[24] In her prayer Hecuba continues to address Zeus in conventional terms: "you who have a seat upon the earth."[25] But then once again she speaks of Zeus in abstract language: "if you are necessity of nature or the mind of mortals." Here again she is addressing Zeus as *aithēr*. Euripides had described the air as the source of human intellection some twenty-five years earlier in his drama *Alcestis*. There the chorus of old men observes, "I have sped through song and up into the air (*metarsios*) and laid hold of many ideas (*logoi*), but I have found nothing more powerful than Necessity" (962–6).[26] Even before Zeus was identified with *aithēr*, poets talked about him as the power that controls everything. At

the beginning of the *Works and Days*, Hesiod describes Zeus as the
power that determines the fate of all human beings (*Works and Days*
3–8); Solon states that "Zeus oversees the outcome of everything"
(fr. 13.17W). As Hecuba concludes her prayer, she still seems to
be speaking of Zeus as *aithēr*: "for as you go along your noiseless
path, you direct all mortal affairs according to justice." Here her
language has become more traditional: that men are unaware
of, and thus surprised by, the ways in which Zeus directs human
affairs is an idea that goes back to Solon, who compares the justice
of Zeus to a sudden spring storm (fr. 13.17–25W). It is this final,
conventional characterization of Zeus' power that will prove to
be most accurate, as the audience knows. Zeus' daughter Athena
and his brother Poseidon will soon punish the Greeks for their
impiety during the sack of Troy, and the justice of Zeus will be
accomplished.[27]

Although it is the abstract language of Hecuba's prayer that
is innovative, rather than the ideas that it conveys, ancient
scholars ignored the context in which the prayer was spoken
and the conventional terminology used in it. Instead, most likely
because they had been influenced, either directly or indirectly,
by Aristophanes' caricature of Euripides, they supposed that the
views expressed in Hecuba's prayer represented not Hecuba's
but Euripides' own personal ideas about divinity. Aristophanes
had made fun of Euripides for regarding *Aithēr* as the origin of
all things, and for praying to *Aithēr* as his sustenance. The ancient
scholia or marginal commentary on Hecuba's speech records
several different points of view about the prayer (schol. *Tro.*
884, II p. 366 Schwartz). The commentators situated Hecuba's
"conveyance of the earth" "in the middle of the air" (*meteōron*),
rather than with Zeus and the *aithēr*, as Euripides himself had
done. Anaxagoras had theorized about *aēr* (as opposed to *aithēr*)
and had said that the air was strong enough to keep the earth in

suspension (*meteōron*, 59A42 DK).[28] The *meteōron* also connected
Euripides with Aristophanes' Socrates, who appeared onstage in
a basket in the air (*aerobatō, Clouds* 227), and had been called by
his enemies a "thinker about the air" (*meteōra phrontistēs*, Pl., *Apol.*
18b). But since Aristophanes does not seem to have made fun of
Sophocles, scholars did not suggest that Sophocles had Anaxagoras'
theories in mind (e.g., 59 B 6, II 35 DK) when he wrote the
prayer that Electra addresses to "sacred light and air (*aēr*) that has a
share equal to earth" (*El.* 87).[29]

Hecuba's next suggestion, that Zeus might be called *nous
brotōn*, elicited several different interpretations, depending upon
whether the ancient commentators on the *Trojan Women* (schol.
Tro. 884, II p. 366 Schwartz = 59A48 DK) understood the phrase
to mean "mind *for* mortals" (objective genitive), or "mind *of* man"
(subjective genitive). The view that it meant "mind *for* mortals"
would be consistent with conventional theology: "Zeus is the
one who placed Mind in humankind, or mind that pervades
everything." But other ancient scholars explained the reference
to *nous* as "mind *of* mortals," citing a line from a lost play, "in
each of us our mind is god" (*TrGF* 5.2, F 1018).[30] In that case, the
reference to *nous* in itself was presumed to be evidence that "these
ideas arose (*hormōntai*) from the writings of Anaxagoras." Other
commentators explained that "either Zeus takes human form, or is
physical necessity, or is such a mind as humans possess. Or god is a
creation of human intelligence." The idea that Zeus is a creation of
human intelligence is the most radical suggestion, but it does not
correspond to anything Anaxagoras himself appears to have said,
since in other fragments and summaries of his works he appears
to have been talking about divine intelligence. The philosopher
Democritus classified human intelligence as a divinity (68 A 74
DK).[31] But the notion that *nous brotōn* means the mind *of* mortals
does not fit the context as well as the reading that it means the

mind *for* mortals, since Zeus is the power who directs human affairs in all the other phrases Hecuba uses to describe him.

Whatever Euripides himself may have intended, his ancient biographers seemed determined to see in virtually any reference he might make to "mind" or "air" a connection to Anaxagoras. When in a lost drama Theseus says "I have learned from a wise man (*sophos*) and have considered for myself in my thoughts and mind (*nous*) misfortunes and exile from my native land and untimely death and other forms of evil" (*TrGF* 5.2, F 964 = 59 A 33 DK), a commentator supposed that he had Anaxagoras (the "wise man" in these verses) in mind, who had uttered similar reflections after he learned that his son had died.[32] Some ancient commentators thought that there was a reference to Anaxagoras in Euripides' *Alcestis* in the passage where the old men of the chorus sing: "I have sped through song and up into the air (*metarsios*) and laid hold of many ideas (*logoi*), but I have found nothing more powerful than Necessity" (962–6).[33] The ancient commentators on this passage interpret Euripides' lines as if the poet were speaking about his own personal experience—"the poet through the persona of the chorus indicates what sort of education he has had"—and paraphrase Euripides' lines as "I have thought about things in the air, have studied astronomy, and have devoted myself to this" (schol. *Alc.* 962–3, II p. 238 Schwartz).[34]

A single Anaxagorean word was enough to establish a connection. In Euripides' *Orestes* Electra sings a monody in which she wishes she could escape to "the rock strung in suspense between sky and earth by golden chains, borne on the breezes, a clod (*bōlos*) from Olympus" (982–3). The idea of a rock chained to Mt. Olympus comes from the *Iliad*, where Zeus threatens to suspend the gods with a golden cord tied around Olympus so that "everything was in the air" (*meteōra*, 8.19–26). In the *Orestes*, however, Electra is talking about a golden chain attached to the

stone that hovers over the head of Tantalus, a punishment he
pays eternally for offending the gods with his "unbridled tongue"
(*Or.* 4–10). Electra is desperate; she has just learned that the
Argives are planning to execute her, along with Orestes. She says
that she wants to go to the chained stone so she can lament to
Tantalus (the progenitor of her family) about all the troubles that
his descendants have brought upon themselves (984–1011). But
an ancient commentator ignored the context of her remarks,
and concentrated instead on the golden chains and the stone
suspended in the air: "Since Euripides was a pupil of Anaxagoras,
he says that the sun is a lump of molten metal (*mydros*), for thus
Anaxagoras taught" (schol. *Or.* 982, I p. 193 Schwartz). In fact
the word *mydros* does not occur in the passage, and Electra is not
talking about the sun, but the stone that hangs over the head of
Tantalus.[35] The commentator (or his source) connected the passage
with Anaxagoras, because Anaxagoras had predicted the fall of a
meteorite, which he said would come from the sun, and because in
the *Phaethon* Euripides called the sun a golden clod (*chrysean bōlon;*
TrGF 5.2, F 783 = D.L. 2.10). Even an isolated reference to the
Sun-god could be interpreted as Anaxagorean, as when Hippolytus
learns about Phaedra's passion for him and cries out "mother
earth and expanses of the sun" (*Hipp.* 601). Characters in drama
frequently call upon the Sun-god to bear witness.[36] Nonetheless,
an ancient commentator on the passage added a reference to the
Orestes passage about the golden chains and its connection with
Anaxagoras (schol. *Hipp.* 601, II p. 76 Schwartz).

However tenuous in reality his connection with Anaxagoras may
have been, in the Hellenistic era Euripides' biographers appeared
to assume without the least hesitation that he had actually studied
with Anaxagoras (*TrGF* 5.1, T1. IA.2, IB.1). According to one
of Euripides' biographers: "he introduced many innovations,
prologues, philosophical discourses, displays of rhetoric and

recognition scenes, because he attended lectures by Anaxagoras, Prodicus and Protagoras and was a friend of Socrates" (*TrGF* 5.1, T 1 IA.2); "after he had studied with Archelaus the natural philosopher and with Anaxagoras he started to write tragedies" (*TrGF* 5.1, T 1 B.2).[37] The third-century BC writer Alexander of Aetolia could speak of "good old Anaxagoras' boarding student" (*trophimos, CA* fr. 7.1) and assume that his audience would know who he was talking about.[38] The first-century BC historian Diodorus of Sicily (1.38.3) says that Euripides refers to Anaxagoras' theory of the sources of the Nile in the prologue to his *Archelaus* (*TrGF* 5.1, F 288) because Euripides was Anaxagoras' pupil.[39] Neither he nor any other ancient writer pointed out that Aeschylus also has characters in two different dramas offer the same account of the origin of the Nile (*Supp.* 559; *TrGF* 3, F 300) even though Aeschylus was too old to have been one of Anaxagoras' pupils.[40]

Since all of the information we now have about Euripides' connection with Socrates and Anaxagoras seems to have been based on what he *wrote* in his dramas, rather than on independent documentation about what he did, we need to ask why biographers looked for the particular words and phrases that would enable them to connect him with these and other sophists, but say little or nothing about the considerable sophistic influence on other prominent intellectuals, such as Sophocles or Thucydides. The most likely reason was that both Anaxagoras and Socrates had been accused of impiety, either onstage or in an actual courtroom. Diogenes Laertius says that the demagogue Cleon indicted Anaxagoras for impiety (*asebeia*), because of his theory that the sun was a fiery coal (*mydros*, Diog. Laert. 2.12). That is virtually the same charge that Meletus brought against Socrates (Pl., *Apol.*, 18b).[41] No one in antiquity seems to have known the outcome of Anaxagoras' trial, since several conflicting versions are given (death sentence, suicide, exile; Diog. Laert. 2.12–4). But whatever actually happened to him, the idea that Anaxagoras was thought to have been tried for impiety became the motivation for his "pupil" Euripides' decision not to become a sophist like his master: "he listened to Anaxagoras' lectures, but he turned to writing tragedy when he saw what dangers Anaxagoras endured because of the ideas he put forth" (Suda, Epsilon 3695).

Euripides was also associated with the philosophers Protagoras and Prodicus because they too were supposed to have been accused of impiety. Diogenes says that Protagoras was expelled from Athens after he read from his book *About the Gods,* which began with the statement "I do not have the ability to know about the gods, whether they exist or they do not exist or what they look like" (Diog. Laert. 9.51 = 80 A 4 DK). Diogenes offers several different accounts of where the reading took place and who Protagoras' accuser might have been.[42] Diogenes says that copies of Protagoras' books were collected by a herald and burned, but actual book-burning seems not to have been added to the story before the last half of the first century BC.[43] In its original context what Protagoras said may not have been all that radical. Humans who have never seen the gods do not have the ability to know for sure whether or not they exist or what they look like, since their information is based on belief rather than knowledge.[44] According to Plato, Protagoras enjoyed a high reputation in Athens throughout his life (*Meno* 91e).[45] It was only his later biographers who claimed that Protagoras suffered the proverbial fate of the impious, shipwreck.[46] Stories about the public reading, his subsequent indictment for impiety, and his violent death appear to have been made up to fit that particular trope. The late-fourth–early-third-century writer Philochorus in his history of Athens (328 *FGrHist* 217) relates that "when Protagoras was sailing to Sicily, his ship sank, and

Euripides hints at this in the *Ixion*" (Diog. Laert. 9.55 = 80 A 2
DK). The term "hints at" (*ainittesthai*) indicates that there was
no explicit reference to Protagoras in Euripides' text (*TrGF* 5.1,
T 1). The *Ixion* was considered to be shocking because its plot
described how Ixion tried to seduce the goddess Hera. According
to Plutarch (*Mor.* 19e), the play was criticized for being impious
and obscene (*asebēs kai miaros*), but Euripides replied that he had
Ixion punished for attempting to rape Hera: "I attached him to
his wheel before I led him off the stage" (*TrGF* 5.1, (33) iii). The
source of the story about impiety in the *Ixion* was almost certainly
a contemporary Athenian comedy, in which a single incident or
reference in a drama could be interpreted in the worst possible
light, and even represented as multiple incidents. For example,
in the *Frogs* (1079) Aristophanes' comic Aeschylus criticizes
Euripides for putting procuresses onstage, presumably because
in the *Hippolytus*, Phaedra's old nurse tells Hippolytus that his
stepmother Phaedra is in love with him! Aristophanes' Aeschylus
then (1080–1) also accuses Euripides of having women give birth
in temples (like Augē, who gave birth to Heracles' son Telephus in
the sanctuary of Athena), and women who have intercourse with
their brothers (Canace with Macareus in the *Aeolus*).[47]

In their eagerness to show that Euripides was a corrupting
influence, biographers also sought to connect Euripides to the
sophist Prodicus of Ceos. The Suda entry on Euripides states
without qualification that "Euripides was a pupil of Prodicus in
rhetoric" (Epsilon 3695). In the *Clouds* Aristophanes links Prodicus
with Socrates as a "thinker about things in the air" (*meteōrosophistēs*,
360–1). The chorus of the *Birds* advises the audience to listen to
them (the Birds) about things in the air (*ta meteōra*) and genealogies
of the gods, and to forget about Prodicus (690–2 = 84 A 4 & 5
DK).[48] Aristophanes also made fun of Prodicus for his bad influence
on the young: "as for this fellow, he has been corrupted by a book

or Prodicus or an idle talker" (fr. 506 K-A, *PCG*, IIIA 54).[49] In his dialogue *Protagoras*, Plato describes how Socrates arrives at Callias' house when the sophists Protagoras, Hippias, and Prodicus were also present. Socrates sees Prodicus lying on a bed, lecturing, wrapped in sheepskins, surrounded by an audience. "And then I saw Tantalus," says Socrates, quoting a passage from the *Odyssey*, where Odysseus sees Tantalus and other men who are being punished in Tartarus for having offended the gods (11.582).[50] Plato has Socrates add that he wanted to listen to Prodicus because "he seemed to me an omniscient and godly man, but the reverberation of his deep voice in the house made his discourse unintelligible" (*Prot.* 315e–316a). Prodicus had left Athens by the time of Socrates' trial, and it is not likely that he would have returned there after Socrates was condemned and executed. Nonetheless, a biographer eventually claimed that Prodicus had "died in Athens by drinking hemlock, on the grounds that he corrupted the youth," exactly like Socrates (Suda, Pi 2365 = schol. *Resp.* 600c, p. 273 Greene = 84A1DK).[51] Popular belief demanded that the impious should die violent and degrading deaths.

Some anecdotes put Euripides on trial for impiety, like his supposed mentors.[52] Aristotle defined impiety as an offence in respect of the gods or of the dead or of parents or of native land (*De virtut. et vit.* 1251a31–3). Any violation of religious practice, such as entry into a forbidden sanctuary or cutting off a sacred branch, would be sufficient grounds for a charge of impiety, and such accusations could be combined with other kinds of court procedures.[53] Hard evidence was not needed to support an allegation. Aristotle tells a story about Euripides' trial for impiety as an illustration of how to dispel slander (*diabolē*):

> when Hygiaenon accused Euripides of impiety (*asebeia*) in an
> *antidosis*, because he composed a verse instructing people to

forswear themselves, "my tongue swore it, but my mind did
not take the oath" (*Hipp.* 612), Euripides said that Hygiaenon
was being unjust because he brought trials from the contest of
Dionysus into the courtroom; it was there (in the theater) that he
had given or would give an account, if Hygiaenon wished to accuse
him. (*Rhet.* 1416a28–35 = *TrGF* 5.1, T N. 98)

An *antidosis* was a procedure in which someone could demand
payment from a man richer than himself.[54] If this Hygiaenon is
the same person who was attacked by the orator Hyperides, he
might as a young man have accused Euripides in his old age.[55]
But it is much more likely that the source of the anecdote was a
scene in a comedy in which Hygiaenon and Euripides appeared as
characters, if only because the charge of impiety is based on the
famous quotation that Aristophanes parodies several times in his
extant comedies.[56] As the ancient commentator on the line from
the *Hippolytus* states, Euripides' first accuser in his trial was not
Hygiaenon, but Aristophanes: "Aristophanes, taking a general
view, says that Euripides committed *hybris*" (schol. *Hipp.* 612, II
p. 78 Schwartz).

Perhaps there was more than one such stage trial. According
to Satyrus in his *Life of Euripides*, Euripides "was prosecuted by the
demagogue Cleon for impiety, as we have already said" (F 6 fr.
39x). Cleon was a favorite figure in comedy. Unfortunately we do
not know which trial or comedy Satyrus was referring to, because
the earlier passage in the dialogue about the trial has not survived.
Satyrus includes the story about the trial for impiety in a discussion
of Euripides' unpopularity.[57] The other supposedly historical data
in that same passage derive from the plot of Aristophanes' comedy
Thesmophoriazusae: "the women assembled against [Euripides]
at the Thesmophoria festival and gathered together in the place
where he was resting." Aristophanes' biographer reports that

Cleon prosecuted Aristophanes for usurping citizens' rights, but that "trial" was based on the plot of Aristophanes' own comedy *Babylonians* (*PCG* III.2, pp. 62–4 K-A).[58]

The question of Euripides' piety was considered a major topic for debate in Aristotle's time and after, because Socrates' trial, and Plato's concentration on it, colored later understanding of the importance of impiety in the fifth century.[59] Aristotle reports that even Aeschylus, whose traditional piety and devotion to Demeter was celebrated by Aristophanes in the *Frogs* (886–7), was tried for not having known that the Eleusinian Mysteries could not be revealed (*EN* 3.2 111a8 = T 93a Radt), a notion so patently absurd that it could only have come from a comedy.[60] According to the fourth-century BC biographer Heraclides Ponticus (fr. 170 Wehrli), when accused, Aeschylus fled to the altar of Dionysus (*TrGF* 3, T 93a,b). The presence of Dionysus in this story suggests that the trial may have taken place in the theater, as in the case of anecdote about Euripides wishing to be tried in the contest of Dionysus in the trial brought against him by Hygiaenon (*TrGF* 5.1, T N. 98). Aristotle often uses scenes from comedy as illustrations without saying so explicitly.[61] Another trial that almost certainly comes from a comedy concerns Sophocles. In an anecdote from Satyrus' *Life of Sophocles* (F 4), Sophocles was accused by his son Iophon before his phratry of having lost his mind in his old age, but the poet proved his competence with the remark, "if I'm Sophocles I'm not out of my mind and if I'm out of my mind, I'm not Sophocles," and then reading the *Oedipus* out loud (*TrGF* 4, T 1 13).[62] Even if these anecdotes did refer to real rather than to theatrical trials, it is clear that there is no contemporary evidence for their content or proceedings. Aeschylus died in 456/5 BC, but revealing the Mysteries appears to have been considered an actionable offense only after 415 BC, when Alcibiades was accused of profaning the Mysteries.[63]

If biographers could find "evidence" in Euripides' dramas that
the poet was impious, it was inevitable that someone should
suppose that he died in an even more degrading manner than his
supposed teachers Anaxagoras, Socrates, Prodicus (execution),
or Protagoras (shipwreck). One of the interlocutors in Satyrus'
dialogues (F 6 fr. 39 col. xxi) claims that old raconteurs in
Macedonia told a tale that after Euripides had come to Macedonia
to produce tragedies for King Archelaus, he had been tracked
down and eaten by the royal hunting dogs.[64] Satyrus' readers
would have understood that hand-me-down information of this
type was not necessarily historical. Plato sent the same kind of
signals to his audience about the nature of the story of the lost
kingdom of Atlantis, by having the tale narrated by the elderly
Critias, who had heard it at the age of ten from his ninety-year-old
grandfather Critias, who had heard it from Solon, who in turn
had heard it from an Egyptian priest (*Timaeus* 21a–23d). Any
reader who was familiar with the plots of Euripides' tragedies
would have seen that the inspiration for the old Macedonian story
of Euripides' death had come from Euripides' *Bacchae*. In that
drama maenads, described as "swift dogs of madness," pursue the
"godless, lawless, unjust" (*atheos anomos adikos*, 977) king Pentheus
and tear him to pieces, because he refuses to believe that Dionysus
is a god and will not allow the women of Thebes to worship him.
As time went on, new narrative details were added to the story of
the poet's death to make it seem more plausible and interesting.
In the version of the story preserved in the Suda (Epsilon 3695),
two poets who were envious of Euripides bribed the king's slave to
release on Euripides the royal dogs "which he himself had raised"
(a quotation from *Bacchae* 338, describing Actaeon, who was eaten
by his own dogs).[65] In another version of the story, the dogs were
descendants of a dog who had been killed and eaten by villagers
with whom Euripides was friendly (*TrGF* 5.1 T 1, II).[66]

If Euripides had actually been torn to pieces by dogs
Aristophanes would certainly have said something about it in the
Frogs, which was produced after Euripides' death.[67] Satyrus has
at least one of his interlocutors express doubts that Euripides
was an atheist, citing a passage from a lost drama that expresses
traditional religious views: "Who seeing this would not think
that the gods exist, and throw aside the crooked deceptions
of speculators about things in the air" (*meteōrologoi; TrGF* 5.2, F
913).[68] But Euripides' biographers and their epitomizers reported
these and other stories about Euripides' impiety as if they were
credible and even factual. They chose to represent Euripides as
more sophistic and impious than other tragedians, such as his
contemporary Sophocles, because they were compelled to rely
on comedy as their primary source of biographical information.
Apparently the same kinds of jokes were not made with such
frequency about Sophocles, perhaps because the characters in
Sophocles' dramas were less inclined to voice opinions about
religion, or employ the kind of terminology that the sophists used.
How and exactly when the jokes began to be taken seriously is
impossible to determine, but eventually even the most outlandish
jokes and scenes were repurposed as biographical data. The
Euripides Vita reports in all seriousness that "women planned to
kill [Euripides] in his cave, where he spent his time writing," and
that "women wanted to destroy him" (*TrGF* 5.1, T 1. III, 2; IV.2).
That story (of course) derives from the plot of Aristophanes'
comedy *Women at the Thesmophoria*.[69]

The principal sources for information about Euripides' links
with Socrates and other sophists come from Athenian comedy.
Comedy is the most likely source of stories about his trials
for impiety, and the story about his death is based on his own
tragedy, the *Bacchae*. Biographers searched through Euripides'
works for verses that seemed to provide corroboration for

these stories. A biographer like Satyrus clearly included some of his conjectures about the poet's life and work in order to amuse his audiences. But later writers appear to have taken the same conjectures seriously and reported them as if they were historical fact. Unfortunately this largely fictional material has had a lasting influence on how Euripides' dramas have been interpreted and received, up to the present day. But if we are prepared to take the idea of a sophistic and impious Euripides seriously, then to be consistent we ought to believe that Aristophanes' *Clouds* presents a more accurate portrait of Socrates than Plato's *Apology*.

In the next chapter I would like to show why the biographers' characterization of Euripides, however distorted and exaggerated, continued to be persuasive and congenial, first to students in ancient rhetorical schools, then to classrooms in Byzantium, and also to modern audiences. Over time, however, the voicing of skepticism and impious thoughts for which Euripides was condemned by the ancients, and which had made him subject to hypothetical trials, came to be regarded as virtues. Jewish and Christian readers in particular were able to regard Euripides as a poet who shared their own negative attitude towards traditional Greek religion, and came to suppose that he was as deeply troubled by it as they were themselves.

2

PIETY AND IMPIETY IN EURIPIDES' *HERACLES*

As we have seen in the preceding chapter, biographers portrayed Euripides as impious and atheistic, as a protégé of Socrates and other sophists. In this chapter I want to show how these interpretations of Euripides' intentions distort our understanding of divine action in his dramas. I have chosen to begin with the *Heracles* because of all Euripides' plays it shows the behavior of the gods in the most negative light. Two gods, Iris and Lyssa, appear *ex machina* in the middle of the play, just after Heracles has rescued his family from being executed by a brutal tyrant. Zeus had forbidden Hera and Iris to harm him while he was completing his labors (827–9). But now, following Hera's orders, Iris directs Lyssa to drive Heracles insane, so that he kills his wife and children. He would have also have killed his mother's husband Amphitryon, had not Athena intervened to stop him. Why did Hera insist on punishing Heracles even though he personally had done her no harm? Why didn't Zeus stop Hera from sending Iris and Lyssa to attack his son Heracles? Why did Athena wait to intervene? Neither his father Zeus nor any other god appears at the end of the drama to explain what has happened and to predict that Heracles eventually will be deified. There is, I believe, an answer to our questions about the Greek gods' inaction and lack of compassion, a terrifying answer: that is how the gods can and do behave towards humans. Mortals cannot expect to receive redemption, salvation, or even assistance from the gods, even when they deserve to receive it.

Zeus is the most powerful god, but since he cannot be everywhere at once, the other gods can act independently of him and of each other. Zeus and his daughter Athena are on Heracles' side, but his wife Hera hates Heracles, because Zeus chose Alcmena (and not Hera) to be Heracles' mother; Homer describes in the *Iliad* how jealous Hera was of Alcmena and Heracles (*Il.* 19.95–133). Lyssa explains that in accordance with "necessity" (*to chrē*) Zeus protected Heracles until he completed his labors (*HF* 827–9). But now that he has completed them, Zeus does nothing to stop Hera (and Iris) from persecuting him. The audience would have realized that something terrible was about to happen when Iris brought along with her the goddess Lyssa (whose name means "wolf-disease," or rabies). Iris says that she has brought Lyssa to make Heracles in a fit of insanity kill his wife and children: "Hera wishes him to shed kindred blood by killing his children, and I wish that as well" (831–2). She wants him "to know what Hera's wrath is like, and to learn what my wrath is like as well: the gods will be nowhere, and mortals will be great, if he is not punished" (840–2).[1] Hera wants to punish Heracles because he has been able to achieve too much. Lyssa objects that Heracles does not deserve to be punished for all the good that he has done for humankind. But Iris tells Lyssa that Hera and she did not care what she thought: "Zeus' wife did not send you here to advise moderation" (*sōphronein*, 857). Lyssa must obey, because she belongs to an older generation of gods who are now subservient to Zeus. Lyssa makes Heracles believe that he is attacking the palace of his archenemy Eurystheus in Argos, and killing his family. But since he is in Thebes, and not in Argos, the family that he kills in his delusion is in fact his own wife and children.[2]

The audience hears the story of the slaughter of Heracles' wife and children from a messenger, who describes in detail how he hunted down two of his sons and then killed his wife and a third son with a single arrow. He then galloped off to kill his father, but

Figure 2.1 Heracles with the goddess Mania (Insanity) looking on from the upper left, prepares to throw one of his children into the fire Paestan calyx-crater ca. 350 BC. Madrid Museo. Credit: Album/Art Resource, NY.

"an image arrived—Pallas [Athena], as it appeared to our view, brandishing her spear; she threw a rock at Heracles' chest, which stopped him from his insane slaughter and sent him into a sleep" (1001–6). Amphitryon and the slaves tied him to a broken pillar. When Heracles wakes up and learns from Amphitryon what he has done, he wants to kill himself. Heracles' friend Theseus, the king of Athens, arrives just in time to try to persuade him to remain alive. Heracles is angry at the gods, and even though Theseus doubts that the gods will pay attention to his threats, Heracles says "the gods can do what they want, and I am doing that to them" by exercising his free will (1243–4). He then tries to explain to Theseus why his life is not worth living. First he wonders if he was not destined to suffer because his father Amphitryon had killed his mother's father; then he says the lines that might have seemed impious to later critics: "Zeus, whoever Zeus is, begot me to be hated by Hera—do not be angry at me, old man, since I think of you as my father rather than Zeus" (1263–5). He also complains about the behavior of Zeus' consort Hera, who was jealous of Heracles' mother Alcmena: "who could offer prayers to such a goddess? Because she was jealous of Zeus' love for a woman, she destroyed the benefactor of Greece [i.e., Heracles himself], who was in no way guilty of any wrongdoing" (1307–10). These lines would not necessarily have been considered impious by Euripides' audience, because they were simply a statement of mythological fact.

Theseus agrees that Hera was the divinity responsible for his ordeal (1311–2). But then Theseus makes another argument on the basis of traditional myth: Heracles ought not to commit suicide because the gods also commit crimes, but nonetheless continue their existence despite their mistakes; if gods do not complain of their misfortunes, neither should mortals. But Heracles denies that the gods can commit crimes: "I do not believe that the gods seek out illicit unions and bind each other in chains; I do not suppose and will not believe that one god is master of another. For a god, if he is truly a god, needs nothing. These [stories] are the miserable tales of poets" (1341–4). Here Heracles seems to be paraphrasing what the philosopher Xenophanes of Colophon had said years before, that Homer and Hesiod ought not to have attributed such immorality to the gods (21 B 11 D-K).[3] In the fifth and early fourth century BC some of the ideas Euripides puts into Heracles' mouth would have seemed radical and contrary to the tenets of traditional religion. We know that because in Plato's dialogue *Euthyphro* Socrates says that he believes that he is being brought to trial because he finds the traditional ideas about the gods' immorality to be unbearable (5d–6a). Socrates was tried for impiety (and convicted) even though he was not the first thinker who refused to believe that the gods were capable of immoral behavior. It was also controversial to assert, as Heracles continues to do in his speech to Theseus: "for a god, if he is truly a god, needs nothing." The idea of "reciprocity," that if you give a god something valuable, you will get something good from him or her in return, forms the basis for the custom of sacrifice.[4] So in the *Euthyphro*, Socrates was asking for trouble when he insisted that the gods cannot get any advantage from offerings made to them by mortals (14e–15a).[5] That idea had been voiced before the Persian wars by Xenophanes, who stated that "none of the gods needs anything at all" (21A25–6 D-K), and Euripides' contemporary Antiphon the Sophist (87 B 10 D-K) said something similar.[6] Sacrifice was such an integral feature of traditional religion that Socrates' defenders Xenophon and Plato insist that in practice Socrates did not fail to offer sacrifices to the gods, as most memorably, in his last request to Crito, to sacrifice a cock to Asclepius (*Phaedo* 118a).

How would the original audience of the *Heracles* have reacted
to Heracles' statement that the gods could not be immoral
and needed nothing? We have no direct evidence, but I think it
is reasonable to suppose that initially at least they would have
been surprised and even confused, like Menelaus in the *Trojan
Women*, when he hears Hecuba address Zeus as "Conveyance of
the Earth" (884), and exclaims: "What is this? You've invented
new prayers to the gods!"(889).[7] Heracles' statement would have
appeared strange if only because he himself was the offspring of
the kind of "illicit union" that he had just said the gods did not
seek out! But soon the audience would have heard that despite
complaints about the poets' "wretched tales" about the gods,
Heracles once again starts talking about how Hera was able
to destroy him and his family and himself "with a single blow"
(1393).[8] In retrospect, the audience would have realized that
Heracles had not suddenly turned into a philosopher proclaiming
a new theology. Rather in his guilt and grief he is trying to deny
an obvious reality.

Poets have their characters express doubts about the gods in
moments of despair and isolation, when the gods appear to have
deserted them. When made in context, the doubts expressed
by the characters are understandable, and elicit the audience's
sympathy. As Robert Parker has written, "the gnawing religious
doubt in Greece, for practical people at least, was much less
likely to be 'do the gods exist?' than 'can one get through to the
gods?' or 'do they care about human beings?' "[9] There is no reason
to suppose that anyone in the original audience would have been
persuaded by Heracles' outburst to abandon traditional religious
beliefs or practices. In later times it was not Heracles' speech but
Athena's action that was remembered in Heracles' hometown of
Thebes. In the late first century AD, the Greek traveler Pausanias
(9.11.2) saw on display at the tomb of his children in Thebes the

"Chastener stone" (*lithos sōphronistēr*) that the goddess was said to have thrown at the great hero.[10]

Even though Heracles for a brief moment sounds as if he had studied with Socrates, no one in the fifth century BC would have accused Euripides of impiety for writing the *Heracles*, except in the context of a comedy.[11] If anyone had done so, Euripides could have been able to defend himself against his accusers by quoting by quoting passages from the *Heracles* that celebrate the actions of the gods (735–9, 772–80, 811–4), which would have made him sound as moral and traditional as Aeschylus in Aristophanes' *Frogs*.[12] Although he made Heracles say "Zeus, whoever Zeus is" (1263), Aeschylus in the *Agamemnon* had the old men who form the chorus state that they do not know how best to address Zeus: "Zeus, whoever he is, if it is pleasing for him to be called by that name, I shall call him that. I have nothing to compare him to, when I consider everything, except Zeus, if I must in truth cast off the vain burden of thought from my heart (*phrenes*; 161–7)."[13] Euripides could then have pointed out that in those lines Aeschylus appeared to be restating what he had learned from his "teacher," Heraclitus of Ephesus, who had written: "the one wise entity wants and does not want the name of Zeus" (22B32D-K).[14] He then could have added that Zeus is the most difficult for mortals to know of all the gods, because he does not intervene directly in human life, except to beget children, and even then he appears in many different disguises (for example, as a bull or swan), since any mortal who saw Zeus as he appears to other gods would not be able to endure the sight.[15] In any case it was his character Hecuba rather than he himself who had uttered the "new-fangled" prayer to Zeus in the *Trojan Women*. Under the circumstances it was only natural that Hecuba and Heracles would not be able to understand what Zeus had intended and what his motives may have been. A dramatist must be able to think in the ways that he imagines that his characters might think, and have them say what he presumes that they might say in desperate circumstances. Even though Aristophanes had written about Euripides that "he is like what he makes his characters say" (fr. 694 K-A, *PCG* III.2, p. 356), Euripides himself did not choose to be identified with any of them![16] He was not a comic poet, who could speak in his own persona in the *parabasis* of one of his productions.

Despite everything Euripides was accused of by Aristophanes in his comedies, he was never tried for impiety in a real court of law, and however and wherever he actually died, he wasn't subjected to a trial in Athens, or convicted of impiety, or forced (like Socrates) to drink the hemlock. Nonetheless, we do know that half a millennium later, in the third century AD, a list of rhetorical exercises on a papyrus includes the topic: "Euripides is being tried for impiety for having staged the *Heracles Mad* at the Dionysia" (*POxy* 2400 = *TrGF* 5.1, T 100).[17] The other exercises in the papyrus list required students to debate moral issues raised by historical actions: should the Athenian politician Cleon be accused of demagoguery for putting the men of Mytilene to death? Should Alexander the Great give the Athenians confiscated Theban land to cultivate? Presumably the *Heracles* was chosen as a justification for putting Euripides on trial, rather than some other play, because by the third century AD the notion that Euripides was impious and even atheistic was well established. Not only was Euripides said to have been killed by dogs (a death appropriate for the atheists); anecdotes based on shocking lines had been mined from his dramas, and stories that associated him with Socrates and other sophists, stories that are faithfully alluded to in the ancient commentaries (scholia) to his dramas and recorded as if historical by biographers like Diogenes Laertius.

Since Euripides was thought to be impious, the third-century AD rhetorical exercise could have focused on the complaints uttered in the *Heracles* about Zeus by Heracles' stepfather Amphitryon and Heracles himself, particularly the lines in which Amphitryon blames Zeus for abandoning Heracles' family, and states that he is superior to Zeus in virtue because he did not abandon Heracles' children: "You do not understand how to save your friends. You are either a stupid god or an unjust one" (339–47). And then there are the lines in which Heracles seems to have doubts about Zeus: "Zeus, whoever Zeus is, begot me to be hated by Hera—do not be angry at me, old man, since I think of you as my father rather than Zeus" (1263–5). No ancient commentary on the *Heracles* has survived. But we can get a sense of the kind of objections that might have been raised in the early centuries AD from an anecdote related by Plutarch. Writing in the late first/early second century AD, Plutarch says that Euripides was the subject of a disturbance (*ethorubēthē*) for having written at the beginning of his drama *Melanippe the Wise* (*TrGF* 5.1, F 480): "Zeus, whoever Zeus is—for I don't know this except from tradition." Plutarch says that Euripides was awarded another chorus and produced a new version of the play in which he replaced the offensive line with the anodyne "Zeus, as it is said in truth" (*TrGF* 5.1, F 481.1). Plutarch relates the anecdote as a means of answering the following question: "what is the advantage of doubting or being uncertain about our belief in Zeus or Athena or Erōs?" (*Mor.* 756b–c). Plutarch's answer is that one ought not to express such doubts. It is of course unlikely that Plutarch's anecdote about the revised first line of *Melanippe the Wise* was historical. Dramas open with statements, not with questions, and in any case the inoffensive replacement line was not newly composed but extracted from another poet's drama, Critias' *Perithous* (*TrGF* 1, 43 F 1.9).[18] Probably the story was based on a scene in a comedy, because that is where the practice of juxtaposing a line from one play with a line from another began.[19]

If in a third-century AD classroom what a character says in a drama could be thought to represent what the poet who wrote them believed, a charge of impiety could have been made against Euripides for being impious, since he allowed Heracles to say "Zeus, whoever Zeus is . . ." (1263). I think it likely that the students who took part in the exercise would have found Euripides guilty, though not because he has Heracles claim that the gods behave according to the conventional standards of mortal morality. Rather, the third-century AD students would have been more concerned about his supposed lack of faith. At a time when traditional beliefs were being threatened by newer, foreign cults, the students of rhetoric might have argued that in letting Heracles speak a line that seemed to suggest that Zeus did not exist, the poet was advocating disbelief in the existence of the traditional gods. The students might also have argued that the gods were punishing Heracles and Amphitryon for their blasphemy.[20] But unlike God in the Old Testament, the Greek gods seemed to allow people to wonder whether or not they (the gods) cared about them. Since Zeus' generation of gods didn't create humankind, most of the time they probably weren't even listening when such complaints were voiced.

The process of singling out statements in dramas that appeared to be critical of Greek religion had begun in the Hellenistic era, with Jewish writers who sought to show that Greek poets had stolen their ideas from Jewish religious writings. These writers looked through the dramas to find passages in which the poet spoke about an unspecified *theos* or *theoi* in general, and discussed them without reference to their original contexts.[21] Following in their tradition, Clement of Alexandria (a convert from paganism) attributed the following lines to Euripides (*Protrepticus*

6.68.3–4): "how should one think of God (*theos*), who sees
everything and yet is not seen himself" (*TrGF* 2, F 622). Euripides
or whoever wrote these lines was almost certainly thinking of
Zeus, or Zeus as the invisible upper air (*aithēr*).[22] Not only did
they try to equate Zeus with their supreme deity, Jewish writers
added lines from other works, or composed new lines to make the
original polytheistic texts appear to support their own system of
beliefs. For example, someone took some lines from Euripides'
Phrixus about the justice of Zeus (e.g., *TrGF* 5.2, F 835), and tacked
onto them some lines from the comic poet Diphilus along with
a couple of new trimeter lines: "God, Lord of all, whose name
is fearful and whom I should not name" (Clem. Alex., *Strom.*
5.14.121). This last statement could only have been made by a
Jewish writer; worshipers of the traditional Greek gods were
not afraid to refer to them by their names! In the early centuries
AD writers continued to search for passages in Greek drama that
were compatible with Christian views about the nature of divinity.
One such anthology was dedicated to the Empress Eudocia
(ca. 401–60) by a certain Orion from Egyptian Thebes (Suda,
Omega 188). Almost all of Orion's quotations from tragedy come
from Euripides, including two quotations that Euripides might
have used in self-defense during his "trial" for impiety (one is
Hippolytus' traditionally pious speech to Artemis; *Hipp.* 73–87).[23]

The same qualities that made Euripides seem impious in a
polytheistic world made him acceptable to monotheists. Euripides
was valued by Christians for the same reasons that certain pagans
distrusted him. They approved of his supposed collegiality with
Socrates and other thinkers who questioned traditional religion,
as well as of his vivid portrayal of the cruelty of the gods, not
to mention the various passages where characters in his dramas
question the nature and existence of the traditional deities. In the
Heracles (and, of course, many other dramas) Euripides depicted

a world in which gods treat human beings cruelly and unfairly.
In the *Heracles* Zeus, the king of the gods, is portrayed as a father
who neglects his mortal children and does nothing to prevent their
suffering. To us, even more than to the ancients, any complaints
that Euripides' characters might utter about the behavior of the
gods have a particular resonance, if only because they seem to
suggest that the great dramatists were capable of asking the kinds
of questions that ordinary people did not dare to ask about the
gods, or at least did not seem to ask (since in fact we do not really
know what ordinary people thought about anything). In the case
of the *Heracles* modern critics have paid particular attention to the
lines (discussed above) in which Heracles asks who Zeus is and
denies that the gods could "seek out illicit unions and bind each
other in chains" (1341–2). Scholars have drawn on these lines
repeatedly to argue that Euripides in his dramas was espousing a
sustained and devastating criticism of the actions of the traditional
gods, and treat the poet as if he were, at least covertly, a religious
reformer.

The Victorians placed a high value on rational thinking, which
they believed was characteristic of their own age, and other high
cultures, such as that of fifth- and fourth-century BC Athens. They
believed that certain superior minds, such as those of Sophocles
and Euripides, and the philosophers, must have questioned the
values and practices of traditional Greek religion, even if they were
unable completely to dissociate themselves from the myths that
they learned in their childhood.[24] In 1905 A. W. Verrall argued that
in the *Heracles* Euripides could not have intended that the more
intelligent members of his audience should understand the action
of the drama literally.[25] To Verrall Heracles' lines are not simply
a rejection of a particular argument; they are a comprehensive
condemnation of all mythology and (in Verrall's words) "a
profession of faith" and "the word for which we have

waited"; "the speaker [Heracles] rejects absolutely, and once for all, such man-like superhuman beings, such deities with the passion of men, as the common legend of Heracles, with its battles of giants and invasions of Hades, requires us to assume as part of the world and of possible human experience."[26] Verrall imagined that Heracles did not do (and may not even believe that he did) any of the deeds that he was commonly believed to have done: "the legend of Heracles, as commonly told, is not to be supposed as part of the story, but replaced by some totally different conception of Heracles, and of his mental and physical history."[27] As first presented in the drama, Heracles is suffering from delusions of grandeur, hallucinating about deeds that no one onstage has actually witnessed. Heracles already shows signs of being out of control in his plans to get revenge against Lycus and all the Thebans who failed to be grateful for his previous good deeds.[28] The fit of madness in which he kills his wife and children is the result of "a burst of cruel fury."[29] The appearance *ex machina* of Iris and Lyssa is an illusion, and like other supernatural figures in Euripides the goddesses are "so placed in the drama that they can, as the dramatist intends, be dropped off."[30] The old men in the chorus only *suppose* that they have seen them.

In his discussion of the drama Verrall did not provide any explicit reasons why he chose to characterize Heracles' statements in this way. He was expressing a point of view that both he and his readers would have found credible and acceptable, if only because they in their own lives believed that the Greek gods (like the Judeo-Christian God) ought to be just and themselves adhere to the standards of morality that they set for humans. As Hugh Lloyd-Jones observed, "Greek religion was the part of Greek culture which the Victorians found hardest to understand. Polytheism and the attribution of human passions to the gods embarrassed them. . . ."[31] Verrall dealt with the problem of Greek religion by denying that intelligent Greeks could have believed in it: "whatever is said by a divinity is to be regarded as *ipso facto* discredited."[32] This approach had the advantage of making the ancient Athenians seem to share the same religious values and preoccupations as Verrall and his readers. Miracles, epiphanies of gods (on- or offstage) were irrational delusions experienced by the characters in the drama, which the intelligent observer would recognize as such. Verrall encouraged his readers to regard references to traditional divinities *ironically*. He claims that there is "a final touch of irony" in the last lines of Heracles' speech to Theseus, when he asks the Thebans to mourn for him and his dead family because "we were all destroyed miserably, struck by a single blow from Hera" (*HF* 1392–3). This irony "warns us that the fierce feelings, and even the insane beliefs which fill the preceding speech [about Heracles' birth and his labors] may possibly still be revived."[33] The presence of irony (Verrall believes) is a "natural touch, given without the least emphasis, and left, as in real life, to be marked or neglected as the observer shall please," which "is vividly characteristic of Euripides."[34]

By insisting that no reference to the gods should be taken at its face value, Verrall made it possible for his readers to make Euripides (or Heracles) mean whatever they want him to have said. As Eduard Fraenkel observed, one of the most effective tools at the modern interpreter's disposal is "the magic wand of irony, by which the commentator converts the sense of a sentence into the exact opposite of what, to the ordinary man, it seems to say."[35] But why should we suppose that Heracles is being ironic when he says that he and his family were all destroyed "by a single blow from Hera" (1392–3), when that is in fact what happened in the course of the drama? Heracles never sought to deny that Hera has been persecuting him. If in his speech to Theseus Heracles claims that the gods do not commit crimes (1340–4), there is no reason to imagine that it is a "profession of faith" on his part or on that of the poet. Rather, Heracles' denial that the gods commit crimes is the proper response that a mortal ought to make when someone tells tries to compare his or her behavior to the conduct of a god or gods.[36] Mortals cannot play by divine rules because they are not deathless, powerful, and ageless. When in the *Hippolytus* the Nurse tries to persuade Phaedra that she can use the gods' immoral behavior as a justification for her own desire to commit adultery (451–9), Phaedra objects that the Nurse's arguments are "too attractive," and that instead of recommending what might give her (Phaedra) pleasure, the Nurse should think of what might enhance her reputation, that is, by persuading her not to do it (*Hipp*. 486–9). Heracles does not tell Theseus directly that his argument is specious, because Theseus is his friend and benefactor; instead he blames the poets for inventing stories that attribute immorality to the gods.

Fraenkel thought that not many people in his day were "willing to believe" in irony. But in practice, then and now, many commentators and translators have persuaded themselves that it is present, especially in cases where they need to account for what they perceive to be cruelty or injustice on the part of the gods. Verrall's ingenious and tendentious methods of exegesis have had a wide influence among Anglophones, not only because they appeal to adherents of monotheistic religions, but also because they allow an interpretative freedom that traditional philology is unable to provide.[37] In effect, Verrall enabled scholars to bring what they supposed to be the wisdom of the superior understanding of their enlightened age to bear upon the ancient text. Certainly Verrall's approach helps to make ancient drama more accessible and familiar to his readers. But unfortunately it does so (as we have seen) at the cost of investing Euripides' words with meanings that he could never have intended. A particularly interesting

example of such rationalistic reconstruction occurs at the end of
Heracles' speech to Theseus, when he asks Theseus to help him
take "the miserable dog back to Argos, so that in my loneliness
I won't suffer some harm because of my grief for my children"
(1386–8). Euripides' audience would have naturally supposed that
in these lines Heracles was talking about Cerberus, the vicious
three-headed immortal dog that guarded the gate to the lower
world and prevented dead souls from returning to the world of
the living. Fetching Cerberus from the lower world was the last
labor that Eurystheus, the king of Argos, had imposed on Heracles,
presumably because Eurystheus hoped that Heracles would never
be able to carry out that mission. When contrary to the chorus'
expectations (428–9) Heracles suddenly arrives in Thebes just in
time to prevent his wife and children from being executed, he
explains that has just come back from the lower world, where he
had fought against and captured the three-headed dog, and left it
under guard in the grove of Persephone at Hermione, a city in the
Peloponnesus south of Theseus' ancestral home of Troezen (615).[38]
The reason why at the end of the drama Heracles asks Theseus
to help him bring Cerberus to Eurystheus in Argos, is because
in his weakened state he might not be able to control the dog
single-handedly.[39]

Verrall in his discussion of this same passage offered a
completely different interpretation, one that would fit in with his
theory that Euripides was seeking to reject traditional mythology.
He argued that Heracles was not talking about the monstrous
Cerberus, but about an ordinary dog that he had found on the
road and wished to have as a companion in his loneliness.[40]
Such sympathy for animals, Verrall suggested, was particularly
Euripidean, and he cited examples of characters in other dramas
who express concern for animals. None of those animals, however,
was a dog. The ancient Greeks used dogs to hunt with, or to guard

the house, but not as companions. There is very little evidence that they shared our contemporary concern for stray animals. In referring to Cerberus simply as "the dog" in this passage and earlier in the drama, Heracles was following the traditional practice of not mentioning his name, because any direct reference to the gods of the underworld was unlucky.[41]

Verrall's approach clearly appealed to the German scholar Wilhelm Nestle.[42] In his book on "Euripides, the poet of the Greek Enlightenment," Nestle took Heracles' refusal to believe that the gods were immoral as a rejection of traditional religion: "to Euripides Athena and Lyssa are nothing more than mythical decoration."[43] Euripides' revisions of the myth of Heracles, according to Nestle, "served the purpose of directing his audience away from traditional polytheistic belief to a correct and pure knowledge of divinity, the world, and humanity."[44] He regarded Hecuba's unconventional prayer to Zeus in the *Trojan Women* as "fundamental to Euripides' theology."[45] Nestle believed that Euripides had characterized Heracles' madness as an epileptic fit, and in support of his argument cited the rationalistic etiology for that disease in the Hippocratic treatise *On the Sacred Disease*, whose author claims that epilepsy is caused not by divine intervention, but by physical forces.[46] In fact, it is much more likely that ancient audiences would have understood Heracles' glinting eyes, foaming mouth, aggressiveness, and delusions (*HF* 868–89, 932–4) as symptoms of rabies (*lyssa*) in both dogs and humans.[47] By including references to ancient scientific and philosophical texts throughout his discussion of Euripides' dramas, Nestle conveys the impression that Euripides was participating in a contemporary intellectual renaissance, even though most of our information about ancient Greek rationalism comes from the fourth century or even later.

In his 1920 book *Greek Tragedy*, Gilbert Norwood argued that Aeschylean certainty had by the last quarter of the fifth century

been undermined by an endemic cynicism, which he considered
to be analogous to the way in which his own generation had
rejected Victorian certainties. Norwood had read Nestle's
book on Euripides, and believed that his readers could better
appreciate "the poet of 'the Greek enlightenment'—or rather
of the Athenian disillusionment—better than most generations
of [Euripides'] readers."[48] Norwood not only accepted most of
Verrall's arguments but took them even further, applying the
appropriate psychological terminology. He thought that Heracles
throughout the drama had been experiencing hallucinations and
in reality accomplished none of the labors that he is credited with.
Heracles only imagines that he went to Hades to get Cerberus
(1276–8), because Theseus only speaks about coming "from the
corpses" (1222), a phrase that could easily apply any subterranean
location, as, for example, a cave.[49] The appearance of Iris and
Lyssa was a dream seen and reported by a member of the chorus.
When Heracles becomes rational, Norwood represents him
as a monotheist. In Greek Heracles says "the god (*ho theos*), if
he is truly a god, needs nothing" (1345–6) without specifying
whether or not he means Zeus or another god.[50] Norwood
translates: "God, if in truth he be God, needs naught," and adds
that this "sober and reasonable speech" repudiates traditional
mythology and shows that "Heracles believes in one God utterly
above human weaknesses."[51] But despite the capital G, Heracles is
not talking about the God of the Old Testament. Heracles' very
existence confirms that Zeus commits adultery; Norwood might
more persuasively have argued that it is Heracles' statement about
divine morality that is delusional, rather than the theophany and
the account of Heracles' visit to the Lower World.[52]

The convention of translating "the god" (*ho theos*) as "God" was
intended to convey to nonspecialist readers the need to recognize
the power and importance of the ancient Greeks' chief divinity.

But the practice was also misleading because it suggested that
Zeus and the Judeo-Christian God could somehow be equated,
and that Zeus shared with God an abiding concern with the
fate of human beings and involvement in their lives. Once we
can assume that Zeus shared some of God's more positive and
humane qualities, then it followed that Euripides could not have
meant "to present the scene between Iris and Lyssa as what in any
sense could be taken as true or possible," as L. H. G. Greenwood
wrote in 1953. Greenwood approved of Athena's intervention
to save Amphitryon as "the one beneficent deed performed by a
divine being." But he wondered why she did not stop Heracles
from killing his wife and children, and suggested that by calling
attention here and in other dramas to the gods' deficiencies,
Euripides was openly satirizing them.[53] Yet if Greenwood and
Norwood and Verrall before him had questioned their own
assumptions about the nature of religion, they might have been
able to see that the reason why they believed that Euripides was
criticizing Greek religion was that they themselves simply could
not accept the possibility that most fifth-century Athenians still
believed the existence of multiple divinities, especially in gods
who (unlike the Christian God) could be both good and evil, who
worked at cross-purposes with one another, and who were not
particularly concerned with seeing that justice was done in the
course of a human lifetime or on a human timetable. Verrall's and
Norwood's interpretations of Greek drama tell us much more
about themselves and Victorian notions of divinity than they do
about what Euripides was trying to portray in his dramas.

Nonetheless, the idea that in the *Heracles* Euripides was
advocating religious reform continues to have advocates. The most
influential of these was Philip Vellacott, who in his 1975 book
Ironic Drama argued that Heracles' insistent belief on "the moral
nature of gods" was an illustration of "the way in which Euripides

encourages his listeners to reject old, incomprehensible notions of divine 'justice' (which include, of course the whole 'logic' of human sacrifice) and to look instead to their own moral sense, however fallible it may be."[54] Like Verrall and Norwood, Vellacott wished to represent the poet as being ahead of his times, with religious sensibilities like those of a modern educated person. But Vellacott explicitly said that he did not believe that most members of Euripides' audience would have understood his sophisticated teachings, and he did not suggest that Euripides was trying to encourage his audience not to believe in the traditional gods. Rather, he thought that the poet wished only to encourage at least some members of his audience to think about alternatives to the traditional religion, and that he would have welcomed "the critical temper" of modern religious thought.

Following in the footsteps of Norwood and his predecessors Nestle and Verrall, more recent critics appear to have assumed that Euripides was more uncomfortable with traditional religious beliefs than either Aeschylus or Sophocles, both because of his supposed connections with the radical philosophers of his day, and because in his dramas he depicts the cruelty of the gods so vividly—the actions of Iris and Lyssa in the *Heracles* are a prime example. At the same time, and for similar reasons, modern critics have singled out passages in Aeschylus that refer to the preeminence of Zeus, and have supposed that he was advocating a kind of monotheism. In a handbook that in the nineteen fifties and sixties enjoyed a wide readership, H. J. Rose observed that "Zeus is particularly prominent in the works of Aeschylus, the greatest theologian of all Greek poets." Rose referred to Aeschylus as a theologian because he held "advanced" religious views (where "advanced" must mean closer to a monotheistic conception of divinity): "Zeus is a dignified figure, always vastly superior to the other gods, and passing without great effort into the God

of a monotheistic, or practically monotheistic philosophy."[55] In
1970 G. M. A. Grube observed that Aeschylus' "emphasis on
the supremacy of Zeus seems to show Aeschylus feeling his way
towards a kind of monotheism."[56] I would agree, but only if we
understand "monotheism" as an attempt to describe the special
emphasis accorded to Zeus by many early Greek writers, because
he is the god who has power over all the other gods, as well as
mortals.[57]

Even in relatively recent times, when we have become at least
nominally more ready to try to accommodate religious traditions
different from our own, critics have been prepared to grant
disproportionate importance to dramatic passages that appear to
express a reformist point of view, particularly lines that appear
to reject the traditional gods in favor of more humanitarian and
moral entities. In her 1985 book *Ritual Irony* Helene Foley saw
Heracles' statement about the gods as evidence of a movement
away from the old anthropomorphic deities towards a religion
that placed greater emphasis on heroes like Heracles who
could mediate between gods and mortals through their cults in
particular communities.[58] Foley claimed that "through the city's
experience of Heracles' imagination, courage, and suffering,
we see that Athens will receive the advantage of the hero's
divine energies in a form more human and predictable than that
embodied in the forces variously called Zeus, Hera, or *tuchē*."[59]
This description of Heracles sounds more like Jesus than the
brutal and determined Heracles of traditional myth. Certainly
Theseus promises Heracles that he will have a hero cult in Athens,
where he will be worshiped after his death. But nothing in the
drama suggests that this cult should or would take precedence
over existing cults of the gods, or that the poet or the characters
in the drama regard Zeus or Hera as "forces" rather than as
anthropomorphic deities. The gods who appear onstage are not

unlike Homer's gods, each of whom has a distinct character and human appearance. In the *Heracles* Euripides has the self-important Iris say "[Heracles'] father Zeus kept me and Hera from doing him harm until he completed Eurystheus' labors; now Hera wants him to shed kindred blood by killing his children and I want that too" (828–32). When Heracles says that he has been struck by *Hēras tychē* (1393) he is not talking about an abstraction, but a specific event, a "blow" of misfortune sent by a god.[60]

In her 1987 book on Euripides, Ann Michelini understood that the action of the drama confirms that Heracles' denial that the gods can be immoral has no validity, at least in what she calls "the play's mimesis of reality." But at the same time she believed that Heracles' statement that traditional myths are "the miserable tales of poets" forces the audience to "consider that the *Herakles* itself, the play we are watching, is also a mere fiction, told by a poet who is lying . . . The mention of lying poets projects outside the frame of the drama, as a self-referential suggestion that our interpretation of the play should not confine itself within the boundary of the fictional 'reality.'"[61] But why should we suppose that an ancient audience would attach greater significance to these lines than to what Theseus said about the gods or any other attempt by mortals to try to comprehend divine behavior? Similarly, in 1988 Harvey Yunis also placed a disproportionate emphasis on Heracles' statement, and went so far as to suggest that Heracles was in fact proposing a "new creed": "[Heracles] "recognizes how perversely the gods repaid his piety, and then renounces the forms and significance of the relationship between himself and the immoral gods."[62] It is certainly troubling that a pious person like Heracles is treated so cruelly by certain divinities. But no one in Euripides' audience would have expected that the gods would place a high value on what Heracles had done for the benefit of humankind, since they subscribed to the traditional belief that what gods seek from humans is not better conditions for humanity, but honor for themselves.

In her 2003 book about Euripides in the context of contemporary intellectual trends, Franziska Egli stated that Heracles' statement about the gods is "an attempt to put the world and contemporary belief of the late fifth century on the stage to contrast with its mythic context."[63] Edith Hall made a similar argument in her 2010 book about Greek tragedy: "Although on one level a religious drama providing a mythical explanation for a traditional hero's place in Athenian cult, *Heracles* radically calls traditional religion into question and replaces it with more human-centered ethics."[64] She sees in Heracles' refusal to believe that gods can commit crimes, and in the commendable compassion shown to Heracles by Amphitryon and Theseus of the drama, the influence of Protagoras. Hall points out that according to Diogenes Laertius Protagoras first read out his book *About the Gods* in Euripides' house (9.54), and she sees the influence of Protagoras in the remarks Euripides puts in Heracles' mouth, by claiming that his book about the gods began with the statement: "Man is the measure of all things" (80 A 1 D-K = Diog. Laert. 9.51). But this emphasis on Protagoras' influence seems to me to be misleading. First of all, Diogenes notes that other sources put Protagoras' reading of his book about the gods in different locations (*TrGF* 5.1, T 40). Another problem is that Diogenes says that the statement "man is the measure of all things" came at the beginning of another book, elsewhere called *Antilogioi* or *Antilogikoi*, in which Protagoras stated that there were two sides to every question; presumably the other side of the statement that man is the measure of all things would have said that everything was determined by the gods. The opening of Protagoras' book *About the Gods* was "I do not have the ability to know about the gods, whether they exist or they do not exist or what they look

like" (80 A 4 D-K = Diog. Laert. 9.51), but that statement does
not have much relevance to a drama like the *Heracles*, where all the
characters and audience had seen Iris and Lyssa appear *ex machina*.

That is not to say that Euripides was unaware of the issues
raised by Protagoras and other sophists when he wrote the
Heracles or any other drama. Of course he did, if only because it
is in the nature of drama to present conflicting ideas and address
issues of contemporary interest; there would be no drama if all
the characters onstage understood in the same way everything
that happens to them. But in any case the question raised in the
discussion between Heracles and Theseus is not whether gods
exist or do not exist (that was *Protagoras'* question), but whether
or not they are capable of acting unjustly and immorally. There
is no doubt about how the gods have behaved during the course
of the drama: some gods, Hera through her agents Iris and Lyssa,
have behaved with the greatest cruelty and inhumanity, and other
gods have done nothing to stop them. Iris and Lyssa made Heracles
murder the wife and children he has just rescued, and neither
Athena nor his father Zeus intervenes to save Heracles' wife and
children. Hera wins, if only for the time being. The humans in the
drama are horrified by the brutal revenge inflicted on Heracles by
Hera, and the audience will instinctively sympathize with him and
the human characters that treat him compassionately.

To allow the audience to see what the gods are like, however,
is not the same as advocating that they should no longer be
worshiped, as some modern critics seem to have supposed. On
the contrary, the demonstration of divine power in the *Heracles*
provides a strong argument for maintaining traditional religious
practice and belief. But the drama also shows that rather than
looking to the gods, mortals must turn to each other for comfort
and compassion. The *Heracles* demonstrates, like virtually all
surviving Greek dramas, that mortals cannot know what will

happen to them in the future. Heracles at the end of the drama has no reason to believe that Zeus cares about him. Neither he nor any of the other characters in the drama knows that at the end of his life Zeus will in fact make him a god, who will come to live with him in Olympus. The drama ends without an appearance *ex machina* by Athena or any other god, or any promises about Heracles' apotheosis in the future. Instead, it is the mortal Theseus who provides Heracles with a sanctuary in Athens, Athena's city.[65] The chorus speaks the last lines, expressing the sympathy that only a mortal can feel for another human being: "we are going in sorrow and with many tears; we have lost the best of friends" (1427–8). No one in the ancient audience would have expected similar compassion from a god, even though the god was the father of a mortal whom another god was persecuting. Here Euripides may be making the point that in certain respects human morality is superior to that of the gods, if only because the inevitability of suffering and death in human existence makes humans better friends and parents.[66] As parents, gods only intervene only when it suits their particular purposes. As the writer of the Aristotelian treatise *Magna Moralia* observed: "People think that there can be friendships with gods and inanimate things, but they are wrong. We say that friendship can exist when it can be reciprocated, but friendship towards a god cannot be reciprocated, and loving in general. It would be impossible to say that one is on terms of friendship with Zeus" (1208b).[67]

No reader of Greek poetry understood the nature of the Olympian gods' behavior better than the Roman poet Virgil. When at the beginning of the *Aeneid*, Venus appears to her son Aeneas, she does so in disguise as a virgin huntress. She tells him that he has landed in Carthage after his ships were wrecked in a terrible storm. Aeneas suspects that she might be a goddess (though she denies it), and recognizes that in fact she is his mother only as she is leaving. He implores her: "why do you trick your son again and again (you also are cruel) with disguises? Why don't you let me hold your hand and hold a real conversation?" (*Aeneid* 1.407–9). Venus leaves without taking the trouble to reply. Euripides (like Socrates) might justly have been accused of impiety, or of inventing "new-fangled gods," had he chosen to portray Zeus as a loving father who communicated privately with his son Heracles, and provided him with personal guidance throughout his life. One reason why Socrates was condemned to death is that he believed that throughout his life he received instructions from a personal deity, which warned him if he was about to do something wrong. No one else could see or hear this "divine spirit" (*daimonion*, Pl., *Apol.* 31d), and so he was accused of "inventing new gods and not believing in the old ones" (Pl., *Euthyphr.* 3b, *Apol.* 24c).[68] To represent a god as a kindly, personal guide was disrespectful of long-standing tradition.

Since modern notions of divine behavior are so profoundly different, scholars (like other modern readers of ancient texts) cannot help being instinctively dissatisfied with the practices characteristic of Greek religion, such as animal and even human sacrifices, and gods who can be either cruel or kind, for reasons that seem to us petty, selfish, and capricious. For that reason they are too ready to assume that that the poet shared at least some of the views and concerns of Socrates, Anaxagoras, and other sophists about the nature of divinity. And like the comic poets and ancient commentators on the dramas, they support their arguments by singling out particular passages, like Heracles' statement about the gods' morality, and discuss them as if they somehow were independent of their dramatic context. But as we have seen, when ancient critics used that methodology, they came up with a portrait of Euripides that was based on conjecture and inference, rather than on historical information gathered independently of his own plays.

Perhaps if Euripides had altered the narrative trajectory of the myths and substituted endings of his own, in which the gods behaved as mortals would wish, and his dramas ended in accord with modern notions of justice, we might be able to assume that he was suggesting to his audience a new form of religion, a "new creed" in which the gods worked with mortals throughout their lives, and promised them future happiness. In that case Euripides would have described Zeus as a version of the Lord God of the Old Testament, who tests Job's loyalty to him by killing his family, but then because Job remains faithful to him, gives Job a new family and new prosperity. This Zeus would have sent his daughter Athena to appear *ex machina* at the end of the drama, in order to predict a future in which Zeus would stand by Heracles' side, and eventually confer immortality upon him. Instead, Zeus in Euripides' *Heracles* behaves like Zeus in the *Iliad*. Although he takes an interest in human life, and sees to it that Troy must fall (*Il*. 1.5), he does not come down to earth to intervene in the fighting, does not try to save his son Sarpedon from being killed by Patroclus, though he weeps tears of blood in his honor (*Il*. 16.458–601). So we should not be surprised if Zeus does not intervene to save his son Heracles. When Heracles says "Zeus, whoever Zeus is," and considers Amphitryon to be his father rather than Zeus, he is simply acknowledging that he has never seen nor heard from the god who engendered him (1263–5). Heracles acknowledges Zeus' power and his lack of empathy, when he adds that Zeus begot him "to be hated by Hera." There is nothing in that statement that expresses skepticism about the existence of Zeus or Hera or any other god, either on his part or that of Euripides.[69] Heracles is simply acknowledging reality, as he perceives it. The

Heracles compels the audience, whether ancient or modern, to ask why the gods do not behave as Heracles would like them behave, and then allows them to realize that the gods will have no particular desire or motivation to supply the answer.[70] David Konstan has argued that the *Heracles* is "a problem play, and forces its audience to confront a contradiction in the classical conception of divinity. The dilemma, in the terms posed by the drama, seems insoluble."[71] I would agree, if by "its audience" Konstan means its *modern* audience. The problem, and the dilemma, are *ours*: how can we come to terms with the fact that the ancient Greeks appeared to believe that their gods could behave as they are described in ancient Greek literature?

3

ATHENA

The god who appears most often at the end of Euripides'
extant dramas is Apollo's half-sister Athena, the daughter of
Zeus and Mētis ("Intelligence"). Of all the Olympian gods
she is the closest to Zeus; in Homer she acts as his confidante
and emissary. That special relationship also gives her unique
destructive powers, because Zeus allows her to borrow his aegis
and his lightning bolt; no other god, not even Apollo, has that
privilege. As we saw in the *Trojan Women*, Athena used Zeus'
lightning to attack the Greeks as they sail back home from Troy,
in order to punish them for their impiety (80–1). In Euripides'
drama *Heracles*, it is Athena, rather than Heracles' own father
Zeus, who intervenes to keep Heracles from killing his beloved
stepfather Amphitryon (1002–6).[1] Euripides gives Athena
a constructive role in many of his dramas because she is the
goddess who is the special protector the city of Athens, and for
whom the city was named. What we now call Greek drama is
specifically an *Athenian* invention, and Athenian poets take every
opportunity to praise the city and her surrounding countryside
for the qualities that the goddess exemplifies, courage in war
and the cultivation of civic values.

In seeking to give contemporary relevance to the narrative of
his drama and in finding new ways to emphasize the importance of
Athenian religious and cultural traditions, the poet was following

an established tradition. In Aeschylus' *Persians*, the earliest of the
Greek dramas that have come down to us (472 BC), a Persian
messenger offers elaborate praise of Athenian piety, courage,
order, and discipline in the Battle of Salamis (388–405), and
later in that drama the ghost of the Persian king Darius advises
his council of elders, who form the chorus, to remember Athens
and Greece (824).[2] In Aeschylus' *Eumenides* (458 BC) Orestes
promises that after his death as a hero he will make his native
Argos prosper if her citizens continue to honor Athens (*Eum.*
762–74).[3] Sophocles has Ajax's Trojan concubine Tecmessa address
the Salaminian sailors who form the chorus as descendants of the
Athenian king Erechtheus (201–2), as if in prehistoric times the
island Salamis had been under Athenian hegemony rather than
independent (as it almost surely had been).[4]

Athena concentrates on Athens when she appears at the end
of Euripides' *Suppliants*. The hero of that drama is Theseus,
the king of Athens, who is willing to go to war with Thebes
to help Adrastus, the king of Argos, recover the bodies of the
six captains who sought to assist Oedipus' son Polynices in his
attempt to reclaim the kingship of Thebes from his brother
Eteocles. After the Thebans defeated the Argives and refused
to release the bodies of the defeated Argive captains, Theseus
went to Thebes with his army, and defeated the Thebans.[5] But
instead of sacking the city, Theseus asks only that the bodies of
the Argive captains be given to him to receive proper burial.
When Theseus returns to Eleusis, the sons of the dead men
arrive from Argos to join their mothers in mourning the dead.
The bodies are burned on the pyre, and their bones returned to
their families. But just before the Argive mothers and children
start to return to their homeland with the bones, Athena appears
and orders Theseus to demand that in return for Theseus'
services to him, the Argive king Adrastus must swear an oath

that Argos will never attack Athens, and that they will come to
help the Athenians in case of a hostile attack (1183–95). The
goddess gives Theseus detailed orders about how the oath-taking
ceremony should be conducted. She predicts that the sons of
the dead captains, as soon as they reach manhood, will conquer
Thebes and take the city. They will be known as the Epigoni and
celebrated in song. In all of this long speech the goddess does
not take time to express sympathy to the mothers for the loss of
their sons, or to the families of the Athenians who lost their lives
in recovering the Argives' bodies. Her emphasis is on the future,
and the protection of Athens.

If anything, the drama seeks to emphasize the importance of
traditional piety. Adrastus delivers eulogies for the dead, and their
mothers and sons lament them, according to long-established
custom.[6] In the *Suppliants* those who refuse to allow enemy dead
to be buried are punished.[7] The drama reminds the audience
of the importance of traditional piety, while also conveying a
relevant political message. In her speech at the end of the drama
Athena gives precise directions for a ritual sacrifice that must
accompany the oath taken by the Argives never to invade Athens
again.[8] Theseus must use a tripod that was given to him by
Heracles. The throats of three sheep must be cut, and their blood
collected in the hollow bowl of the tripod on which the words of
the oath must be inscribed. Athena specifies that the tripod with
its inscription must be taken to the shrine of Apollo at Delphi.
Theseus must bury the knife used to slay the sacrificial animals, so
that it can be shown to the Argives to frighten them if they return to
Athens with any hostile intentions.

No version of this treaty appears to have existed in written
form; rather, it is a symbolic re-creation of the actual alliance
between Athens and Argos in the fifth century.[9] Similar
references to the alliance between the two city-states are made by

mythological figures in other dramas. For example, in Aeschylus'
Eumenides, performed in 458 BC, Orestes swears that in gratitude
for his acquittal by the court of the Areopagus, after his death
he will punish the Argives if they try to invade Athens, but will
make them prosper if they continue to honor the city of Pallas
Athena (*Eum*. 762–74).[10] Since Euripides' *Suppliants* was probably
produced in 423 BC, Adrastus' oath would have provided the
mythological background for an actual detente that was recognized
soon afterwards by a formal treaty that was enacted between the
Athenians, Eleians, Argives, and Mantineans in 420, and renewed
in 416.[11]

   After the appearance of a god at the end of a drama, the mortals
agree faithfully to follow the instructions they have been given.
Theseus thanks the goddess for her advice, promises to make
Adrastus take the oath, and hopes for her continued protection
of Athens. Athena does not describe what participation in the
ritual will require of the men who must perform the sacrifice,
but she demands that "if they abandon the oath and attack Athens
[Adrastus] must pray that the land of Argos perish miserably"
(1193–4). In Athens, as the audience of the *Suppliants* would
have known, anyone taking an oath that specifically calls for
self-destruction would be required to dip his hands in the blood
of the sacrificial sheep, while standing on the animals' severed
testicles. The ritual was meant to represent what would happen
to the oath-takers if they did not observe the terms of the
oath: destruction to themselves, their families and households.[12]
The text of the historical treaty between Athens, Elis, Argos, and
Mantinea of 420 BC (as recorded by Thucydides) also does not
describe the details of the sacrificial ritual, stating only that they
"shall each swear the oath which in the cities of the contracting
parties is considered the greatest over full-grown victims" (Thuc.
5.47.8).[13]

Contemporary speculation about the nature of divinity and ritual practice seems to have no place in this drama. There are only a couple of passages that have been thought to show the influence of current philosophical theories about life after death, both involving the role of the *aithēr*. Speaking of the dead captains, Theseus says "let their bodies be covered in earth, and let each thing go to the light from which it came, the spirit to the sky (*aithēr*) and the body to the earth" (532–4). His words imply that the souls of the dead by being absorbed into the *aithēr* have attained a kind of immortality, while their bodies have been reclaimed by the earth below. Franziska Egli suggests that the idea that souls and bodies become immortal by being reabsorbed into the earth and sky reflects the thinking of Anaxagoras, who died in 428 BC. Anaxagoras said that "the Greeks do not have an accurate understanding of being born and dying. Nothing is born or dies, but is intermingled or divided. They might more accurately speak of being born as intermingling and dying as division" (59B17 D-K).[14] But such statements about creation and death are less revolutionary than they might seem. In effect Anaxagoras has restated in abstract language a belief which had for some time been a commonplace, especially in expressions of consolation. By the second half of the fifth century, *aithēr* was regularly described as Zeus' home and considered to be the source of human intellection.[15] The idea was familiar enough to have been used in a public inscription honoring the Athenians who died in the siege of Potideia in 432 BC: "the *aithēr* holds their souls (*psychai*) and the earth their bodies."[16] Towards the end of the *Suppliants* the chorus attempts to comfort the children of the dead Argive captains by saying that "the sky (*aithēr*) holds them now, melted in the fire's ash. With wings they have reached Hades" (1139–41). Egli suggests that the word "winged" (*potanos*) implies that Euripides means that Hades is located in the air, which might fit with Anaxagoras' theory of death being an intermingling.[17] But it is much more likely that here the poet means that the smoke from their bodies is in the air, while their souls are making the traditional journey to the Lower World. In the *Odyssey* the souls of the dead suitors are compared to bats flying (*poteontai*) around a cave, when Hermes comes to guide them to Hades (24.1–10).[18]

In general, there seems to be no reason to suppose that in the *Suppliants* Euripides had any intention to undermine traditional religion. Nonetheless, some scholars have tried to show that the poet must have meant what he wrote to be interpreted ironically, as a satire on conventional views of divinity and patriotism. In 1953 Greenwood argued that the few other supernatural events mentioned in the drama, including Athena's epiphany at the end, were not "essential parts" of the drama. He faults Athena for her lack of compassion and criticizes Theseus for not being sufficiently aware of her deficiencies: "When Athena's cruel speech to the Argive boys is immediately followed by Theseus' words of complete trust in her and devotion to her (1227–31), the intelligent and humane spectator may feel that Theseus might with advantage have had less piety and more intelligence and humanity."[19] Presumably Greenwood himself, like his "intelligent and humane spectator," could not accept that a poet supposedly as sophisticated as Euripides could have found meaning in a bloody sacrifice or could have believed in the existence of a goddess who is more interested in the preservation of her city than in the particular mortals who inhabit it.[20] Similar doubts were expressed in 1970 by R. D. Gamble, who thought that Theseus' willing acceptance of Athena's commands and expressed gratitude for her guidance looked "more like a 'cri-de-coeur' than an avowal of confidence . . . if Euripides cries out for some means by which life can be guided, he entertains little hope of finding it in the traditional gods of Greece, even if he can offer no alternative."[21]

But why should Gamble have supposed that Theseus did not mean what he said, since the goddess had intervened in order to protect his city in the future? What passages in the drama suggest that Euripides was crying out for a new guide to human life, rather than seeking to recognize and portray the cruelty and pain of war, during a time when his city was almost continually involved in war?

How then should we understand the purpose of Athena's epiphany at the end of the *Suppliants*? Writing in the wake of the Second World War, G. Zuntz thought that Athena's appearance strengthened the drama and gave it meaning: "only the goddess could resolve its sorrow into trust and its novelty into belief." He argued that "the *Suppliant Women* could be read, without much violence to its basic purport, as a piece of pacifist propaganda."[22] But in a book written while the United States was planning to retaliate for a terrorist attack on New York City, Daniel Mendelsohn found evidence of militarism in the drama, and regarded Athena's role as "perverting Demetrian gestures and themes" of peace and fertility appropriate to Eleusis, where the action of the drama takes place.[23] "The warlike, man-like goddess promotes future violence . . . Her victory over Demeter is complete. Her presence and her words valorize the vengeful and self-interested ethos that brought ruin to all the play's characters except Theseus."[24] In Mendelsohn's view, when Theseus promises to obey Athena's orders the drama becomes a warning against further aggression: "Like Theseus in the play, the Athenians were beguiled. Like him they chose badly."[25] The goddess, he implies, was their guide.

Where Zuntz saw Athena as resolving future conflict and promoting a lasting detente, Mendelsohn found only hints of menace. But in order to provide evidence of belligerence in Athena's words, Mendelsohn puts an emphasis on Demeter's

role in the drama that cannot be found in the text. Theseus'
mother Aethra invokes Demeter in her opening speech (1–2),
and just before the chorus of Argive women appears onstage,
Aethra is making a sacrifice for the plowing of the earth at
the temple of Demeter and Kore, where the first grain on
earth was believed to have appeared (33–4).[26] Adrastus,
believing that Theseus will not help him, invokes Demeter
Torchbearer—the epithet refers to the torch the goddess
carried while searching for her lost daughter Persephone.[27]
Nothing explicit is said about Demeter in her role as the
goddess of peace and prosperity, or about any conflict that
she might have had with Athena. Mendelsohn seeks to draw
an unfavorable comparison between Euripides' Athena in the
Suppliants and Aeschylus' Athena in the *Oresteia*: "the pact
that she demands [in the *Suppliants*], complete with elaborate
ritual details and sacred sanctions, makes a mockery of
Athena's decisive role in bringing the *Oresteia*'s violence to
a close."[28] Certainly it is true that in the *Eumenides*, the last
play in Aeschylus' *Oresteia* trilogy, Athena puts an end to the
series of revenge killings in the house of Atreus by casting the
deciding ballot that allows Orestes to be acquitted of murder.
She also offers the Erinyes, Orestes' persecutors, a home
where they can receive honors from her people, and protect
the city rather than seek to damage it. But the reason why she
can bring about a constructive resolution to the drama is that
she is also (to use Mendelsohn's words) "a warlike, man-like
goddess" who gets her way because she has access to superior
force and is prepared to use it. She is able to persuade the
angry Erinyes to accept her offer without much trouble
because (as she reminds them) she alone of all the gods has the
keys to the house where Zeus keeps the lightning with which
he defeated the generation of Titan gods to which the Erinyes

belong (827–8). Athena prefers to use persuasion rather
than coercion because she wishes to protect her city and its
people from the destruction that the Erinyes could cause.
In Aeschylus' *Eumenides*, as in Euripides' *Suppliants*, Athena
seeks by her intervention to protect her city by exacting a
demanding promise from a potential enemy. In both plays her
aim is to defend her city.

Modern readers seek to contrast Aeschylus' characterization
with Euripides' because we have only a limited amount of
comparative material to draw on. But we have no way of knowing
whether or not an ancient audience would have found such a
comparison natural or even useful, because they would have seen
Athena onstage in many other plays that are now lost to us. Since
the *Suppliants* refers to no particular contemporary event, in
practice the *Suppliants* is no more overtly "political" than dramas
like Sophocles' *Antigone*, which stresses the importance of burial
of the dead, or the *Oedipus at Colonus*, which contrasts Athenian
democratic principles with Theban autocracy. If instead we
consider Euripides' *Suppliants* on its own terms, we might more
accurately regard it as neither pacifistic nor belligerent but rather
as celebratory. The drama affirms the value of traditional piety: the
custom of proper burial of the dead is preserved, even at great
personal and national cost. The rescue of the bodies of the Seven
became a standard topic in Athenian oratory.[29] The religious values
that all Greeks share are recognized, but as always in Athenian
drama, democracy (with benevolent leadership) proves to be
superior to tyranny, and the gods support the pious. Athena's
last-minute appearance makes it clear to both the Argives and the
Athenians that the gods approve of Theseus' actions. But the main
reason that she intervenes is to ensure that Athens receives some
material benefit from Theseus' piety; hence her insistence on
the oath that will guarantee that Argos will be allied with Athens

in perpetuity. Here again Euripides has portrayed Athena as the goddess of Athens, determined to protect her *polis*.

Euripides also has Athena proclaim aetiologies at the end of his drama *Erechtheus*. No ancient information about the precise date of the play has come down to us, but stylistic patterns suggest that it was written after the *Suppliants*, perhaps in 422.[30] Only excerpts of the *Erechtheus* survive, some in quotations by later authors, others on a fragmentary papyrus that was first published only in 1967, including what remains of Athena's speech *ex machina* at the end of the drama (*TrGF* 5.1, F 370). During the preceding part of the drama, the king of Athens, Erechtheus, learned from the oracle in Delphi that he would have to sacrifice one of his daughters in order to defeat an attack by an army of Thracians, led by Eumolpus, a son of Poseidon. Erechtheus' wife Praxithea agreed to the sacrifice in a speech that was remembered and recited many years later (*TrGF* 5.1, F 360). One of her daughters gave her consent (to be effective, sacrificial animals always had to be willing). But this daughter and her two sisters appear to have made some sort of pact, because after the one sister was sacrificed, the other two also were sacrificed or killed themselves.[31] Erechtheus himself was killed in the fighting, but Athens defeated the Thracians and Eumolpus was killed. In the final scene of what must have been an exciting drama, Poseidon sought to avenge the death of his son by causing an earthquake beneath the Athenian Acropolis (*TrGF* 5.1, F 370.34–54). Praxithea is terrified and desperate, but just at that moment Athena appears *ex machina* to defend her city and orders Poseidon to stop his attack on the city (55–62). It is only because the goddess intervenes that the characters are able to survive the earthquake, which would have killed them and destroyed the buildings on the Acropolis. But after putting a stop to impending violence, Athena concentrates on religious observance, as she does at the end of the *Suppliants*.

Athena directs her remarks first to Praxithea: she must bury her daughter where she died and her two sisters along with her in "the same tomb of earth," because of their nobility in keeping their oath to die along with her (65–70). Athena comforts Praxithea by assuring her that she has given their souls (*psychai*) a home in the *aithēr* (71–2), rather than in Hades. That action bestows on them the kind of immortality that heroes win in battle.[32] The goddess also ensures that the daughters will have the kind of immortality that comes from remembrance. She will give them a name that is famous in Greece: people will call them "goddesses, daughters of Hyacinthus" (73–4), thus indicating that they will be worshiped as heroines.[33] Only a few words of the next few lines survive, but they may have been intended to explain why that name is appropriate for them, which has something to do with "the gleam of the hyacinth" (76). Athena says that the Athenians in future will offer yearly sacrifices to them, maidens will dance in their honor, and boys will offer sacrifices to them before battles, using for their libations a mixture of honey and water rather than wine (77–86).[34] Their sanctuary will be "untrodden," inaccessible to those who are not taking part in the ritual. Also, like other hero cults, the site will offer protection to those who dwell nearby. No enemy will be allowed to enter, since if enemies were allowed to offer sacrifices there, they might be able to ensure victory for themselves and suffering for Athena's city (87–9).

All the information that we have about the cult of the daughters of Hyacinthus derives from sources that postdate Athena's speech in the *Erechtheus*, but it seems quite likely that this drama is the source of the idea that the daughters of Erechtheus were identified with the Hyacinthides.[35] The three sisters were sacrificed on a hill called Hyacinthus, which appears to have been located above the *Sphendonai* ("Slings"), to the west of the Acropolis, just beyond the city wall, near what in historical times was known as the Hill of the Nymphs.[36] After instructing Praxithea to bury her daughters where they died on Hyacinthus hill, Athena orders the Athenians to honor Erechtheus by building a precinct in the middle of the city that is enclosed by stones, offering him sacrifices of oxen, and addressing him as Poseidon Erechtheus.[37] This structure was the precursor of the temple built on the Acropolis around the time this play was produced, known as the Erechtheum (90–4).[38] Praxithea will become the first priestess of the cult of Athena Polias, in charge of burnt sacrifices on behalf of the city (95–7). The rest of the text of Athena's speech in the *Erechtheus* is too fragmentary to provide any context (107–8), but one line contains the word Hyades. According to an ancient commentary on the Hellenistic poet Aratus in his poem about the visible signs in the stars, "Euripides in his drama *Erechtheus* said that the three daughters of Erechtheus became the Hyades" (*TrGF* 5.1, p.418). Being memorialized as stars would have provided yet another enduring recognition and reminder of the daughters' heroism. Euripides is the earliest author we know of who made this particular association.[39]

During her epiphany in the *Erechtheus*, as in the *Suppliants*, Athena appears to say almost nothing about the role played by her citizens in war against Eumolpus. Instead she concentrates on the protection of her city through its religious rituals, which she represents as having existed from this time forward.[40] Her emphasis in her speech is on the eternal, and on the honors the city must pay to the gods who can protect it. She makes it clear that Athens needs to retain Zeus' support in order to survive and prosper. Also, as in the *Suppliants*, Athena gives specific instructions about the nature of the sacrifices offered to the daughters, and in a final innovation, appears to have stated that their heroism will receive a permanent memorial in the stars, as the constellation Hyades.

Athena plays a less overtly partisan role in Euripides' drama *Iphigenia among the Taurians*. She appears *ex machina* in the last scene of the drama, just in time save Agamemnon's daughter Iphigenia, her brother Orestes, and his friend Pylades from being captured as they try to escape from Tauris, a barbarian country located in modern Crimea. Orestes had come to Tauris because he had been instructed by the oracle of Delphi to take a sacred statue of Artemis to the land of the Athenians. This statue was believed to have fallen from the sky into the temple of Artemis in Tauris, where years earlier, Iphigenia had been taken by Artemis at the start of the Trojan War.[41] The goddess had rescued her just before her father Agamemnon was about to sacrifice her in order to ensure favorable winds so the Greeks could sail to Troy. In Tauris Iphigenia served as priestess at the temple, presiding over human sacrifices. Fortunately she recognizes Orestes, and instead of sacrificing him, she decides to trick Thoas, the king of the Taurians, into letting her take the statue of the goddess out to sea in order to purify it along with the Greek captives (Orestes and Pylades) before she sacrifices them. She prays to Artemis, who rescued her at Aulis to help her in the present crisis, assuring the goddess that it is not right for her to live in Tauris when she could dwell in Athens, "a city favored by the gods" (1082–8, 1230–3). For a while, the plot works perfectly; the Greek ship that had brought Orestes and Pylades to Tauris comes to get them, while they are in a boat taking the statue to be washed. But before they can leave the harbor, a wave drives their ship back towards land. Iphigenia prays to Artemis and the Greek sailors pray to Apollo. Nonetheless, the ship is driven close to the shore and the Taurians are able to surround it. But before Thoas can leave the palace and capture them, the gods intervene to calm the sea and see that Iphigenia and Orestes are able to escape.[42]

Surprisingly, the goddess who appears *ex machina* is Athena, not
Artemis. She orders Thoas to stop his pursuit of Iphigenia and the
cult statue. She explains that Apollo had ordered Orestes to come
to Tauris, and to bring the statue back to her country. She tells
Thoas that he could not capture Orestes even if he tried, since
Poseidon will make the sea smooth for Orestes' passage back to
Greece. Athena also orders Thoas to send home the Greek women
who accompanied Iphigenia to Tauris and promises Orestes that he
will be acquitted in his trial on the Areopagus at Athens.[43] Thoas
agrees to obey the goddess' commands. Athena commends him,
commands the winds to send the ship on its way, and leaves to join
them in accompanying Iphigenia and Orestes to Athens. Athena
does not say explicitly why it is she, rather than Artemis, who has
intervened to rescue Iphigenia and Orestes. Perhaps, like Apollo
in the *Ion*, Artemis did not wish to be reproached by the mortals
for the suffering she had caused them. Earlier in the drama
Iphigenia despairingly criticizes Artemis for her "faulty reasoning"
(*sophismata*, 380) and the ignorance (*amathia*, 386) that led her to
demand human sacrifices. Iphigenia had believed that her father
was going to cut her throat with his sword as he held her over the
altar, until the goddess suddenly rescued her; but then the goddess
made *her* preside over the slaughter of other human victims.[44]

But the reason why Artemis does not appear probably has
more to do with Athena than it does with Artemis. Athena needs
to instruct the mortal characters about the future because she
is the goddess of Athens, where both Iphigenia and Orestes are
now heading. Athena presides over the religious affairs of her
country and will oversee the trial of Orestes on the Areopagus.
As soon as Athena has stopped Thoas from pursuing the fugitives,
she addresses her remarks to Orestes and Iphigenia in their ship,
heading for Athens: "you can hear a goddess' voice although you
are not here" (1447). Her directives to them, like her instructions

to Theseus in the *Suppliants*, concern religious ritual. She tells Orestes to bring the statue of Artemis to Halae, a town on the east coast of Attica, and build a temple there to house it.[45] Artemis will be worshiped there with the title Tauropolos in a ritual named for the country of Tauris and his experiences there. At the cult festival a sword will be held at a man's throat and blood will be spilt, in recollection of the sacrifice Orestes might have undergone at Tauris, had he and Iphigenia not recognized each other and planned their escape. Iphigenia will serve as priestess at Artemis' temple in Brauron. She will be buried there, and robes will be dedicated to her by women who have died in childbirth.

In this drama, as in the *Erechtheus*, the goddess' speech creates a mythic connection between cults that were originally unrelated. Athena tells Orestes to bring the cult statue of Artemis that he has taken from Tauris to Halae and "to build a temple and set up the statue in it, named for the Tauric land and your sufferings" (1453–4). She adds that "in the future people will celebrate Artemis in song as Artemis Tauropolos" (1456–7). The similarity in sound suggests that the two words had a common origin. But in reality the epithet *tauropolos* had nothing to do with the country Tauris in the Crimea. The temple at Halae and other cults of Artemis in Greece required the sacrifice of bulls (*tauroi*).[46] Euripides and other dramatists frequently make such associations between sound-alike names, because puns were thought to reveal the true meaning of words.[47] By connecting the cults at Tauris and in Attica, Euripides brings out an important contrast between Athenian culture and that of their counterparts in Scythian Crimea, where humans rather than bulls were sacrificed to the goddess. Athena states that it will be the custom at Halae to go through the motions of a human sacrifice, by placing a sword at a man's throat and drawing blood. The ritual allows the goddess to receive blood in recompense for the blood she did not receive because Orestes was not sacrificed. The unusual ritual also demonstrates that the Athenians are ethically superior to barbarians like Thoas.[48] Euripides also emphasizes the humane values of Athenian culture by having Athena proclaim that Iphigenia will become the chief priestess (*kleidouchos*) of Artemis at Brauron, where she will no longer be required to preside at a ceremony involving the sacrifice of human beings. In addition, she will be honored by the Athenians after her death, and thus no longer be isolated, "without marriage, children, city, and family," as she was when she was living in Tauris (*IT* 220).

Athena's speech ends with a further prediction that brings credit to the Athenian *polis*. In the future the Athenians will honor Iphigenia as if she were the representative of the goddess whom she served as a priestess. Iphigenia will be buried at Brauron, and robes will be offered to her that had belonged to women who died in childbirth.[49] At Brauron and in cults elsewhere in Greece, including the Athenian Acropolis, inscriptions recorded that women dedicated robes to Artemis in gratitude for their recovery from childbirth and women's diseases.[50] Perhaps Euripides thought it appropriate to create a connection between Iphigenia (who in some myths was sacrificed to Artemis) and women who died in childbirth, because women who died untimely deaths were sacred to Artemis.[51] It would not have mattered to Euripides' audience if the rituals Athena describes did not exist in their day, since they believed that cult practices could change over time and vary from *polis* to *polis*. Here, as in the *Suppliants*, the *Erechtheus*, and the *Ion*, it was the goddess' declared intention that mattered, and the celebration of piety and ethical values of Athens.[52]

By monotheistic standards the gods behave relatively well in the *Iphigenia among the Taurians*. Artemis did not allow Iphigenia to be sacrificed at Aulis. Athena ensures that she will have a home in Attica and that Orestes will receive a fair trial. Athenian humanism is compared favorably to the barbarian savagery, as evinced in the practice of human sacrifice. Iphigenia refuses to believe that any god could be evil, but blames the murderous people of Tauris for attributing their own meanness (*to phaulon*) to the gods (389–91), echoing what the philosopher Xenophanes had said half a century earlier about poets who created gods in their own image, stealing, committing adultery, and deceiving others (21 B 11, I 132 D-K).[53] As long as Orestes thinks that he will be sacrificed to Artemis he believes that the gods are no more reliable than "winged dreams" (570–1), but after he discovers that Iphigenia is still alive he believes that Apollo never would have ordered him to bring his sister Artemis' statue from Tauris to Athens if Artemis had raised any objection, and that therefore the gods intended that he and Iphigenia would be able to return to Greece (1011–6). Orestes' obedience to Apollo is rewarded.

Anne Burnett understood that the triumphant conclusion of the drama is "a gift from god," consistent with traditional piety, a story "that Solon or Pindar might have heard with full approval."[54] But at the same time, she suggests that the play "becomes a kind of parable, as satyr drama sometimes did, in which providence and prophecy overcome chance and dreams, and Apollo slays a new dragon in the form of the Tauric cult." But characterizing the drama as a parable deprives the last scene of the drama of its meaning, by shifting the focus away from Athena and Athens and giving Apollo the kind of importance he had in the *Eumenides*, even though he is not a character in the *Iphigenia among the Taurians* and does nothing in the course of the drama to put an end to the cult of Artemis in Tauris. In portraying the drama as escapist and lacking in tragic seriousness, Burnett appears to be concerned about what seems to her to be a shift in dramatic emphasis. Although in other dramas Euripides portrays humans trying to overcome the terrible challenges fortune, fate, or the gods impose upon them, Burnett seems to believe that in this drama the gods make the mortals' triumph over chance (*tychē*) too easy, by preventing a wave from washing their boat back to shore and allowing them to continue on their journey to Attica. The humans are diminished because the drama "concludes with a demonstration of the power of the gods."[55] It is as if Burnett found it hard to believe that that on occasion the gods could reward pious mortals and see that they received the recognition and support that they deserved.

Although his book *Ironic Drama* appeared only a few years after Burnett's *Catastrophe Survived* was published, Vellacott was even more unwilling to give any credit to the gods for the good outcome of the drama. To him Orestes' attempt to see a divine purpose in events (*IT* 1012–6) was similar to Heracles' reluctance to believe in the face of divine malice that the gods could be immoral (*HF* 1340–6).[56] In Vellacott's view, "the whole tenor of Euripides' work seems to me to deprecate such an attitude as groundless, harmful, and undignified."[57] But Vellacott's comparison between Orestes' and Heracles' speeches is not particularly apt. Heracles was criticizing the poets' attribution of human faults to the gods, as Iphigenia does when contemplating her role in the cult of Artemis at Tauris (389–91). Orestes, however, was suggesting that gods must have been at work because chance alone could not have made events work in their favor. Vellacott apparently did not suppose that in the *Iphigenia among the Taurians* Euripides could have intended to show that Orestes' trust in the gods turned out to be fully justified.

Francis Dunn also did not seem to believe that the audience of the *Iphigenia* could have taken Athena's speech seriously, because they would have known that not everything Athena says about the cults of Artemis in Attica could literally have been true. In his view, too many questions are left unanswered, for example: "How

does bringing a statue of Artemis to Athens cleanse the Argive
[Orestes] of matricide?" He thought that the drama ought to have
ended by connecting the past to the present, but instead "it fails
to deliver on such an end, not just by marking the gap between
past and present, but by confusing them."[58] Euripides' "fabricated"
aetiologies "exact our complicity with their outrageous claims
even as they make us aware of, and reflect on, their status as
rhetorical untruths."[59] The gods, and particularly Athena in
her several appearances, involve the audience in a process of
"mystification." Euripides invented new cult aetiologies in order
to get his audience to question their assumptions about reality,
and sought to get them to play "a self-conscious game, drawing
attention to rival accounts that his aetiology seeks to upstage."[60]

But why would an ancient audience have considered Euripides'
new aetiologies to be "outrageous"? Would Dunn have supposed
that Euripides was trying to get his audience to recognize that
Athena was lying to them by fabricating aetiologies, had Euripides'
biographers not characterized him as an atheist and friend of
philosophers who questioned the existence of the traditional gods?
Sophocles also appears to have invented aetiologies, but no one has
accuses *him* of trying to manipulate his audience or getting them
to suppose that the gods would seek deliberately to mislead them,
because since antiquity Sophocles has always had a reputation for
piety.[61] Sophocles in his drama *Oedipus at Colonus* refers to a *heröon*
that no one has ever been able to locate. According to Homer
Oedipus had a tomb in his homeland of Thebes (*Il.* 23.678–9), but
in the *Oedipus at Colonus* the aged Oedipus is said to have died and
to have been buried somewhere in Colonus, a deme northwest of
the Athenian Acropolis, where Sophocles himself was born. Like
Euripides, Sophocles changed aspects of traditional narratives
to suit his own particular purposes.[62] In the *Oedipus at Colonus*
Sophocles describes how Oedipus comes to Athens, and asks for

refuge there, promising Theseus in return that if buried there
he would be able to save the city (460) and bring her prosperity
(478).[63] Oedipus promises that his grave will protect the city
from her enemies, and he predicts that if Thebes goes to war
with Athens, his "corpse, sleeping and hidden, although cold will
someday drink their warm blood" (621–2).[64] He describes himself
as a resident (*oikētēr*) of Athens (627).[65] At the end of the drama,
when the gods summon him to die, Oedipus allows only Theseus
to know where in the area of Colonus his grave will be located. He
instructs Theseus to reveal the site only at the end of his life to the
most prominent man in Athens, who in turn will reveal it to his
successor (1522–34).

Since presumably no one besides the legendary kings of Athens
knew where in Colonus the grave of Oedipus was located, it
has never been found and no ancient inscriptions refer to it.[66]
Pausanias saw a tomb of Oedipus on the Areopagus, and was told
that his bones had been brought there from Thebes. Pausanias says
explicitly that he did not believe Sophocles' account of Oedipus'
death (1.28.7), because according to Homer, Oedipus had died in
Thebes (*Il.* 23.679–80).[67] Normally, a hero would be interred in a
public place, such as the agora or the sanctuary of a divinity, where
people could congregate to offer sacrifices and libations.[68] For
example, in Euripides' *Heraclidae*, Eurystheus, the legendary king
of Argos who persecuted Heracles, states that he is fated to lie in
front of the temple of Athena at Pallene (*Hcld.* 1030–1). That grave
also has never been found, and is mentioned by no other ancient
author.[69] In practice, however, it did not matter where exactly
Eurystheus or Oedipus or any other hero or heroine was supposed
to have been buried, or if he or she was thought to have been
buried at several different sites. Memory counted for more than
reality, and Sophocles' dramas were better known throughout the
ancient world than any physical monuments. Even in the second

century AD the orator Aelius Aristides could speak of "Oedipus lying in Colonus" as one of the divinities (*daimones*) that protect Greece.[70]

To return to the issues raised by Dunn in his discussion of the *Iphigenia among the Taurians*: there is no reason to suppose that the audience of that drama, or any of Euripides' other dramas, would have understood his new aetiologies as "fabrications" or "playing a self-conscious game" with them or the other poets with whom he was competing.[71] It is not as if there ever had been a single orthodox account of how these or any other cults had been established. New versions of any myth could always be devised to suit a particular purpose or occasion. In the *Trojan Women* Euripides' follows Homer's account in the *Iliad* and has Helen go to Troy with Paris. In the *Helen* Euripides followed a very different narrative according to which Helen never went to Troy but was represented there during the whole of the war by a wraith. She remained in Egypt until she was rescued by Menelaus seven years after the war had ended.[72] In Euripides' *Orestes* Menelaus brings Helen directly back from Troy to Argos.

In presenting different versions of traditional narratives, Euripides and other dramatists were not seeking to deceive their audiences. Rather, they were finding new and ingenious ways to entertain them, and at the same time, to represent as vividly as the conventions of the theater would allow them to do the extraordinary range of the gods' powers. When angry, Athena can be ruthless, as she is in the *Trojan Women*, asking Poseidon to punish the Greeks by sending a storm to destroy their ships on their way home from Troy. But more often she acts in the best interests of the citizens of her city, as she does in the *Ion* when she intervenes to make sure that both Creusa and Ion understand what Apollo has done to ensure the future of Athens. In the *Suppliants* she arrives at a critical moment to see that the Athenians in perpetuity will have the Argives as their allies, and in the *Erechtheus* she comes to make sure that the Athenians have her own cult as well as that of Poseidon on their Acropolis, to protect them in future wars. In the *Iphigenia among the Taurians* Athena arranges that Artemis will be properly worshiped at Brauron and be favorable to the inhabitants of Attica and Athens.

In addition to celebrating the values of Athenian civilization, Athena's intervention at the end of the *Iphigenia among the Taurians* provides yet another illustration of the versatility of the powers of the gods. "Necessity (*to chreon*) has power over both humans and gods," as she says to Thoas (1486). In the context of the drama, Athena helps her father maintain "necessity," in this case by providing through her intervention a secure future for Orestes, who will return to rule Argos, and by giving Iphigenia a new home and enduring honors in Brauron. In granting them this respite from their previous troubles, the goddess does not apologize for the suffering that necessity has imposed upon them; the gods take it for granted mortals must suffer and remain ignorant of the gods' intentions and nature. It is perhaps natural for readers who associate divinity with providence to suppose that divine "necessity" is aleatory or random in nature. Poulheria Kyriakou, for example, equates necessity with happenstance (*tyche*). In her view, the drama's ending offers a sad testimony to the inadequacy of the gods: "With its silences, its ambiguities that are left unresolved, the glimpses of the role of chance and the need for last-minute intervention it provides, Athena' s speech confirms the opaque, non-deterministic nature of human-divine interaction that has become apparent throughout the play."[73] But as we have seen in the drama, the gods can take deliberate actions that the mortals affected by them regard as miraculous. The gods can and did save the lives of a few individuals, even if they remain unable or unwilling to alter or improve the lives of most human beings.

4

APOLLO

The other god who plays an important role in Euripides'
dramas is Apollo. He appears *ex machina* in two dramas, and
works behind the scenes in several others. But because of
the nature of his character, his motives and intentions are
harder for mortals (and mortal audiences) to understand.
Through his oracles and prophets Apollo gives mortals an
opportunity to seek divine approval for their enterprises and
to inquire about the future, so they can learn if they have the
gods' support for their enterprises. It is, however, up to the
mortals to try to understand what Apollo tells them through
his intermediaries, and (unfortunately) the god's predictions
as relayed to them are not easy to interpret.[1] Mortals call the
god Loxias, the slanted or ambiguous one, because most of
the time they cannot understand him.[2] In traditional myths,
he makes love to mortal women and begets mortal children,
whom he seeks to protect, but he also helps mortals who
honor him and carry out his wishes. The dramas in which
Apollo appears were produced at either end of the poet's
career. The *Alcestis* is almost certainly Euripides' oldest
surviving play, produced in 438 BC, when according to
his ancient biographers the poet was forty-two years old.
Particular stylistic and metrical patterns in the *Ion* suggest
that the drama was produced towards the end of his career,

around 410.[3] The *Orestes* was performed in 408 BC, about two years before the poet died. But the way in which Euripides portrays the god does not change significantly during those thirty years.

The prologue of the *Alcestis*, like that of the *Trojan Women*, is a dialogue between two gods, Apollo and Death. First Apollo appears, explaining who he is and where he is for an ancient audience that had no programs or subtitles to supply such basic information. Apollo says he has spent a year working as a hired laborer on the estate of Admetus, a king in Thessaly. The year of exile from Olympus was a punishment given to Apollo by his father Zeus. Zeus had killed Apollo's son Asclepius with his thunderbolts for bringing a man back to life, and in revenge Apollo had killed the Cyclopes who made Zeus' thunderbolts. For a god a year spent as a shepherd, working for a mortal man, is a punishment, because the gods, as Homer put it, "live at their ease" (e.g., *Il.* 6.138), that is, they do not work for food or shelter; all the means of life are supplied for them. So it is only natural that Apollo would leave Admetus' house without regrets. Instead of nectar and ambrosia, he explains that "in this house I had to accept a slave's fare, although I am a god" (1–2). But nonetheless he has great respect for Admetus, his master during this year. He has protected his house, because he is "dutiful" himself (*hosios*); Admetus is also "dutiful" (*hosios*), and each repays the other for his kindness (9–10).[4] For this reason Apollo was willing to save Admetus' life. Admetus had been fated to die during this year, but Apollo beguiled the Fates into letting Admetus find someone who would be willing to die in his stead. The only person who was prepared to do so was Admetus' wife, Alcestis, who must die on this very day. Apollo himself must leave before she dies, in order to avoid the pollution of death (as his sister Artemis for the same reason needs to abandon her dying companion Hippolytus; *Hipp*.

1437–8). When the god Death arrives to claim Alcestis, Apollo tries to reason with him and persuade him to postpone her death. When Death refuses to cooperate, Apollo predicts that Heracles will soon come to take Alcestis away from him before he can bring her to the Lower World, and then restore her to her husband.

This prologue, although brief, provides a vivid illustration of the character of both the gods who appear in it. Death is implacable and relentless. As a god, he is entitled to rewards, and he has come to claim Alcestis, the person that the Fates have offered him. Apollo is willing to help Admetus. He respects Admetus because he has treated him with due honor, but nonetheless the god is not prepared to empathize with his mortal host in any way. He does not delay in returning to the life of the gods on Mt. Olympus. He does not remain to comfort Admetus when his wife is dying. But he seems kindly when compared to Death, who has no sympathy for his victims and cares only about claiming the honors to which he is entitled (53), for example, the greater reward he will get by claiming the life of a young person (55). But the prologue also demonstrates that despite his character Death is less powerful than Apollo. Death has reason to hesitate when he sees Apollo with his bow.[5] Apollo is powerful because he is the son of Zeus, and in any contest the god most closely connected with Zeus will win.[6] Apollo also has the power to see into the future, which Death apparently is unable to do. When Apollo tells Death that Heracles will wrestle with him and take Alcestis back to Admetus, Death does not believe him, and as a result suffers defeat at the hands of Heracles. Death's lack of foresight is shared by the mortals in the drama, who suffer unnecessarily because they have no way of knowing what will happen next. Admetus does not believe that Alcestis has returned from the dead until he sees her standing before him at the very end of the play. He thanks Heracles for having brought her back to him, but does not seem to realize that Alcestis' rescue would not have been possible without divine intervention: how else could Heracles have arrived at Admetus' house at precisely the right moment, just after Admetus has buried Alcestis, but before Death has come to take her to the Lower World? Such precise timing is always a sure sign that Apollo is at work behind the scenes, as we will see in the other dramas discussed in this chapter.

Apollo does not appear as a character in Euripides' *Ion*, but his actions, past and present, determine the fates of the mortals involved in the drama. We might have expected that Apollo himself would have spoken the prologue to a drama involving mortals with whom he had had a significant relationship. But strikingly, it is not he who appears but his half-brother the god Hermes, another son of Zeus, but by another mother. Hermes explains that Apollo "had by force joined in a union" with Creusa the daughter of Erechtheus, the king of Athens. After taking her to a cave, where he raped her, Apollo went away. Nonetheless from a distance he kept her father from noticing her pregnancy. She gave birth to a son in the cave where Apollo had taken her, and left the baby there to die. Apollo, however, sent Hermes to bring the baby to Apollo's shrine at Delphi and leave it on the steps of his temple, where a priestess found it. She was about to remove it from the temple precinct, but once again Apollo intervened: "the god worked along with her so that the child would not to be thrown out of his temple" (48). When the god's son became a young man, he became the steward of the temple. Now (Hermes explains) Apollo is directing the course of events (67–8) so that the child's mother Creusa will come to the temple with her husband Xuthus, in the hopes of learning how they might have children. Apollo will give Xuthus an oracle that will allow Xuthus to suppose that he is the father of the son Creusa had abandoned.[7] But Creusa will know the secret truth, i.e., that the young man Xuthus thinks is his son is in fact the child she bore in Athens to the god. This son will be called Ion, and become the ancestor of the Ionians, the Greeks who in ancient times lived on the coast of Asia Minor.

In this story Apollo protects Creusa and their son Ion with ingenuity and efficiency, but without any display of empathy. He abandons Creusa after he has raped her, but when she in turn abandons her child and leaves him to die in the cave where she was raped by the god, the god does not come to rescue his child himself, but sends his brother Hermes to bring the baby to Delphi. Apollo's son grows up without a family or any knowledge of his true identity. As the poet describes it, Ion seems happy enough with his simple life, sweeping the steps of Apollo's temple, and threatening with his bow and arrows to kill the birds which foul the shrine. But to Creusa her encounter with Apollo has brought only anguish. She has not been able to bear children with her husband Xuthus, and after her husband comes to believe that Ion is his son, she feels that she has been betrayed by the god (878):

> You came to me, your hair glittering with gold, when I was gathering saffron flowers in the fold of my dress, and closing your hand on my white wrists, with no sense of shame, you led me to a bed in the cave, as I cried out "mother," a god sharing my bed, as a favor to Aphrodite. In my misfortune I bore you a son, and in fear of my mother I threw him on your couch on the bed of sorrow where you yoked my poor self, in my misfortune. (887–901)

Creusa says that the god acted "without any sense of shame" (*anaideiai*), because he did not ask for her consent. He put his hand on her wrist, a gesture that an Athenian groom would make when leading his bride to his house, but then disappeared. Gods usually offer gifts to the women they seduce, and tell them about the child or children they will bear, but Apollo says nothing to Creusa about the future. After she comes to Delphi with her husband Xuthus, the god does not stop her from supposing that the young steward of the temple is the illegitimate son of her husband Xuthus, who has adopted him and named him Ion (661). In a fit of jealous rage she gives her old tutor two drops of poisonous Gorgon's blood to place in Ion's wine. Again the god is forced to intervene, although indirectly; before the young man can drink the wine, a bird tastes it, and dies in agony. The Delphians sentence Creusa to be stoned to death. But again the god sees to it that Creusa will discover Ion's true identity before either her son or the Delphians can kill her. The priestess who found Ion on the temple steps now reveals the chest in which she found him, with his birth tokens. Creusa recognizes the chest and without looking at it is able to tell Ion its exact contents. So Ion realizes that Creusa is his mother and states "this is the work of the god" (1456).

The perfect timing is also a sign the god's intervention, even though the characters in the drama do not recognize it for what it is.[8] But such last-minute shifts of fortune, although they serve as brilliant demonstrations of divine power, are not in any way designed to spare the feelings of the mortals in whose lives a god has intervened. Ion says:

> The god has been good to me, but during the time when I should have been coddled in my mother's arms and getting some enjoyment from my life, I was deprived of my dearest mother's nurture. But my mother was also miserable; she endured the same sorrow, because she lost the joy of her child. (1375–9)

When he learns from Creusa that Apollo (rather than Xuthus or some other mortal) was his father, Ion still wishes for confirmation: "either the god speaks truly or in vain; Mother, understandably, this troubles my mind" (1537–8). We might expect that the Apollo would appear at the end of the drama, to offer an explanation for his behavior in the past, and explain what he had done to protect Ion up to the present moment. But just as Ion is about to go into the temple to ask Apollo if he is indeed his father, another god appears *ex machina*. Ion recognizes that a god is present from the brightness of the god's countenance, but he knows that it is wrong to look at a god's face, unless he has been given permission (1551–2).

The god, however, is Athena, not Apollo. She explains that Apollo sent her because he was afraid that Ion would reproach him for "what happened in the past" (1558). She assures Ion that Creusa is his mother and that he should not tell Xuthus that Apollo is his real father, so that as Xuthus' son he can rule over Athens; Ion will have four sons, and Xuthus and Creusa will together have other children. These sons will be the ancestors of the Ionians; "this," the goddess says, "will give strength to my land" (i.e., Athens) (1584–5). They will be called Ionians, and their dominion will include land in both Europe and Asia, since they will settle on both sides of the straits leading into the Black Sea. Athena then states that Xuthus and Creusa will have two other sons: Dorus, after whom the Dorian people in the Peloponnesus will be named, and Achaeus, who will give his name to the peoples who live on the western side of the Peloponnesus. Here Euripides appears to have revised the traditional genealogy, by making Dorus Xuthus' son rather than his brother, as in the sixth-century epic *Catalogue of Women* (fr. 9 M-W).[9]

Athena concludes her speech by predicting that from now on both Creusa and Ion will have "a fate that is blessed by the gods" (1605). After both Ion and Creusa express their gratitude, Athena replies that "although the gods move slowly, in the end they are not without power" (1615). She promises to accompany them back to Athens, where Ion will take his place upon the ancient throne

(1619). The chorus of Athenian women who have accompanied
Creusa from Athens are happy for Creusa and Ion. They bid
Apollo farewell, and advise that anyone whose family is beset
by misfortune should honor the gods: "in the end good people
get their reward" (1622). But although in the end the gods have
brought good fortune to Ion's family, Athena in her speech has
kept her focus on the distant future and the legendary history of
the Athenian empire. She offers no apology to Creusa for all the
years during which she lamented the loss of the child she thought
she had abandoned, or to Ion for the time he spent working as
a temple slave. Although she assures Ion and Creusa that her
intentions towards them are kindly (*eumenēs*; 1554), neither she
nor any other god spends enough time among humans to bear
witness to their mental anguish or make any apology for it. From
the gods' point of view it is the final outcome that matters, and for
Creusa and Ion that outcome is very good indeed.

In the drama's final lines, the chorus bids farewell to Apollo,
and offers reassurance to the audience that the gods' justice
triumphs in the end: "Anyone whose house is assailed by troubles
should take heart and worship the gods. In the end the good shall
get their reward. The evil, since they are evil, will never prosper"
(1620–3). These lines remind the audience that even the people
gods favor can expect to suffer during their lifetime. As Achilles
says to Priam in the *Iliad*, Zeus allows mortals to have lives with
good and bad mixed, or all bad (24.527–33). All good is not a
possibility. Creusa might have been less unhappy, if she had kept
in mind that the children of gods are always superior to ordinary
mortals. But since Apollo gives her no information about what will
happen to her or her child in the future, both she and Ion suffer,
and in their ignorance, almost kill each other.

It is not unrealistic to depict a world in which gods seem to
pay only intermittent attention to human beings. Sometimes

gods who seduce mortal women treat them kindly, so that they too get some pleasure from the experience, and even let them know that the child or children they will bear will be in some way remarkable.[10] Apollo, by contrast, forced himself on Creusa and left her without information about her child's future, although as the god of prophecy, he knew exactly what would happen to their son.[11] In the dramas, human beings expect the gods to be kinder and gentler than they actually are. But even if they learn about the god's plan through a dream or an oracle, they almost always doubt or misconstrue what they hear, or suppose that they can somehow avoid what was prophesied, like Priam who when Hecuba dreamt she had given birth to a firebrand, did not destroy the baby as soon as it was born (918–22), and so let his son Paris live to bring about the destruction of Troy.[12]

Anne Burnett understood that "Apollo's divinity is the essential point of this play," and she recognized that it was in his nature not to be able to understand the passions of the human heart or appreciate how Creusa or Ion must feel.[13] But as she observed, other modern critics have found Apollo's interventions to be too mechanical, and the god's behavior to be irresponsible. "This attitude," Burnett argued, "springs from the modern inability to think mythically, and from the modern assumption that Euripides must have shared with us the limitation of imagination which we call 'healthy skepticism.' "The gods' reticence about their plans, their constant failure fully to explain to uncomprehending mortals why they do what they do, encourages modern readers of Greek drama to regard divine interventions as having an ironic meaning, or to imagine that the audience is meant to suppose that the poet deliberately has presented them in ways that will emphasize their cruelty and indifference.

Norwood had claimed that the play proved the validity of Verrall's theory of the poet's method.[14] He regarded the *Ion* as "the one play in which Euripides attacks the Olympian theology beyond all conceivable doubt," and stated that it was certain that the poet did not believe in the existence of Apollo or Hermes. He accepted Creusa's evaluation of the god as "uncomprehending" (961) and her old tutor's assessment of the god as "bad" (952), without regard for the context in which the characters voiced those criticisms.[15] But as Desmond Conacher observed, this "rationalistic" approach "spoils almost every dramatic effect in the play." Yet Conacher nonetheless still thought that the poet wished to criticize the god's behavior towards Creusa: "shadowing the golden Apollo of Creusa's glorious 'mythological picture' and the (politically) all-provident one of Athena's epilogue is the background impression of a rather furtive, shabby, and inefficient god, which leaves its mark even when the official defense has rested."[16] This type of interpretation continued to carry conviction. For example, R. F. Willetts, who translated the *Ion* for the influential Chicago *Complete Greek Tragedies*, observed: "Athene's answer to Ion's question about his paternity is 'completely farcical.' Apollo now becomes contemptible . . . Only Athene, Hermes, and Creusa seem satisfied that Apollo has 'managed all things well.' Certainly no reader of the play can be." Willetts adds the stage direction "(*ironically*)" to his translation of Ion's brief but gracious speech to Athena at the end of the play. He believed that "[Ion's] continued silence after apparent acceptance is indication enough of his attitude."[17]

Undoubtedly Conacher and Willetts described what many modern readers may feel about Apollo when they have finished reading the *Ion*, but there is no evidence that ancient audiences would have understood it in this way, or that there is any irony in Ion's speech.[18] If the poet portrays Ion as silent after he expresses his thanks to Athena, it is out of respect in the presence of a deity, and consideration for his mother; he is the youngest person present. Ion in particular would not have expected that the god would ever have provided him with a kingship and a prosperous life, and the ancient audience would not have expected the gods to have given the mortal characters greater gifts than what Athena offers.[19] As David Kovacs observes: "Though both Ion and Creusa praise Apollo, the impression remains that, as in the first book of the *Iliad*, the world is run by gods on Olympus who do not understand the human condition. That is a good image for the tragedy of human life."

Apollo worked behind the scenes in the *Ion*, and left it to his brother Hermes and his sister Athena to tell mortals what he had done on behalf of his son Ion and his human family. Similarly, in all but the last few minutes of Euripides' *Orestes* there is no indication that the god is playing any active role in what happens onstage. As in Aeschylus' drama the *Libation Bearers* (*Choephoroe*), Apollo through his oracle at Delphi had told Orestes that he must avenge his father's death by killing both Aegisthus and his Clytemnestra.[20] No god or mortal disapproved of Orestes killing Aegisthus, who was a cousin of his, but not a parent. But Orestes understandably hesitates to kill his own mother, and only does so when Pylades (who had not spoken up to that point) asks Orestes "then in the future where will the oracles of Loxias be, the ones given at Pytho, and the trusted oaths taken: count all men your enemies rather than the gods" (*Cho*. 900–2). But even though Orestes then does what the oracle had told him to do, he is nonetheless pursued by the Erinyes, his mother's avenging deities, until he is rescued by Apollo and Athena in the third play of the trilogy, the *Eumenides*.[21]

When Euripides' drama *Orestes* opens, Orestes is lying on his bed, miserable and delirious after killing his mother. Both he and his sister Electra believe that the gods have deserted them. Electra complains that "the unjust god gave unjust orders" (163) and that "Phoebus has sacrificed us" (*exethuse*, 191) in order to

Figure 4.1 Orestes with Apollo and Athena, red-figure column krater (475–25 BC), Credit: © RMN-Grand Palais/Art Resource, NY.

see that Agamemnon's murder was avenged. When Orestes sees his mother's avenging Erinyes, "bloody-faced snaky maidens," attacking him, he calls on Apollo and reaches for the bow made of horn that the god Apollo gave him. Apollo does not appear, but nonetheless Orestes succeeds in driving them off, telling them that they should lay the blame for his mother's murder not on him but on Apollo's oracle (277).[22] When his uncle Menelaus arrives and blames him for murdering his mother, Orestes pleads that he was following the god's orders. His father Agamemnon would

have asked him not to kill his mother, because of the suffering it
would bring upon him (285–9). When Menelaus states that Apollo
"has no understanding of what is good and just," Orestes replies
"we are slaves to the gods, whatever the gods are" (417–8).[23] But
Menelaus is still unwilling to believe that Apollo had sanctioned
the murder. The citizens of Argos also refuse to believe Orestes
and vote to stone him to death, but allow him to commit suicide
instead. Orestes' friend Pylades persuades him first to kill Helen,
as a means of revenge against her husband Menelaus, and then to
seize Menelaus' and Helen's daughter Hermione as a hostage.

But just as Orestes is about to strike Helen, she disappears
(1494–5). Orestes then seizes Hermione, while Electra and his
friend Pylades begin to set fire to Agamemnon's palace. It is only
now, at this critical point in the drama, that the god Apollo enters
ex machina and immediately brings about a peaceful resolution to
Orestes' desperate and misguided display of violence. The god
begins by telling Menelaus not to be angry at Orestes, and instructs
Orestes not to kill Hermione. Orestes supposed that he had killed
Helen, but he was "mistaken" (*hēmartes*; 1630). In fact Apollo
himself had rescued Helen, because his father Zeus (who is also
Helen's father) ordered him to save his daughter. Instead, Helen
will become a goddess, like her brothers Castor and Polydeuces
(1633–7). Orestes is to go into exile for a year, and to be tried
in Athens and acquitted for his mother's murder. He is to marry
Hermione (whom he was just about to kill), and his sister Electra
is to marry Pylades; Orestes will then return to rule over Argos,
and Menelaus will return to Sparta, now free from Helen and the
trouble she has brought him. Apollo even promises to "set things
right" with the Argives who had wanted to kill Orestes (1664–5).

Because (like all mortals) Orestes had only an incomplete
understanding of what was happening, he had believed that
Apollo had deserted him. Now he immediately agrees to do

what the god tells him: "Prophetic Loxias, you did not prove
to be a false prophet of your own oracles, but a true one.
I had begun to fear that I was hearing some god of vengeance
rather than your voice. But all is well in the end. I shall obey
your commands" (1666–70). Menelaus also immediately
agrees to do what the god says; he addresses his wife Helen as
a divinity, promises his daughter Hermione to Orestes, and
ends his quarrel with him: "one must obey" (1679). Apollo
then prepares to leave the scene, instructing them to honor the
goddess Peace, and taking Helen with him to Olympus to join
her brothers Castor and Polydeuces as a patroness of mariners.
Here the play ends, with a final prayer for victory in the
dramatic competition. By waiting until the last possible moment
to make his appearance, Apollo illustrates in the most vivid
manner possible the difference between the divine and mortal
understanding. Until this final moment the human characters
in the drama had only a partial grasp of what was happening
to them. Their ignorance led them to make bad decisions that
would have turned out to be disastrous, were it not for the
god's last-minute intervention.[24] Apollo promises Orestes a
secure and honorific future: he will be tried in Athens not by
men but by the gods, and acquitted by a majority vote: "the
gods as justices for your case will split their vote most
righteously; for there you are fated to win" (1650–2).[25] Having
the gods serve as judges is a striking departure from Aeschylus'
version of the story. There Athenian men voted to condemn him
by a majority of one, forcing Athena to cast a vote in his favor,
so that the votes for and against him are even, causing him to be
acquitted, as was customary in Athenian law (Aristotle, *Ath. Pol.*
69.1). In the *Orestes* Euripides makes the gods the benevolent
purveyors of justice, as if they alone were capable of putting a
stop to human violence.[26]

Apollo's sudden intervention also prevents Orestes and his family from destroying one another, and guarantees that Agamemnon's palace remains standing. Just before he returns to Olympus, Apollo advises Orestes and his family: "Depart then on your journeys, and honor Peace, fairest of goddesses" (1682–3). This special emphasis on peace suggests that in his depiction of the violent and disloyal behavior of Orestes and other members of his family, Euripides may have had in mind the moral deterioration characteristic of the Peloponnesian War, as vividly described by his contemporary Thucydides (e.g., 3.82), and exemplified particularly by the Athenian politics in the last desperate years of that conflict.[27] During that war, soldiers of all ranks believed evidence that the gods could help them. The Spartans supposed that Athena intervened to help them in the siege of Lekythos, in 424/3 BC (Thuc. 4.116), and some thought that Castor and Polydeuces had appeared to support the Spartans at Aegospotami (Plut., *Lys.* 12.1).[28]

Apollo is the god who is also portrayed as a powerful interventionist on the West Pediment of the Temple of Zeus at Olympia, which was built in the second quarter of the fifth century.

There the god is shown using the authority of his father Zeus to bring an end to the *hybris* of the Centaurs. He appears in the center of the pediment standing taller than the mortal figures, staying above the action and not wielding a weapon himself. He is pointing, giving the physical equivalent of a verbal command. As Heraclitus said, "the lord, whose oracle is in Delphi, does not speak or conceal, but sends a sign" (22B 93 D-K).[29] The god depicted on the Temple of Zeus is recognizably the same god as Homer's Apollo: powerful, but generally contemptuous of mortals; Apollo prefers to work from a distance rather than converse with mortals directly. So also in the *Orestes*, by

Figure 4.2 Apollo at Olympia, American School of Classical Studies at Athens, Alison Frantz Photo Archive, no. 162.

intervening just in time to prevent Orestes from killing Helen and Hermione, Apollo stands above the human characters and gets them to make peace with one another. Apollo's intervention is unquestionably benevolent and effective, despite its abruptness and the god's lack of empathy for the mortals involved.

First performed in 408 BC, the *Orestes* became Euripides' most popular drama. Socrates was said to have wanted the first three lines of the play to be repeated because of its accurate description of human experience: "There is nothing so dreadful to speak of, no suffering or disaster sent by the gods, of which human existence might not take up the burden."[30] The play was restaged repeatedly after its author's death, not just in Athens but elsewhere the Greek-speaking world.[31] In antiquity it was quoted more frequently than any of Aeschylus' or Sophocles' dramas, and was still being read in the Byzantine era.[32] It was one of the ten dramas selected around 250 AD for reading in schools.[33] Many more papyrus fragments of the *Orestes* survive than of the plays that are most often performed in the modern world, such as the *Bacchae, Medea*, or *Trojan Women*. The same is true of Euripides' drama *Phoenissae*, which though it was also one of the ten plays selected for schools, is no longer considered to be one of his most important plays.[34] But the two dramas have some features in common that may help to account for their relative popularity. Both have the distinct advantage of being based on familiar myths. As Aristotle observed, the best tragedies focus on a few families, including those of Orestes and of Oedipus, which "have either suffered or done terrible things" (*Poet.* 1453a 17–32). In addition, the plots of both the *Orestes* and the *Phoenissae* are unusually fast-moving and innovative, and each involves an unusually large number of famous characters. The *Phoenissae* is set in Thebes at the time when it is being attacked by the Argive army led by Oedipus' son Polynices. The blinded Oedipus and his wife/ mother Jocasta are still living in Thebes when Polynices and the Argive army arrive, and Jocasta kills herself over the bodies of her two sons (not, as in Sophocles' *Oedipus Tyrannus*, immediately after she discovers that she has been married to her own son). In the *Orestes* Pylades plays a pivotal role, but in Aeschylus' *Choephoroe* he spoke only a few lines, and he remains silent in both Sophocles' and Euripides' versions of the *Electra*. Euripides also manages to

include Helen, Hermione, Menelaus, and Tyndareus in the plot of
the *Orestes*, and instead of using a conventional messenger's speech
brings in a Phrygian slave to deliver a sensational narrative.

Despite its popularity in ancient times, the *Orestes* has had its
critics. In fourth-century BC Athens, Aristotle was troubled by the
ethics of the *Orestes*. He believed that characters in drama ought
to be good (*Poetics* 1454a17), and that the tragic poet ought to
portray characters "better than ourselves," and who should be
honorable (*epieikeis*), whatever their faults (*Poet.* 1454b11–5).
In particular, Aristotle did not approve of the way in which
Euripides portrayed Menelaus in the *Orestes*, citing it as an example
of unnecessary "evil" (*ponēria*) in a character (*Poet.* 1454a28–9,
1461b19–21). The compiler of the scholia on the *Orestes* continued
that line of criticism. He said that "the drama employs a comic
resolution" and that "while the play was one of the most highly
regarded for its staging, it was the worst in respect to its ethics;
with the exception of Pylades the characters in the *Orestes* are not
noble but common (*phauloi*)" (*Hypothesis,* I p. 93 Schwartz). At the
end of the drama the compiler observed that the play ended not
with lamentation and suffering, but "with truces and solutions"
like the *Alcestis*, and that there was a "recognition scene" at the
end, as in Sophocles' (now-lost) *Tyro* and often in other tragedies
(sch. *Or.* 1691, I 241 Schwartz). We don't know exactly how the
lost *Tyro* ended, but the compiler may have thought that the *Orestes*
and *Alcestis* ended in similar ways because both plays have a happy
outcome that comes as a surprise to the mortal characters.

Even at the time that the scholia were compiled, the doubts
that the characters express about the gods had affected the
interpretation of the scene where Orestes sees the Erinyes
coming—he even thinks that Electra is one of them. Electra says
"oh poor me—what help can I get hold of, since we have the
power of the gods against us?" Orestes replies: "give me the bow

made of horn, a gift to me from Loxias; Apollo told me to use
it against the goddesses" (i.e., the Erinyes, 266–9). The scholia
on the passage provide some interesting information about
how actors performed this scene (schol. Eur. *Or.* 268, I p. 126
Schwartz = Stesichorus fr. 218.24 Finglass): "Euripides follows
Stesichorus in claiming that [Orestes] has received a bow from
Apollo. Accordingly the actor ought to take up the bow and
shoot. But those who play the hero today ask for the bow, but do
not receive it and pretend to use it." Like the actors described
in the scholia, most modern commentators think that Orestes is
suffering from hallucinations.[35] But certainly in the *Eumenides* the
Erinyes he saw were real and appear as characters in the drama.
Suppose for the moment that the bow Apollo gave Euripides'
Orestes was a real bow, and (as the text seems to imply) he
believed that it worked?[36] Why did the actors (and why do we)
need to doubt that Apollo gave him the bow? Are we too ready to
believe that Apollo has deserted him, and that Electra is justified in
exclaiming that "we have the power of the gods against us"?[37]

In the second half of the twentieth century many scholars
were prepared to suppose that the play was intended to criticize
the gods.[38] Not only was Apollo's bow considered to be a
figment of Orestes' imagination; William Arrowsmith supposed
that Euripides' audience would have understood the ending
of the drama as "illusory," so great is the contrast between the
brutal actions of the characters and the unrealistically mythical
intervention of the god. He concluded that "Euripides had
deliberately inverted the *deus ex machina* to show that no solution
was possible; not even a god could halt the momentum of these
forces in their sweep toward inevitable disaster."[39] Arrowsmith did
not explain why he considered Apollo's arrangements (and that of
other Euripidean gods) to be "stupid." In fact, the outcome of the
drama varies only in a few details and in its timing from Aeschylus'

version of the myth. And how could the god's command that the
characters should "honor peace" (1682–3) have been meant to
show that "no solution was possible"? Hindsight perhaps lends
some credibility to Arrowsmith's notion that Apollo's speech
predicted the outcome of the Peloponnesian War. But in the
years before the performance of this drama in 408 BC how could
Euripides and his audience have been certain that Athens was
going to lose?

Anne Burnett also was disgusted by the violence of Orestes'
actions, not to mention the ignoble behavior of the other
characters in the drama. To her the *Orestes* resembled a satyr
play, in which cowardly beast-men are rewarded: "If there
is a hint of caricature in the speed and the perversity of this
salvation scheme, it is because Apollo's smile must stretch to
a grimace to take these creatures in, for they would try the
patience of a god."[40] She points out that the compiler of the
Byzantine commentary thought that the passage where the
Phrygian slave fails to understand Orestes' reference to the
myth about the Gorgon's head was "comical and low" (schol.
Or. 1521, I p. 230 Schwartz). Menelaus does call Orestes
and Pylades "a pair of lions, not a pair of men" (1555). But at
the time that the *Orestes* was performed, that is, in wartime,
ruthless behavior was not extraordinary. Burnett even doubted
that the audience could have supposed that Apollo had the
power completely to change the direction of the drama's
action: "could this god by these means put a permanent stop
to this sequence of violent acts and could he save this group of
mortals, according to the play's own evidence?"[41] If by evidence
she means obvious indications that the god would eventually
intervene, it is indeed true that the god is noticeably absent
until he suddenly appears at the very end of the drama, and
that he did not send an omen or signal to assure Orestes that he

had not deserted him. But Euripides' Athenian audience knew that Orestes did not kill Helen or Hermione, and that Apollo would see that in the end Apollo would save Orestes from persecution by the Erinyes. She and the other critics might also have observed that in the *Orestes*, Apollo only needed to stop *intended* violence. Even actual violence would not have been a challenge for him, neither would mortal weaponry, as anyone who knew the story of the Lapiths and the Centaurs would have known, and anyone who looked at the statue of the unsmiling and powerful Apollo on West Pediment of the Temple Zeus at Olympia would immediately have seen.

Vellacott, however, agreed with Burnett's assessment that the audience would not have put much faith in the god's intervention and used her interpretation to support his assertion that the drama's ending is ironic. He thought that Apollo's supposed "goodness" is explicitly denied in the first half of the play and that the end of the play is a "mockery." Vellacott interpreted the speech in which Orestes offers his thanks to the god (1666–72) as "a piece of irony which seems to challenge even the most obtuse to work out its implication."[42] In his view, "Orestes joins Apollo in disowning every acknowledgement of truth and humane value which he, Electra, and the chorus expressed in the early part of the play, before Ares assumed leadership in the person of Pylades." Here Vellacott attributed to Euripides an additional divine intervention that is not mentioned in Euripides' text.[43] It is as if Vellacott supposed that anything connected with the gods must inevitably be destructive or meaningless and that Apollo's final instruction to the mortal characters, that they should honor Peace, is devoid of any real hope.[44] In that way even the god's constructive and beneficent advice can be understood to mean the opposite of what Euripides actually had him say.

The "ironic" view of the play's ending has been widely influential. Peter Euben accepted the notion that the ending of the drama was illusory, arguing that it confirms and celebrates an inability on the part of both poet and his audience to believe in the traditional gods, and that Euripides was trying to warn his audiences about the moral deficiencies of their religion.[45] Other scholars call attention to the incongruity between the chaotic action of the preceding part of the drama and the god's precise attention to arrangements at the end of the play. In the *Cambridge History of Classical Literature* Bernard Knox stated that the ending of the *Orestes*, like that of Euripides' *Electra*, is an "artistic failure," where the final arrangements "seem incongruously out-of-line with the desperation portrayed in the body of the play."[46] Deborah Roberts described Apollo's instructions as "tying up loose ends with an exaggerated completeness, answering questions we would not even have thought to ask." The excessive precision (which as we have seen is characteristic of this god), according to Roberts, "suggests the arbitrariness and artificiality of endings."[47] Francis Dunn gave the title "No Way Out" to his discussion of the drama's ending, in which he argued that device of the *deus ex machina* "may be the proper and familiar outcome, but it has nothing to do with the play that has just been enacted. Only a god has the power and authority to impose a 'resolution' that resolves nothing, to prescribe a conclusion that is totally oblivious of all that has gone before."[48] Or as Bernd Seidensticker describes it, ". . . the intervention by Apollo (which puts the derailed connection back on its traditional mythical tracks) has no meaningful connection with the dramatic action that precedes it; rather, by the glaring absurdity of the 'solution' that it represents, this intervention only serves to intensify the general impression of senselessness and futility."[49]

But how can it be said that the god's intervention resolves nothing? Certainly the god does not punish Orestes (or Pylades or Menelaus) for the harm that they *intended* to do. As in the *Ion* (and the *Alcestis*) Apollo sees to it that that despite all the sound and fury, no one—not even the Phrygian slave—was killed or even injured during all the action at the end of the drama. The god's last-minute intervention kept the mortals from carrying out their destructive plans, by proposing a simple solution to the complex problems they had created for themselves, namely, that they must all make peace with one another. Meanwhile, Apollo will see to it that Orestes will be exonerated by the gods and allowed to return to Argos. Far from offering them "No Way Out," the god in fact has resolved all outstanding issues for all the characters involved in the dramatic action, as gods characteristically do when they appear *ex machina* at the end of a drama.[50] If Apollo had sent Athena to represent him at the end of the *Orestes* instead of showing up himself, she would have been justified in saying, as she does at the end of the *Ion*: "Apollo has done all this well" (1595). So he has, from the gods' point of view. That is not to say that everything is resolved from the mortals' point of view; it never can be, because even when lives are spared, as they are in the *Orestes*, the gods have not done anything to stop human suffering or keep the mortal characters from making serious errors in judgment. The mortals have survived, not because they have behaved well, but because it has served the gods' purposes for them to do so.

The ending of the drama is not illusory or artificial. I would suggest that if it *seems* "forced,"[51] it is because of the suddenness with which it occurs and Apollo's aloofness from the human emotions that have fueled the action of the drama up to the moment he appeared *ex machina*. Perhaps more than that of any other surviving drama, the ending of the *Orestes* illustrates the nature of the gulf between the confusing world mortals are

compelled to live in and the isolated and insulated world occupied
by the gods. As Donald Mastronarde has observed: "the power, the
ease, and the immortality of the Olympians render them unsuited
to the appreciation of the human condition. . . ."[52]

Once again, it seems, interpretive notions about the nature
of divinity make it difficult for modern audiences to understand
that the ending of the *Orestes* is a miracle, a demonstration of the
justice of Zeus, and an illustration of the limitations of human
understanding. Mortals think that a proper god ought to care
about our suffering, and that evil deeds should be punished
precisely and swiftly. From a human point of view, the gods are
often too slow to act.[53] In the *Ion*, Athena says "although the gods
move slowly, in the end they are not without power" (1615–6).
As Orestes says to Menelaus: "[Apollo] is on his way; that is what
gods are like" (420). Euripides' audiences understood that the
gods were on a different schedule.[54]

In the *Ion*, Hermes lets the audience know in advance what
Apollo has done and intends to do, and swift changes of fortune
throughout the drama also give the impression that a divine
presence is at work. In the *Orestes*, however, there are no such
perceptible manifestations of intention by the god or one of his
delegates, and there are no overt indications during the course of
the drama of a divine presence. But if Apollo works behind the
scenes and remains undetected by any of the mortal characters,
that is how that particular god prefers to act, avoiding any close
emotional connection to the mortals whose lives he has been
responsible for changing. In the *Alcestis* he knows that Heracles will
save Alcestis from Death, but he does not convey this information
to Admetus or do anything to stop him from lamenting the
apparent loss of his wife. Ion and Creusa also believe that he has
forgotten about them, but meanwhile he has been looking after
them through his delegates, immortal and mortal. He sent his

brother Hermes to rescue his son Ion when his mother Creusa abandoned him. He saw to it that Creusa did not poison her son, and he kept the people of Delphi and Ion from killing Creusa. Although Apollo does not appear himself at the end of the *Ion*, he makes sure that Creusa and Ion realize what he has done for them by sending his sister Athena to represent him; as Athena says, "Apollo has done all this well" (1595).

In Aeschylus' *Eumenides*, Apollo may appear to be more engaged with Orestes than in Euripides' *Orestes* because he plays a larger role in the action, but Aeschylus' characterization of the god bears a close resemblance to Euripides' portrayal of Apollo in the *Orestes*. In the *Eumenides* Apollo first appears *ex machina* after the terrifying entry of the Erinyes, who have pursued Orestes to Apollo's temple in Delphi. But Aeschylus also portrays him as distant and lacking in empathy. Apollo tells the exhausted Orestes: "I shall not betray you, but I shall be your guard through to the end, standing near you or at far distance, and I shall not be kind to your enemies" (64–6). Orestes still seeks more reassurance and assistance from the god: "Lord Apollo, you know how not to do wrong. Since you have that skill, learn not to be neglectful. You are strong, you can help me" (85–7). Apollo tells Orestes not to be afraid, but rather than escort Orestes to Athens himself, he sends Hermes to protect him on his journey.

Minimalist interventions are characteristic of this god, who prefers not to spend more time in the world of mortals than suits his immediate pleasure. In the *Eumenides* when Orestes gets to Athens, it is Athena (not Apollo) who immediately comes from Troy to protect Orestes from the Erinyes (398) and makes arrangements for his trial on the Hill of Ares at Athens. It is only when the trial begins that Apollo arrives, just in time to defend Orestes (579). He does so effectively, but bases his arguments on abstract reasoning rather than on the particulars of the case, claiming that the father is the more significant parent of the child, and that the mother's life is worth less, on the grounds that she is merely the soil in which the seed is planted (660–2). He does not speak directly to Orestes during the course of his trial and does not comfort him during his ordeal or do anything to stop his suffering. It is Athena who persuades the Erinyes not to punish the Athenians, but instead offers them honor in perpetuity so she can protect her city.

In the *Iliad* also Athena is more willing to speak with mortals than is Apollo. In Book 5 she rides in his chariot with Diomedes, and lifts the mist from his eyes so that he can see the gods in action on the battlefield. Apollo, however, appears only when needed. After Diomedes wounds the Trojan hero Aeneas, Diomedes also wounds Aeneas' mother Aphrodite when she comes to rescue him. Apollo comes to defend Aeneas, and delivers a succinct warning to the aggressive Diomedes not to try to oppose him or to have any illusions about their comparative strength: "do not wish to think yourself equal to the gods; since the race of the immortal gods is not the same as that of men who walk on the ground" (*Il.* 5.440–2). The god carries Aeneas to his temple in Troy, to be cared for by his own mother Leto and sister Artemis, and he creates an image of Aeneas to remain on the battlefield, for the Greeks and Trojans to fight over (449–53). In the *Orestes* Apollo silently takes Helen away just as Orestes is about to kill her (1629–30). Certainly if Apollo had spoken to Orestes and Electra he might have saved them and the other characters in the drama considerable agony. But as in the *Iliad* and the *Ion*, Apollo has little interest in mortals' suffering, but intervenes only to achieve a particular result.

In two of Sophocles' dramas, as in the *Ion*, Apollo directs the action, but always offstage. In Sophocles' *Electra*, Apollo through his oracle at Delphi told Orestes that he could avenge

his father's murder by stealth, without the help of an army
(32–7). Clytemnestra believes that he is dead, so although she
had been warned in a dream (417–27), she does not suspect that
Orestes has returned. When Orestes tells Electra that he is alive,
Clytemnestra does not hear her cries of joy. Aegisthus happens
to be away, so Orestes is able to kill Clytemnestra without
encountering any resistance. When Aegisthus comes back, Orestes
can catch him off guard, because he thinks that Orestes is dead.
Orestes' plans and timing work perfectly, even though the god
himself never appears or sends a sign of his presence.

   The same exact timing is characteristic of the action in
Sophocles' *Oedipus Tyrannus*.[55] Oedipus was told by the oracle at
Delphi that he would kill his father and marry his mother.[56] He
thought he could avoid his fate by not returning home to Corinth.
But by heading for Thebes, he fulfilled the prophecy. As soon as
he tries to discover who killed his father, he is able to learn the
truth in a single day. He refuses to listen to the prophet Tiresias,
who knows the truth that Apollo is planning to harm him (376–7).
The rapid unfolding of events reveals that the god is at work.
When Oedipus finally realizes who he is, "in his frenzy some god
showed him" (1258) where to find Jocasta's body. Only after he
has blinded himself does he finally realize that the god had seen
to it that the oracle was fulfilled: "It was Apollo, my friends,
Apollo, who brought about these evils, my evils, my suffering"
(1327–30).[57]

   In Euripides' dramas, as in Sophocles', Apollo seems to want
to keep his distance from the mortal characters and to enter their
world only when it is absolutely necessary for him to do so. His
speech directing the mortals to make peace with one another
is lacking in warmth or sympathy. But even though his remarks
are brief, and the content of his speech surprising, the mortal
characters immediately follow his directions, without expressing

any doubts or pausing to wonder at the reversal of their intentions and fortunes. Modern readers should follow their lead, however unanticipated and even artificial the intervention may seem to them. Greek audiences were accustomed to such last-minute epiphanies. At the end of Euripides' *Helen*, Helen and Menelaus are trying to escape from Egypt, but the king Theoclymenus is planning to murder the messenger who wants to keep him from killing his sister Theonoe, because she helped them plan their escape. But before anything can happen, Helen's brothers, the gods Castor and Polydeuces, suddenly appear *ex machina*. Speaking for both himself and Polydeuces, Castor orders Theoclymenus to stop, give up his plans to murder Theonoe and to marry Helen; instead he must allow her to return home with Menelaus. Castor's speech of intervention is about the same length as Apollo's in the *Orestes*, and the poet gives no hint in the preceding part of the play that he would appear at the end. At the beginning of the drama, Helen did not even know that he and Polydeuces had now become "gods who resemble stars" (140). Yet despite the suddenness of Castor's unanticipated appearance, no modern commentators doubt that he has the power to protect Helen from Theoclymenus or that he can convey to her and Menelaus the will of Zeus.

Unlike Apollo in the *Orestes*, who lets Orestes make his own way on to Athens (1643–8), Castor and Polydeuces do not leave Helen and Menelaus to sail back to Sparta unassisted. Castor promises that they will have a favoring breeze on their journey home, and that he and Polydeuces will accompany them on land back to their home in Sparta. Even though he is a god, he has some understanding of the human condition, because he had been a mortal, with two mortal parents, until Zeus allowed Polydeuces to waken him from death and made him a god.[58] If Apollo had been as solicitous about Orestes as Castor was about Helen, he would probably have seemed to be more credible to some of his modern critics, who were brought up on the notion that gods should care about mortals. Also if the mortal characters in the *Orestes* throughout the course of the drama had been trusting and steadfast in their belief that the god would defend Orestes, and if they had never complained about Apollo or doubted that he was prepared to help them, it might have been easier for modern readers to believe in the reality of his epiphany and its stunning and immediate effectiveness.

5

OTHER GODS

The other gods who appear *ex machina* in Euripides' dramas
do so because of their connections with particular mortals.
Aphrodite sees that Hippolytus will die because he refuses
to honor her; but Artemis comes to pay tribute to the dying
Hippolytus, and promises to avenge his death and ensure
that he will be remembered in ritual. In Euripides' *Bacchae*,
Zeus' son Dionysus punishes his own aunt, Agave, and her
son and his first cousin Pentheus for refusing to acknowledge
his divinity. He even sends his grandfather Cadmus into
exile: "long ago my father Zeus approved this" (1349).
Castor and Polydeuces come to help to their mortal relatives
in the *Electra* and the *Helen*. Hermes in Euripides' lost drama
Antiope intervenes to stop Amphion and Zethus from killing
Lycus, the king of Thebes. The only one of these gods who is
not a child of Zeus is the sea-goddess Thetis, who intervenes
in the *Andromache* to save the life of her great-grandson
Molossos, and to promise him a bright future. Thetis
belongs to a previous generation of gods who are now no
longer in command of the universe, but Euripides' audience
would have known her from the *Iliad* as Zeus' close ally
and benefactress; she kept Zeus from being overthrown, by
letting him know that the other gods were plotting against
him (*Il*. 1.396–406).

But the Olympians who intervene in drama do not always come in order to carry out the will of Zeus.[1] As in the Homeric epics, even within Zeus' monarchy the gods act independently of him and of each other. To some extent, at least, this lack of coordination helps to explain why pious actions on the part of mortals do not always receive due recompense from the gods. It also allows individual gods to inflict disproportionate punishment on particular mortals who have not given them sufficient honor. In Sophocles' drama *Ajax*, Athena drives Ajax insane and mocks him in his delusions. In the *Trojan Women*, Athena asks Zeus' brother Poseidon to help her destroy the Greek fleet. The author of the *Rhesus* has Athena pretend to be Aphrodite in order to mislead Paris. In Euripides' *Hippolytus* (428 BC) Aphrodite comes to punish Hippolytus, a mortal whom she regards as an enemy. She does not say that she is Zeus' daughter or that she is following his orders.[2] Instead she introduces herself to the audience by stating how famous and important she is throughout the known world, and identifying herself as the goddess Cypris—an alternative name that derives from her cult at Paphos in Cyprus.[3] She states that she respects those who honor her and destroys those who reject her. She explains that she wishes to punish Theseus' son Hippolytus because he is not willing to give her the honor she feels she deserves. All mortals who look upon the sun respect her power, and she harms anyone who does not honor her: gods enjoy being honored by mortals (5–8). It is only after she has reminded the audience of her importance that she describes what she plans to do. Hippolytus, Theseus' son by the Amazon Hippolyta, refuses to honor her and declines to have any part in sex or marriage. Instead he honors the maiden goddess Artemis, and spends his days in her company, hunting. Aphrodite says she does not resent his honoring Artemis; but he should also show proper respect to her. Because he has not done so, she will get her revenge on this very day.

The goddess has already set everything in motion, and has little more to do. She explains that she made Theseus' young wife Phaedra fall in love with Hippolytus when he came to Athens from his great-grandfather's home in Troezen to participate in the Eleusinian Mysteries (24–8). Theseus has now brought Phaedra and their children to Troezen; he had been banished from Athens for a year because in the course of claiming his throne in Athens he had killed his cousins. Now that Phaedra is living in the same house as Hippolytus, she has been trying to kill herself rather than betray her husband. Phaedra has behaved piously towards Aphrodite; after the goddess caused her to fall in love with Hippolytus, Phaedra built a temple to her on the south slopes of the Athenian Acropolis, within sight of the land of Troezen on the northeast coast of the Peloponnesus; "in time to come people will call it the goddess (i.e., her cult statue) set up near Hippolytus" (30–3).[4] But despite this act of piety, Aphrodite does not care about what happens to Phaedra. Getting revenge against someone who does not honor her is more important to her than protecting someone who does: "I do not place a higher value on the harm done to her than on punishing my enemies and bringing satisfaction to myself" (49–50). The goddess now prepares to leave, since she sees Hippolytus coming. Her last words remind the audience of the extent of human ignorance: "he does not know that the gates of Hades have been opened, and he is looking on the light for the last time" (56–7). Her speech makes it very clear that mortals have no choice other than to honor her, and even when they do, they cannot expect from her any kind of recompense, compassion, or forgiveness.

As Aphrodite departs Hippolytus enters with his hunters, singing a short hymn in praise of Artemis "daughter of Leto and Zeus, the most beautiful of all the maidens" (64–6). He offers her a crown made from flowers that he has picked in a meadow where flocks have never grazed, and which only the most noble and chaste can enter. He alone of mortals has the privilege of speaking with her, even though he cannot see her (86). He prays to end his life as he began it. As he finishes praying, an old slave urges him to make an offering also to Aphrodite, whose statue stands in front of the gates to his grandfather's house. But Hippolytus refuses to take the slave's advice; he says he will greet the goddess from a distance, because he is chaste (102). The slave reminds him that Cypris is an important god, but Hippolytus says that he prefers not to honor divinities that are adored at night (106), and bids the goddess farewell (113).[5] The old slave asks the goddess to pardon him because he is young and proud: "Pretend not to hear him; gods should be wiser than mortals" (119–20). But the audience knows already that the vain and powerful goddess has no intention of following the slave's advice and pardoning Hippolytus; she has already seen to it that Hippolytus will die because he has not honored her.

With the exception of Hippolytus, all the mortal characters in the drama are aware of the terrible power wielded by Aphrodite and her son Eros, and realize that all mortals and immortals or subject to her (e.g., 447–50).[6] The women of Troezen who comprise the chorus wonder if Phaedra is ill because she has learned that Theseus has a new concubine. Phaedra cannot forget that her sister Ariadne had fallen in love with Theseus, and her mother Pasiphae had fallen in love with a bull (337–41). Phaedra's old Nurse and the chorus are horrified when she reveals that she is in love with her stepson. The old Nurse tries to persuade her to give in to her passion, because Aphrodite is in the *aithēr* and the waves of the sea: Zeus fell in love with Semele, the goddess Dawn with Cephalus, but nonetheless they continued to exist (447–61). Phaedra objects to the Nurse's speech because it appeals to her emotions rather than to her reason and her desire to do what is morally acceptable. But the real problem with the nurse's argument is that she is talking about gods. Why does she suppose that a mortal woman could get away with such behavior?[7] In an attempt to cure Phaedra's passion the Nurse tells Hippolytus that Phaedra is in love with him, swearing him to secrecy. He is horrified, and disparages all women. Phaedra hears him shouting, and decides to kill herself, but to protect her reputation she writes a letter to Theseus accusing Hippolytus of raping her. When Theseus returns to find his wife dead and reads her letter, he immediately uses one of the three curses his father Poseidon gave him to kill his son on that very day. Hippolytus insists that he is innocent, but cannot tell his father about Phaedra's passion for him because that would mean breaking his oath to the nurse. As Hippolytus prepares to leave Troezen, he says farewell to Artemis. The chorus is in despair, and cannot understand why an innocent man should be punished: "When thoughts about the gods' concerns come to my mind, they greatly relieve my sorrow. I hold some hope within me, but I am lost when I look at what happens to mortals and their accomplishments. One thing comes after another; the life of men changes and is always drifting" (1102–6).[8] Soon they learn from a messenger that Hippolytus' chariot was wrecked by a bull that appeared in a wave of the sea and frightened his horses.

Then, without warning, Artemis appears *ex machina*, blaming Theseus for refusing to discover what actually happened, and for acting without full knowledge: "You have been found to be evil in your father's sight and in mine, because you did not wait for proof or for the words of prophets; you didn't wait for a time to consider, but more quickly than you should you released the curse on your child and killed him" (1320–4). Nonetheless, he can be pardoned for what he has done, because Cypris had wanted this to happen, in order to satisfy her anger. "There is a custom among the gods: no god wants to oppose what another god wishes; instead we stand aside" (1330–1). Artemis could not intervene to help the "man who was most dear to her" because she was afraid of Zeus. "Your ignorance," she says, "releases you from the charge of wrongdoing" (1338). Nonetheless Artemis regrets that she could not intervene in order to save him: "the gods do not rejoice when pious mortals die; but we destroy the evil ones, along with their children and houses" (1339–41).

Although the goddess is still present when Hippolytus is brought in and witnesses his agony, he still cannot see her, but before she can speak to him he senses that she is present: "a divine breath of fragrance."[9] Divine law (themis) does not allow Artemis to shed a tear (1397), when Hippolytus reminds her that he can no longer be her huntsman and her servant, her horse-tender and caretaker of her statues. Artemis explains that the "Cypris the evil-doer devised these troubles," because "she blamed you because of her honor, and hated you because you were chaste" (1400, 1402). At last Hippolytus recognizes Aphrodite's power: "I realize she was the divinity who destroyed me" (1401). Artemis cannot save him, but she promises him that even in the darkness below the earth he will have his revenge; she will use her inescapable arrows to kill the mortal Cypris loves most.[10] She also states that Hippolytus will be remembered in ritual. Young women in Troezen will dedicate a lock of their hair to him before their marriage, and in time to come he will "reap the harvest of their tears," and maidens will remember him in their songs; the story of Phaedra's passion for him will not be forgotten. In the third century BC there was a gymnasium of Hippolytus at Troezen, and in the second century AD Pausanias saw a precinct and a temple dedicated to Hippolytus with a very old statue and a priest.[11]

Artemis concludes her speech by assuring Theseus that it was Aphrodite who was responsible for Hippolytus' death: "For when the gods give them the opportunity, humans usually make errors in judgment" (*examartanein*; 1433–4). She advises Hippolytus not to hate his father, and prepares to take her leave: "divine law (*themis*) does not allow me to look at the dead or defile my vision with dying breaths; and I see that you are near that evil" (1437–9).[12] Artemis can leave without shedding a tear or offering final comfort to the dying man because she is a different species of being, immortal and ageless. Hippolytus says nothing about the goddess' plans for revenge, or about the hero cult that she has promised him, even though it is an honor to be remembered in song and worshipped in cult as a hero. Instead he speaks to her about what has meant most to him during his short lifetime, their past relationship: "Farewell to you, blessed maiden; but you leave this long friendship easily" (*rāidiōs*; 1440–1). It is hard for him to part from her, because of the great satisfaction he derived from speaking with her, being her companion in the hunt, and from tending her cult. But what seems to Hippolytus to be a "long friendship" is only a brief interlude in the goddess' endless existence. She can leave "easily," because gods do everything at their ease.[13]

Hippolytus uses the few minutes of life remaining to him to follow the goddess' advice, and immediately forgives his father. As his son dies, Theseus exclaims "glorious land of Erechtheus and Pallas, what a man you have lost!" (1459–60). The chorus echoes Theseus' lament in their closing statement: "all the citizens share this sorrow, which has come unexpectedly" (1462–3). The idea that Hippolytus' death would be a loss for Athens as well as for Troezen would not have been surprising to an ancient audience, because Athens was where Theseus and his family lived when he was not in exile, and where Phaedra wished that her children would have a good reputation (421–2). In mythology Troezen was also part of Theseus' hegemony, since its ruler Pittheus was the father of

Theseus' mother Aethra. Theseus might have wished to bring his
son back with him to Athens after he returned from his year of
exile. In historical times, after the Persian Wars, the Athenians had
occupied Troezen, and in 430, two years before the *Hippolytus* was
performed, the Athenians had raided Troezen and other cities in
that part of the Argolid (Thuc. 2.56.4).[14] It was around this time
that the first inscriptions that mention the sanctuary of "Aphrodite
near the tomb of Hippolytus" on the Acropolis at Athens were
put up.[15] But the reference to Athens at the end of the play is not
necessarily political in nature. It also serves as a reminder to the
audience that the action of the drama expresses a basic theological
truth: no one, however noble his or her intentions, can pick and
choose the gods he or she prefers to honor; all gods, no matter how
uncongenial they may seem, demand respect and devotion from
mortals. One of Euripides' last dramas, the *Bacchae*, makes a similar
statement, with even more devastating consequences to the mortals
involved.

Hippolytus would have seen nothing wrong in Artemis'
desire to punish Aphrodite, since it was considered ethical to
help friends and harm enemies. One of the few ways in which
one immortal could hurt another was to kill a favorite mortal
or mortals. But the goddess' inability to help Hippolytus has
troubled some modern critics. Certainly, as Helene Foley has
observed, the goddess' promises of retaliation and a future cult
in Troezen do not bring relief to Hippolytus' present suffering.[16]
According to Francis Dunn, any "perverse pleasure" that we might
get from the witnessing the success of Aphrodite's plan to destroy
Hippolytus "does not carry us forward to a new understanding
or a heightened awareness, as does the destruction of Oedipus,
but simply plays out its violent and destructive spectacle."[17] Even
the ritual of remembrance that Artemis describes appears to
Dunn to be an empty promise, because there is no archaeological

evidence that a cult of Hippolytus in Troezen had existed before
the production of Euripides' drama. Artemis' description of the
"greatest honors" that she will bestow on him seems anomalous. In
other known cults young women before their marriage offer locks
of their hair to heroines or goddesses, not to a male hero.[18] As the
one exception to that rule, Scott Scullion suggests, interpreting
the hero cult of Hippolytus is "a typical example of Euripidean
ritual irony."[19]

The concept of ritual irony differs from that of simple irony,
in that it offers a more sophisticated and culturally sensitive
approach to the questions raised by the actions of the gods in
Greek drama. It allows the poet to show respect for traditional
religious practices while simultaneously calling attention to the
deficiencies of conventional theology. As Foley characterizes it,
"Euripides seems to be drawing on ritual as metaphor and symbol
while his own ambiguous art liberates itself from subordination
to actual practice."[20] But there is no particular need to suppose
that Euripides was being ironic when he had Artemis promise
Hippolytus that she would establish a cult in his honor that may
not have existed at the time of the performance. In the context
of a drama, the promise of such a cult would have been sufficient,
whether or not it ever became a reality, as it seems to have been
in the case of the oath in Euripides' *Suppliants*.[21] Also, Euripides
would not have needed to employ irony or any other form of
verbal dissimulation if he wished to portray Artemis (or any other
god) as lacking in empathy.

Artemis does not have the power to save Hippolytus' life or to
grant him immortality (only her father Zeus can do that).[22] But
she can ensure that he will be remembered in perpetuity. The
"greatest honors in Troezen" promised by Artemis are not fixed
in time. The first of these honors, that girls before marriage offer
Hippolytus locks of their hair and "the greatest sorrow of their

tears" (1425–7), would have been familiar to Athenian audiences from the festival of the Adonia.[23] Although in the Near East Adonis was worshiped as a god, in Greece he was regarded as a hero.[24] The cult of Hippolytus, both at Athens and at Troezen, also appears to have been connected with that of Aphrodite.[25] Adonis was one of Aphrodite's lovers, but the custom for Hippolytus is different because he has "a virgin spirit" (*parthenos psychē*; 1006) and was not married, like the girls who will offer him cuttings of their hair. The chorus of Euripides' lost drama *Hippolytus Crowned* sings of him: "Blessed hero Hippolytus, what honors you have won because of your chastity (*sōphrosyne*). Mortals have no power greater than virtue, for sooner or later there is a noble reward for piety (*eusebeia*)" (*TrGF* 5.1, 446).[26] The girls weep for Hippolytus as they leave their maidenhood behind, because unlike themselves, he must remain unmarried for eternity, and never have the children who could bury him and help to keep his memory alive by tending his grave.[27] It is for that reason that Artemis grants him the second honor: maidens will always sing of Phaedra's passion for him, and consequently, his innocence and nobility of mind will always be spoken of (1428–30). That promise has certainly been fulfilled, if only through the medium of Euripides' drama.

In depicting Aphrodite Euripides drew on epic tradition, but his model is not the Aphrodite of the *Iliad*, who comes to rescue her son Aeneas, is wounded by Diomedes, and rushes to her mother to be healed (5.318–62). Instead his portrait of the goddess seems rather to have been inspired by the *Homeric Hymn to Aphrodite*, which depicts the goddess as powerful, deceitful, cunning, and indifferent to human suffering. The poet who composed the hymn also emphasizes the limitations of human knowledge, a theme prominent in the *Hippolytus*, in which neither Hippolytus nor his father are sufficiently aware of how little they understand. The hymn begins by celebrating Aphrodite's power over all living

creatures, mortal and immortal, with the exception of the three
maiden goddesses, Athena, Artemis, and Hestia. Nonetheless,
Zeus caused her to fall in love with a mortal man, so that she
could not boast that she alone had not borne a mortal child. After
visiting her temple at Paphos on the island of Cyprus, Aphrodite
seduced the Trojan prince Anchises by changing her appearance
to that of a maiden. Anchises at first thinks she is a goddess, but
Aphrodite assures him that she is a mortal princess brought to him
by Hermes. So Anchises, a mortal, "slept with the goddess, clearly
without knowing" what he was doing (167).[28] After they have
made love, Aphrodite dresses and appears to him as a goddess,
towering over him, and with immortal beauty shining from her
face, taunts him by asking if she now appears to be the same as
when he first laid eyes on him (178–9), reminding him of the
limitations of his human understanding that the poet emphasized
in his description of Anchises' state of mind as he took the goddess
to bed. She says that she will bear him a son, called Aeneas because
of the pain (*ainon achos*; 198–9) she endured by falling into a
mortal's bed. She also explains why she will not ask Zeus to make
Anchises immortal. She assures him that he will have nothing to
fear if he follows her orders: her son will be brought to him when
he is five, but she warns him never to reveal that he slept with her,
lest Zeus strike him with his thunderbolt. And with that threat the
goddess goes back to Olympus, never to return.

The same characteristics of divinity, desire for honor,
self-importance, cruelty, deceptiveness, and transformative power
are all present in Euripides' portrait of the god Dionysus in his
drama the *Bacchae*. As in the *Hippolytus*, the god punishes those who
refuse to honor him. But instead of allowing mortals to do his work
for him, Dionysus comes to Thebes himself in disguise and without
any apparent effort accomplishes his goal. In constructing the plot of
the drama Euripides drew on themes inherent in earlier narratives

about Dionysus. Homer relates the story of Lycurgus, who pursued the "insane (*mainomenos*) god" and his nurses with an ox-goad; "Dionysus in terror dove into the sea and Thetis took him to her bosom" (*Il.* 6.132–7). But Lycurgus' victory was short-lived and illusory. Because he dared to fight with the gods, Zeus blinded him, and he did not live a long life (138–40). The writer of the *Homeric Hymn to Dionysus* also describes how anyone who refuses to believe in Dionysus' divinity must perish. When the god appears on the sea shore in the form of a fine young man, pirates kidnap him and take him on board their ship in the hope of being able to sell him. When the bonds they put on the god do not hold, the helmsman warns the others that the young man must be a god, but the captain and the other pirates refuse to believe him. Once they set sail, the god performs miracles: wine flows through the ship; ivy grows up the mast; garlands cover the thole-pins. Then the god becomes a lion, and creates a bear; the lion attacks the captain, and the other pirates jump into the sea and become dolphins. But Dionysus saves the helmsman and explains to him who he is: "Dionysus, the loud-thunderer, whom my mother Semele, daughter of Cadmus, once bore to Zeus" (55–7). An ancient audience would have recognized that this identification is in itself another miracle, because Semele and her father Cadmus were mortals. Normally a god's parents must also both be gods.

Dionysus himself delivers the prologue to the *Bacchae*, disguised (as he explains) as a mortal. He identifies himself by describing the miracle of his birth: "I have come, the child of Zeus to the land of Thebes, Dionysus, whom Cadmus' daughter Semele once bore, delivered by the flame of lightning" (1–3). The god points out the funeral monument for his mother that was set up in the place where the lightning struck her while she was alive, near her house; her father Cadmus has made it a shrine, and the god himself surrounded it with ivy. He explains that the site is an "undying

outrage on the part of Hera against my mother" (9). Dionysus did
not need to explain to the ancient audience that Hera was always
jealous of the women to whom her husband had made love, and
sought to harm them in some way; her treatment of Heracles
is another example. He does not describe how Hera tricked
Semele into making Zeus promise to come to her as he would
to Hera, and her body "could not endure the heavenly tumult"
of his lightning and "was burned by the gift of his intercourse,"
as the Roman poet Ovid describes it (*Met*. 3.308–9).[29] Instead
Dionysus calls attention to the story of how he was born from
Zeus' thigh because it explains why he is now immortal, and not
just an extraordinary mortal, like Apollo's son Asclepius.[30] As
the chorus soon relates (88–98), when Semele was destroyed by
Zeus' lightning bolt, Zeus took the fetus and concealed it in his
thigh until it was time for the baby to be born, from his immortal
father rather than from a female womb, like his half-sister Athena,
who was born from Zeus' head. Since anyone who refuses to
believe this story will doubt that Dionysus is a god, most myths
about Dionysus include some form of resistance to his worship
on the part of mortals, followed by demonstration of his divinity
by means of miracles, and then violent punishment for anyone
who still refuses to worship him as a god. The present drama is no
exception.

Dionysus informs the audience that after establishing his cults
throughout Asia, and the Greek cities of Asia Minor, he has come
to Thebes, setting up dances and establishing his rites "so that
I might be a god visible to mortals" (20–2). Thebes was the first
of all Greek cities that he made resound with the ritual cries; he
made the city wear the fawnskin and carry the thyrsus, "a missile
of ivy" (25). He did this because his mother's sisters—who of all
people ought to have believed the story of his birth—refused to
acknowledge that his father was Zeus, but said that Semele made

the story up to cover up a liaison with a mortal man. So he drove his aunts mad and sent them to the wilderness on Mt. Cithaeron, wearing fawnskins and carrying thyrsi, and sent all the women of Thebes along with them: "this city must learn, even if it doesn't want to, that it has not been initiated into my Bacchic rites, and I must speak in defense of Semele by appearing as the god she bore to Zeus" (40–3). Dionysus now explains that Cadmus handed over the kingship to his grandson Pentheus, who "fights against divinity" and rejects his worship and will not pray to him or make offerings. So Dionysus will demonstrate to him and to all the Thebans that "he was born a god, before going on to another city" (47–9). If the Thebans try to bring the women back from the mountains with violence, he will make war against the men on their behalf—that is why he has made himself appear to be a mortal. He then summons the women who have followed him from Asia to beat their drums around Pentheus' house, so that the city will see them, while he himself goes to join the Theban women in the mountains.

From what Dionysus says in his opening speech it is clear that the Thebans in particular have had trouble accepting the fact that he is a god because they know that his mother was a mortal. His aunts in particular refuse to believe that his father was a god. His first cousin Pentheus, the son of his mother's sister Agave, is now the king of Thebes, but he also refuses to believe in Dionysus' divinity and denies him even the basic honors to which gods are entitled. The choral song that follows shows that there are other reasons why the royal family has resisted Dionysus' cult: it is foreign, and disrupts the established pattern of life in the city. The chorus describes how the god's devotees go to the mountain in order to perform his rites, carrying the thyrsus (a fennel stalk) and wearing crowns of ivy on their heads, singing and dancing. They sing of the god's birth, how the lightning bolt brought on his mother's labor pains, and the god took the baby and concealed him in his thigh, securing it with golden pins, hidden from Hera. The chorus speaks of the drums that they use, which were invented by the ecstatic Corybants, who celebrated Zeus' birth in Crete, and describes life in the mountains, and the night rituals led by the god, with the milk and honey the god brings forth, and the freedom of running "like a colt with its mother" (163–6). The ancient audience did not need to be told how different these ecstatic rites were from those that they followed when they were worshiping the other Olympian gods, such as solemn processions leading up to a carefully programmed animal sacrifice; the feasting afterwards, all within a sacred space marked off by the community, with established procedures that must be carefully followed, like the sacrificial ritual prescribed by Athena at the end of Euripides' *Suppliants*.[31]

As the chorus finishes their song, the prophet Tiresias enters to summon Cadmus to join the celebration. The two old men are carrying *thyrsi* and wearing fawnskins and ivy crowns: "We must honor my daughter's son Dionysus who has appeared to mortals as a god and to make him as great as we can" (181–3). They are prepared to dance, even though they are old, and Tiresias advises Cadmus not to ride a chariot to the mountain, because by walking they give greater honor to the god (192). But then Cadmus' grandson Pentheus enters and tries to persuade the two old men not to participate. Like Hippolytus, he is a young man with decided opinions and a deep distrust of women. He is angry because all the women have left the city to honor Dionysus ("whoever he is") and because (or so he claims) the women have gone to the mountains in order to drink wine, dance, and sneak off to sleep with men. He wants to find and kill the stranger, "a sorcerer (*goēs*), enchanter (*epōidos*) from Lydia, with scented hair, a face red with wine, and the pleasures of Aphrodite in his eyes" (234–5).[32] He believes that the stranger spends his days and nights with the young girls. Pentheus is particularly outraged by the stranger's claim that Dionysus is a god, who was sewn into Zeus' thigh—[Dionysus] who was burned up by the fire of the thunderbolt along with his mother, because she lied about her union with Zeus: "These ideas are dreadful, worthy of hanging, whoever this stranger is, to commit these outrages" (hybreis; 248). He then criticizes Tiresias and Cadmus for wearing the god's costume and for trying to join the drunken women. He even suggests that Tiresias is joining the god's devotees in order to collect fees from burnt offerings. The chorus accuses Pentheus of impiety (dyssebeia; 263).

Tiresias tries to reason with him, first by claiming that Demeter and Dionysus are the two gods who do most for humans, Demeter by her gift to them of grain, and Dionysus by providing a way to make mortals stop grieving, sleep, and forget about the evils of the day. He addresses the problematic issue of Dionysus' miraculous birth. But instead of advising Pentheus simply to accept and believe, he tries to rationalize the story: when Zeus brought the baby up to Olympus, Hera wanted to throw it from heaven, but Zeus broke off a section of the aithēr that circles the earth, and gave it to Hera as a hostage (homēros). Later mortals said he had been sewn into the thigh (mēros) of Zeus (289–97). Tiresias then speaks of the powers that come to men from the god's madness: he gives them the ability to prophesy and to rout armies; he is present even in Apollo's Delphi. Finally, Tiresias urges Pentheus not to suppose that his power is greater than that of the god. The prophet's advice is sensible, but it appeals only to reason, and not to emotion, which the god also desires to hear expressed by his worshipers.[33] Cadmus also urges Pentheus to join them, and again appeals to reason: even if Pentheus does not believe that Dionysus is a god, he should say that he is, because it will

bring honor to their family. He reminds him of what happened
to his cousin Actaeon, who was torn apart by his own dogs after
he boasted that he was a better hunter than the goddess Artemis.
Cadmus' advice is sensible, but neither he nor Tiresias appears to
understand what the ritual means to the women who take part
in it, their feelings of joy and release, of being in nature, "away
from their looms and their shuttles" (118). Pentheus is unwilling
to listen to the old men, because he views the cult as a threat to
the established pattern of life in his city. He is convinced that the
reason why the women of the city have abandoned their homes
and families to participate in the cult is so that they can drink and
"serve the beds of men" (221–3, 353–4). He still believes that
by using force he can control the problem. He orders his men
to destroy the place where Tiresias makes his prophecies, and to
find the stranger, so he can be punished by being stoned to death
(356–7).

The stranger, who is of course Dionysus disguised as a
mortal, then performs a series of miracles that happen offstage
but are reported to Pentheus by his slaves. Bonds cannot hold
the stranger or the women. Still, Pentheus is so determined to
do what he himself supposes to be right that he does not hear
that the stranger's answers to his questions are ambiguous, and
indicate that he is something more than he says he is. Pentheus
imprisons the stranger. The chorus once again sings of the story
of the god's birth, describing how the spring of Dirce received
the baby in her waters, after Zeus snatched him from the undying
fire, and cried out "come Dithyrambus, enter my male womb!
Bacchus, I reveal you to Thebes to call by this name" (521–9). [34]
As the women of the chorus finishes their song about the god's
powers, they hear Dionysus' voice calling to them, asking the
goddess Enosis ("Earthquake") to make Pentheus' palace fall to the
ground, and commanding the flame burning on Semele's tomb

to set the palace on fire. The chorus falls to the ground, but then
the stranger enters and reassures them—he has set himself free
from prison. He had made Pentheus delusional, so that he tied up
a bull instead, and slashed the air with his sword, while his palace
burned to the ground. Despite all that has happened, Pentheus still
does not understand the power of the god, and orders the gates of
the city to be shut, as if by that means he could stop the god from
escaping. A herdsman then comes and reports how the women
in the mountains attacked and defeated Pentheus' army, and begs
him to receive the god and his rites into the city. The disguised god
again tries to persuade him to believe, and even offers to bring
the women back from the mountains. But when instead Pentheus
orders his servants to bring him his weapons, Dionysus breaks off
the discussion with a sudden shout; from this point on he sets
out to lead Pentheus to his death (810–1).[35] The god persuades
him to don women's clothes so that he can spy on them; like
them, Pentheus will wear a fawnskin and carry a thyrsus. The god
explains to the chorus that he has put "a light madness" (*lyssa*) into
Pentheus, so that he will wear woman's dress. Not only will he
be mocked by the Thebans, he will be killed by his mother, and
"realize that Dionysus is the son of Zeus, who is a full god, most
terrible to mortals and the kindest" (859–61).

Like Aphrodite in the *Hippolytus*, Dionysus does not harm
Pentheus directly, but lets mortals do the work for him. His
method, however, is to alter their perceptions of reality; it is
that ability, of course, that explains why he is the god both of
wine and of the theater. The god leads the willing Pentheus to
the mountains, where he imagines that he will be able to spy on
the women unperceived. But the god makes sure that his mother
and aunts can see him, and that they imagine him to be a wild
animal. With the powers given to them by the god, the women
tear down the tree in which Pentheus has been hiding. Pentheus

suddenly comes to his senses and tears off his veil so his mother can recognize him. He touches her cheek, and identifies himself, begging her to have pity on him and not to kill him because of his mistakes (*hamartiai*; 1118–21). But Agave and her sisters tear him apart with their bare hands.[36]

His mother Agave returns to Thebes with her son Pentheus' head on her thyrsus, supposing that she is a huntress who has killed a lion. Her father Cadmus slowly brings her to her senses, and explains that like Pentheus she was punished for not worshiping the god (1302). Grieving and powerless, Cadmus concludes: "if there is anyone who thinks he is superior to the divinities, let him look on the death of this man and believe in the gods" (1325–6).

It is at this point that Dionysus appears as himself *ex machina*. The first part of his speech is lost, but he concludes it by letting his grandfather and Pentheus' mother know what Zeus' prophecy has in store for them. Cadmus and his wife Harmonia will become

Figure 5.1 Red-figure cup showing the death of Pentheus. ca. 480 BC. Credit: Kimbell Art Museum, Fort Worth, Texas / Art Resource, NY.

snakes.[37] Cadmus will lead a vast Asian army, which will have a bad homecoming because they have sacked Apollo's oracle. But another god, Harmonia's father Ares, will rescue them and they will live in the land of the blessed, the Elysian Fields. Again the god reminds the mortals that he was born a god: "I, Dionysus make this proclamation because I have not sprung from a mortal father, but from Zeus. If you all had been sensible, when you didn't want to be, you would have had good fortune with the son of Zeus as your ally" (1340–3). Cadmus admits that they have done wrong, and asks for mercy, but the god does not change his mind, because they insulted him. Cadmus replies: "gods ought not to be like mortals in their temperaments" (1348), making the kind of plea that the old servant makes to Aphrodite in the *Hippolytus*, in an attempt to secure her forgiveness: "gods ought to be wiser than mortals" (120).[38] But Dionysus is not moved: "long ago my father Zeus agreed to this" (1349). Even if the audience had not already seen many manifestations of Dionysus' divinity, this lack of empathy alone would have identified him as a god.[39] Agave, along with her sisters, and Cadmus must now go their separate ways into exile, never to see each other again.

The mortals' repeated expressions of affection for each other help to set into clear relief the stark contrast between the natures of gods and of mortals. The portrayal of their affection for one another allows the audience to see some the ways in which humans can try to overcome even the most terrible aspects of their fate simply by enduring and caring for each other. While acquiring such knowledge can hardly be considered something as positive and glorious as a triumph, it does at least offer the partial consolation of understanding, and make the mortals aware of the value of their affection for one another, which can help them to survive the suffering imposed upon them by the god.[40] Jenny March suggests that Euripides may have meant the last scene of the *Bacchae* "to hold in it more of comfort, even of healing, than we, almost two and a half thousand years on, are capable of seeing."[41] But if there is such a message, no hint of it is conveyed to the audience by what Euripides has the characters in the drama say. Cadmus can only visualize the worst features of the god's prediction, metamorphosis into a snake, leading a foreign army against the altars and tombs of Greece, never being able to cross the stream of Acheron, and finding rest in the silence of death (1355–63). He seems to derive no comfort from the god's promise that he and his wife will eventually go to the Elysian Fields. Agave's one consolation is that she and her sisters will be able to go where "polluted" Mt. Cithaeron will never see her again and she will not see Cithaeron or any memorial of the thyrsus.

Cadmus and Agave have been able to bring some comfort to one another, but like Amphitryon and his son Heracles at the end of Euripides' *Heracles*, they must now go into exile and never see each other again. Heracles at least can rely on the support and friendship of Theseus, who offers him not only companionship and compassion, but asylum in Athens and the promise of a hero cult there after his death. At the end of the *Bacchae*, however, there is no promise of a Theseus or an Athens awaiting Cadmus and his daughters, and no prospect of refuge or compassion in Greece or anywhere else. If the drama conveys any particular theological truth, it is to respect the demands of divinity, no matter how bizarre or irrational they may seem to mortal comprehension. As Tiresias tells Pentheus, Dionysus does offer mortals a great gift, temporary forgetfulness of the evils of the day (278–83). But even this gift is in essence an illusion. Neither Dionysus nor any other god does anything to change the reality of human suffering.

As we have seen in other dramas, gods have no compunction about seeing that their enemies are destroyed, but they also do not seem to be concerned when innocent people perish along

with them: Phaedra was pious towards Aphrodite, but the goddess
does not spare her because it is necessary that Phaedra die in
order for Aphrodite to get her revenge. In the *Bacchae* Euripides
makes Dionysus behave with even greater cruelty. Although he is
Cadmus' grandson, and Agave's nephew, he shows no compassion
for the mortal members of his family, nor does he offer them any
forgiveness, even though Cadmus was willing to participate in
his cult and tried to persuade his grandson to join him. The god's
treatment of Pentheus and Agave is even more brutal: before he
leads Pentheus to his death he mocks him by making him put on
women's clothing, and sees to it that before he dies Pentheus is
able to understand that he is being murdered by his own mother.
Euripides may have invented these aspects of the drama's plot.
In the standard version of the myth Pentheus is portrayed as an
armed man trying to attack the god and his women followers, as in
the story of Lycurgus (*Il.* 6.132–7), who tried to attack the god's
nurses with his ox-goad. On vase paintings Pentheus is shown
hiding in the woods dressed in conventional clothing and carrying
a sword.[42]

Gods do little to mitigate hardship for mortals, even when they
come to offer the human characters safe conduct or the promise
of future happiness. But even though they cannot interfere with
another god's plans, they can and will intervene on behalf of their
mortal families and friends. In the *Andromache*, a drama that
was performed not long after the *Hippolytus*, the goddess Thetis
manifests herself only when there seems to be no hope for the
innocent and virtuous. After Thetis' mortal son Achilles had
died in the Trojan War, his son Neoptolemus had won Hector's
wife Andromache as his prize. He brought her to his home to
Thetideion, in Thessaly, and made her his concubine. The town
was named for Neoptolemus' grandmother, the goddess Thetis,
who had been compelled by Zeus to marry the mortal Peleus; but

after their son Achilles was born Thetis left Peleus and returned
to her home in the sea. As the drama begins, Andromache has
taken refuge at the altar in the shrine of Thetis outside of the
house, because Neoptolemus' wife Hermione is jealous of
her, and Hermione's father Menelaus is threatening to kill her.
Neoptolemus cannot protect Andromache or their son because
he has gone to Apollo's shrine in Delphi to make amends for his
irrational behavior in the past, when he demanded that the god pay
recompense to him for murdering his father. Menelaus manages to
get Andromache to leave the altar by threatening to kill the son she
has borne to Neoptolemus, but as soon as she leaves the sanctuary
he goes back on his word and prepares to kill both Andromache
and her son.

Suddenly old Peleus enters and rescues her and her son; he
still commands an army and can protect them. Menelaus leaves;
Hermione wants to kill herself, but before she can do so her
cousin Orestes arrives and promises to rescue her. Although Peleus
and Andromache are unaware of it, Orestes has already made
plans to see that Neoptolemus will never return from Delphi.
Orestes states that Apollo reverses the fortunes of men who
"think great thoughts," supposing that they can tell the gods what
to do, as Neoptolemus tried to do when he asked Apollo to pay
him compensation for the death of his father Achilles (1005–8).
Peleus returns to find that Hermione has left the house and that
Orestes has gone to Delphi. But before Peleus can have word sent
to Neoptolemus warning him about Orestes, a messenger arrives
and says that Neoptolemus has been murdered at Delphi; Orestes
had allies in Delphi who spread the rumor that Neoptolemus had
come to steal treasures from the sanctuary. He was ambushed
while entering the temple so that he might pray to Apollo.[43]
Although Neoptolemus defended himself bravely, he managed to
hold off his attackers until "someone cried out from the middle

of the sanctuary something dreadful and terrifying," in order
to encourage his enemies to renew their attack. The Delphians
stabbed and mutilated Neoptolemus' body, and threw it out of
the sanctuary.[44] The messenger assumes that it was Apollo who
cried out, and considers the god responsible for Neoptolemus'
death: "that is how the god who prophesies to others, who
administers justice to all humankind, punished Achilles' son; he
remembered an old quarrel, like some low-born man—how then
could he be wise?" (1161–5).

Like Cadmus in the *Bacchae*, Peleus laments the death of his
grandson and the destruction of his house, since he now has no
hope of legitimate descendants. He throws his scepter to the
ground and calls on his absent wife the goddess Thetis to witness
his fall into destruction. Like the messenger who asked how
Apollo could be wise if he behaves like some low-born man,
Peleus does not understand that in fact the gods have not forgotten
about him. As soon as he stops speaking, the chorus sees a divinity
coming through the upper air. It is Thetis herself, who tells
him not to "grieve too much." She too has lost her son Achilles,
although she is a goddess and if she had had a god as husband, she
could have given birth to immortal children whom she would
have had no need to weep for.[45] Then, like other gods *ex machina*,
she gives Peleus explicit instructions: he is to take Neoptolemus'
body to Delphi and bury it at the altar of Apollo's temple, as a
reproach to the people of Delphi, who allowed Neoptolemus to be
murdered.[46] Andromache will leave in order to marry the Trojan
seer Helenus in Molossia, and her son by Neoptolemus will be
the ancestor of the kings of that country: "for the race could not
be cut off in that way, not yours nor mine nor that of Troy, for the
gods also care about Troy, even though that city fell because that is
what Athena wanted" (1249–52). Finally she tells Peleus that she
will free him from mortal suffering and make him an immortal

and un-aging god; he will dwell with her in the sea, but be able to walk out with dry feet (!) to see his son Achilles on the White Island in the Black Sea. After going to Delphi with Neoptolemus' body, he is to wait for her in a cave on the promontory of Sepias near the port of Iolcos. He must follow these instructions, which had been decreed by Zeus. "Stop your grief for the dead. This is the vote the gods have cast for all mortals, and they must pay their debt" (1270–2).

As Charles Segal observed, Thetis' last words to Peleus "point back to, and reaffirm the larger community of mortals."[47] But awareness of shared suffering can only be a partial comfort. The future is not what Peleus had hoped for. The gods have promised that neither his race nor that of the Trojans will die out, but their survivors will live on in an obscure place and with a different name; it is an outcome that is tinged with regret for a more glorious past and hopes that will never be fulfilled. Zeus has seen to it that Peleus arrived in time to save Andromache and her son (Peleus' great-grandson) from death (such precise timing is almost always a sign of divine oversight). But neither Zeus nor Apollo does anything to protect Neoptolemus when he returns to Delphi; in fact the voice that comes from Apollo's temple turns the tide of battle against him.[48] Thetis cannot protect her grandson from the hostile intentions of another god, just as Artemis could not save her favorite mortal, Hippolytus. By mortal standards, divine justice will always seem excessive and unforgiving, especially when it is meted out by one of the more powerful gods, like Athena or Apollo.[49] No one familiar with the *Iliad* could be surprised; because Apollo is angry at the way Agamemnon has treated his priest, he kills many men in the Greek army, and even their animals. Such disproportionate revenge is characteristic of the gods. In the *Bacchae* Dionysus is determined in every way he can to demonstrate to his mortal relative that he is a divinity, completely without the empathy or compassion that derives from loss and suffering. His connection with mortality was burned away by the lightning that killed his mortal mother. The goddess Thetis, as both Homer and Euripides portray her, has some understanding and sympathy for humanity; she had a mortal husband, and she saw her son Achilles die in war. But neither she nor any other god can offer any of the mortals in the drama a completely happy ending.

What Thetis brings instead of a happy ending is information that Peleus could never have acquired during his lifetime: his line will survive through his great-grandson and rule over Molossia. In addition, he has the benefit of knowing that he will become immortal. Gods alone can provide mortals with a glimpse into a future that is otherwise invisible to them.[50] Athena must intervene at the end of Euripides' *Suppliants* in order to ensure that the alliance between Athens and Argos will endure long after the death of the mortals who enact the treaty between the two city-states. The epiphany of the twin gods Castor and Polydeuces at the end of Euripides' *Electra* serves a similar purpose. The twin gods appear after Orestes has killed Aegisthus in a particularly brutal way, and he and his sister Electra have killed their mother Clytemnestra by luring her to the hut where Electra has been living, by telling Clytemnestra (falsely) that Electra has just had a baby. As soon as Clytemnestra enters the hut, Orestes tries to kill her, at first dropping his sword, and then covering his eyes with his cloak, so he could drive the sword into her throat. Electra urges him on and holds the sword with him (1221–6). Suddenly, Orestes and Electra are covered with blood and horrified at what they have just done. But as they start to cover their mother's body, the god Castor appears *ex machina* with his twin Polydeuces.[51]

The twin gods have come because they saw that Orestes had murdered his mother, their sister, and they do not approve: "She has received justice, but you did not act justly" (1244). Castor

is about to criticize Apollo for demanding that Orestes kill
his mother, but stops because Apollo is a more powerful
god: "Phoebus, Phoebus—but he is my lord, and I remain silent"
(1245–6). It was wrong to ask a son to kill his mother, but Castor
understands that Orestes had no choice but to follow Apollo's
orders.[52] Because Castor had begun his life as a mortal man, and
experienced pain and death, he understands how much Orestes
will suffer because of the god's command.[53] Orestes must do what
Destiny (*Moira*) and Zeus demand. By killing Aegisthus Orestes has
violated the laws of hospitality, which is an offense against Zeus.
He has shed kindred blood, so he must leave Argos. He will be
pursued and driven insane by the dog-faced goddesses known as
the *Kēres* (here equated with the Erinyes) until he comes to Athens
and grasps the knees of the statue of Athena, who will protect
him with her aegis (1252–7).[54] Orestes will be tried by the court
of the Areopagus, and acquitted, again through the intervention
of a god. At the trial, Apollo will take the blame for the murder
himself, because he ordered Clytemnestra's murder through his
oracle (1265–7). Orestes will leave Athens and found a city in
Arcadia, which will be named for him. The citizens of Argos will
bury Aegisthus, and Menelaus will bury Clytemnestra. Electra
will marry Pylades and live with him in Achaea. Orestes will find
happiness after his trial in Athens.

Unlike Peleus in the *Andromache* and Theseus in the *Suppliants*,
who promise to carry out the instructions they have received,
the characters of the *Electra* still have questions. Orestes asks
Castor and Polydeuces why they did not come sooner and fend
off the *Kēres*. Castor answers: "Fate and Necessity were leading to
what must be, and the unwise demands of Phoebus" (1301–2).[55]
Electra asks: "what sort of Apollo, what sort of oracles ordained
that I should become my mother's murderer?" (1303–4). Castor's
answer is brief and unsympathetic: "Your acts were shared, your

destinies shared; a single ancestral wrong (*atē*) has torn you both"
(1305–7)—the audience would have understood from what the
chorus had said earlier in the drama that Castor was referring
to the series of crimes committed by their ancestors, Tantalus,
Pelops, and Atreus (1175–6, 699–746).[56] Orestes and Electra
now realize that they will never see each other again. Castor tells
Orestes to have courage, because he will find justice in Athens,
but Orestes asks his sister to embrace him, and to "sing a dirge
for me as if I were dead, at my tomb." Here Castor suddenly cries
out: "Alas, alas, what you have spoken is painful even for gods to
hear—for both I and the other immortals have pity for mortals
and their many sorrows" (1325–30). But although the gods can
express compassion, they do nothing to stop human suffering.

After Orestes and Electra have said their farewells, Castor once
more assumes the authority of a god. He urges Orestes to flee to
Athens, because he can see the hounds of revenge coming, with
their serpent arms and dark skin. He and Polydeuces will now go
to the Sicilian Sea to protect ships: "We do not help the defiled,
but those who in their lives love piety and justice—we rescue
them from harsh toils. So let no one wish to commit crimes or sail
with men who have broken their oaths. Since I am a god I speak
thus to mortals" (1350–6). So the drama ends with the characters'
questions left unanswered: why did Electra need to take part in
her mother's murder? Why did Apollo demand that Orestes kill
his mother, when (as Castor says at the end of the play) the gods
come to the aid of those who care for piety and justice? Castor's
response begs rather than answers the question: Apollo, although
wise, gave Orestes an unwise oracle (1246). As Artemis explains,
she could not stop Aphrodite from punishing Hippolytus: "There
is a custom among the gods: no god wants to oppose what another
god wishes; instead we stand aside" (*Hipp.* 1330–1). In the
Andromache Thetis could do nothing to prevent Neoptolemus from

being killed at Delphi, because the sanctuary there belonged to Apollo.

Castor also appears *ex machina* at the end of the *Helen*, once again to rescue a member of his family: his sister Helen. Helen had been in Egypt during the whole of the Trojan War, under the protection of Proteus, that country's king; the gods sent a wraith to accompany Paris to Troy. Helen had heard a prophecy from Hermes that someday she would return to Sparta with her husband Menelaus (56–61), but meanwhile Proteus has died, and his son Theoclymenus wants to marry her. Helen has taken refuge at Proteus' grave, but before Theoclymenus can contrive how to get her to leave her place of sanctuary, Menelaus appears—the precise timing is, of course, a sign of divine intervention. Menelaus had been shipwrecked nearby; he had been wandering at sea for seven years, unable to return home to Sparta, because whenever he got close, a wind drove him back. He supposes that the gods do not want him to come home (403), but he does not understand why.[57] It takes some time for Menelaus to realize that the woman he is speaking with is in fact his wife, because he thinks that he has brought Helen back with him from Troy and does not realize that the "Helen" who had been in Troy was only a phantom.

After the two finally manage to recognize each other, Helen devises a plan for their escape. King Theoclymenus' sister, Theonoe (who has prophetic powers) also realizes that Menelaus has come. She knows that the gods are now debating what to do about Helen; Hera is on Helen's side, and Aphrodite is against her (878–84). Theonoe can save Helen by making sure that her brother does not know that Menelaus is there. After listening to their entreaties, Theonoe promises to keep silent and tells them to pray to Aphrodite and Hera. Helen prays to Hera to release her from her sufferings, and implores Aphrodite to allow her to return to Sparta (1093–106). But neither she nor Menelaus has any idea whether

or not the goddesses will answer her prayers. As the chorus of
Spartan women who have come with her to Egypt asks: "how
any mortal can find out and say what is a god or not a god or
something in between? The furthest you can get is to see that the
gods' actions leap here and there and back again with vague and
uncertain outcomes" (1137–43).[58]

When Theoclymenus learns that the Greeks have escaped, he
wants to kill his sister; it is at that point that Helen's immortal
brothers Castor and Polydeuces appear *ex machina*, and Castor
commands Theoclymenus to stop. Castor says that Helen must
remain married to Menelaus, and commends Theonoe for
honoring the wishes of the gods and the injunctions of her father
Proteus. He also explains why they did not intervene before this
time, even though an earlier intervention would have saved all the
human characters considerable anguish and effort: "We would
have saved our sister long before now, since Zeus had made us
gods; but we are less powerful than fate and the gods, who thought
that things should be as they are" (1658–61).[59] Castor then speaks
to Helen; he and his brother will accompany them back to Sparta.
Helen will become a goddess, and like her brothers be honored in
cult: "that is the wish of Zeus" (1669). An island off the southeast
coast of Attica will be named for her, since it was from there
that Hermes took her to Egypt, so that Paris might not have her.
Menelaus will go to the Islands of the Blest. As in the *Electra*,
Castor, the former mortal, expresses some sympathy for what they
have been compelled to endure, and offers Helen and Menelaus a
partial explanation for their struggles: "The gods do not despise
the nobly born; but their sufferings are greater than those of the
uncounted [masses]" (1678–9).[60] Theoclymenus immediately
obeys, as does Thoas at the end of the *Iphigenia among the Taurians*.

The ending of the *Helen* has seemed to some critics to be
perfunctory.[61] Deborah Roberts claims that "in *Iphigenia among*

the Taurians and in *Helen*, the gods step in almost unnecessarily to accomplish what human beings had been accomplishing already."[62] But who other than a god could have intervened so swiftly and efficiently to stop Theoclymenus from killing the messenger and Theonoe, or to have kept the ship carrying Iphigenia and Orestes from being driven back to shore? In these dramas, as in the *Ion, Hippolytus, Andromache*, and *Electra*, divine intervention is needed to keep the mortals in their ignorance from doing more harm than they have already done.[63] The gods also can provide the mortals with a glimpse of what will happen to them in the future. Helen will have a cult in Sparta, and the naming of the island off of the coast of Attica will provide a reminder to Athenians that she had after all retained her virtue.

But even though these divine interventions manage to tie up almost all of the loose ends of the plots, they do not provide anything other than palliative answers to the questions about why the gods did not intervene sooner to save human beings from disaster.[64] These same questions are raised every time a *deus ex machina* appears.[65] Unlike the orthodox monotheistic religions, ancient Greek theology permits and even encourages the raising of questions, but does not necessarily attempt to offer answers.[66] Why (as Castor claims in the *Helen*) do the gods take it for granted that human beings must endure hardship? Why are they prepared to allow the nobility to face greater challenges than ordinary people? One reason is that the gods discussed in this chapter lack the authority to change a status quo. In the *Andromache*, Thetis cannot save her grandson Neoptolemus, when Apollo is hostile towards him. Castor does not think Apollo should have ordered Orestes to murder his mother Clytemnestra (Castor's own sister), but he must defer to the wishes of the more powerful god. What these less powerful gods can offer, although only in a limited way, is empathy, but it is the gods that have the closest ties to mortals,

such as Thetis and Castor, who are more inclined to express it.
Even Dionysus says that he would have been prepared to help his
relatives. He explains to Cadmus and Agave that they would have
had him as an ally, if they had "been sensible" (*sōphronein*) when
given the opportunity (*Bacch.* 1341–3). As Euripides characterizes
them, it is the gods who are more closely connected to Zeus,
Apollo, Athena, and Hermes, who do not take the trouble to
offer such explanations or apologize to the mortals whom they
are addressing. At the end of the *Ion* Athena can state that "Apollo
has done all this well" (1595), because she is a goddess, and she
keeps herself remote from human suffering. So we should not be
surprised that she makes no reference to the suffering that Apollo
inflicted on Creusa and also on Ion.

6

GODS BEHIND THE SCENES

In Euripides' dramas some mortal characters imagine that
they (rather than the gods) can determine or influence what
happens in their lives. But the gods are always involved in
what happens, even though the mortal characters in the
drama may be unaware of them. In twelve of his extant plays,
as we have seen, Euripides makes sure that his audience is
aware of the gods' power by having divine figures appear *ex
machina*.[1] But gods do not need physically to be present in
order to determine the course of events. The *Medea*, perhaps
more than any other extant play, illustrates how gods can
be at work indirectly even when none of the characters
onstage appears to be aware that they have intervened.
The drama also illustrates how human beings are capable
of doing irreparable harm, which the gods might easily
have prevented, had they chosen to do so. Medea is better
able than most mortals to take decisive action when she
has the opportunity, because as the granddaughter of a god
she has extraordinary powers. She can predict the future;
she knows how to use poisons and magic drugs. Medea
assures the king of Athens, Aegeus, that she will be able to
cure his childlessness (716–8).[2] At the end of the drama she
prophesies how Jason will die a coward's death, struck on the
head by a piece of his famous ship, the Argo (1386–8).[3]

Medea behaves with a self-assurance more characteristic of a child of a god than a descendant (she is the Sun-god's grandchild).[4] Children of gods also behave with indifference to the suffering of the innocent. Heracles destroys a city in order to get Iole as his concubine (*Hipp.* 545–54). In the *Iliad*, because Achilles becomes angry at Agamemnon, he withdraws from fighting; many innocent people die as a result of his anger, including his dearest friend Patroclus. Such ruthlessness is characteristic of the gods. In Euripides' *Hippolytus*, although Phaedra has built a temple to honor her (30–1), Aphrodite without any apparent regret is prepared to let Phaedra die so that she can punish her "enemy" Hippolytus (48–50).[5]

In defending her honor as the Sun-god's granddaughter, Medea is ready to hurt anyone who has wronged her. In her view the practice of helping friends and harming enemies is a sign of strength and a guarantee of glory (807–10). Her enemies are Jason, who is leaving her in order to marry the daughter of the king of Corinth; the king, who has decided to banish her, and his daughter, whom Jason is about to marry. When the king comes to banish her from Corinth, she tries to persuade him to let her stay. He refuses, but admits that he loves his children more than his country (329). Medea then sees that she might get him to relent by begging him to let her remain one extra day so she can take care of her own children. The king agrees, though he realizes that he is making a mistake (*examartanōn*), but he supposes that she cannot do "something dreadful" in that amount of time (356). When he leaves, Medea explains that she would never have appealed to him had she not thought he would relent and give her the extra time she needed "to make three corpses of my enemies," the king, his daughter, and her husband (374–5).[6]

Surprisingly, at least to modern readers, is that the gods appear to be ready to help her in her plans to punish Jason. After she fails to persuade Jason to change his mind, King Aegeus of Athens appears, suddenly and without prior explanation. Aegeus has traveled to Delphi in order to inquire how he can have children (669). He tells Medea that he has come to Corinth on his way to Troezen in order to consult his father-in-law and ally Pittheus (Hippolytus' grandfather) about the oracle he received at Delphi. Medea interprets the oracle for him, and in return gets him to promise her asylum in his homeland of Athens. Medea seems to realize that the gods have intervened on her behalf: "Zeus and Zeus' Justice and the light of the Sun, now we shall be victorious over our enemies! We have started down the road; now there is hope that my enemies will pay the penalty" (764–7).[7] Aristotle thought that the Aegeus scene could be justifiably criticized, presumably because it was not anticipated or alluded to earlier in the drama, and Aegeus was not associated with accounts of Jason's life by other poets (*Poet.* 1461b20–1). But such unanticipated events are characteristic of divine action, as the chorus says in its concluding lines to this drama and several other plays: "the gods bring many things to pass beyond our expectation; what people think will happen does not come to pass" (1417–8).[8]

Although at first Medea had thought she could get revenge on Jason by killing him, along with his new bride and her father the king (374–5), Aegeus' desire for children gives Medea the idea that instead of killing Jason himself she should kill their two sons, because childlessness would be a greater punishment for him (792–3).[9] Now Medea has a precise plan of action: she will tell Jason that she is reconciled to the idea of his new marriage, and she will send her children with gifts to Jason's new bride. The gifts will be poisoned, so that anyone who touches them will be destroyed by them. "With the god's help Jason will pay the penalty" (802) for betraying her: he will lose both his sons and his bride.

After Medea has persuaded Jason that she has forgiven him, and
sent her children off to bring the gifts she has prepared for Jason's
bride, the children's tutor asks why she is crying. Unlike a god, she
cares about her victims, and is horrified by her own intentions.[10]
Nonetheless, as she prepares to break the laws of nature, Medea
speaks as if she understood herself to be working alongside of the
gods: "I have every reason," she says: "for this is what the gods and
I, with evil intentions, have planned" (1013–4).[11] She believes that
she has no choice but to kill her children, not just to punish Jason,
but also to keep them from being murdered by the Corinthians
and not given a proper burial in revenge for the death of Jason's
bride (1060–1, 1239).[12]

When Medea goes into the house to find her children and kill
them, the chorus calls upon the Sun-god to hold her back and stop
her: "for the children are descended from your race of gold, and
it causes fear if the blood of the gods is spilled by mortal men"
(1255–7). But Helios makes no effort to stop Medea from killing
her sons, even though they are his own great-grandsons. When
Jason comes to kill Medea, because the poisoned robe Medea
sent has killed the princess and her father the king, the chorus
informs him that she has also killed their sons. He demands to
be let in to see their bodies and confront Medea, but suddenly
Medea appears above the stage building, out of Jason's reach,
in the location customarily reserved for the appearances of the
gods. She informs Jason that her grandfather the Sun-god has
given her a chariot that will allow her to escape from him and
her other enemies in Corinth.[13] Earlier in the drama Medea had
several times mentioned Helios the Sun-god but not in any way
that suggested that she was in contact with him or was counting
on him to intervene on her behalf.[14] But since Aegeus had insisted
that Medea find her own way to Athens, a supernatural means of
transport would undoubtedly have been the safest option.[15]

Medea's sudden appearance in the Sun's chariot is a brilliant piece of theater, simply because it is a device that (to use Aristotle's terms) was not anticipated and does not arise logically from the preceding action. Aristotle was thinking as a philosopher and not as a dramatist when he stated: "It is clear that the denouements of plots should be drawn from the myth itself, and not as in the *Medea* from a device" (*mēchanē; Poet.* 1453a37–1454b2). The last-minute intervention by the Sun-god would not have seemed as artificial to the original audience as it does to us (or did to Aristotle), because it is in fact "drawn from the myth itself."[16] In traditional epics the Sun-god was believed to be able to see all things on earth (e.g., *Hom. Hym. Cer.* 69–70), so he would have been aware without the need of any messages from witnesses on earth that his descendant Medea needed to be rescued. In a vase (Fig. 6.1) that was painted in southern Italy around 400 BC (about thirty years after the first performance of the *Medea* in Athens) Medea appears above Jason and other characters in the play in a chariot drawn by snakes, surrounded by a disk with rays emanating from it.[17]

The disk with rays clearly represents the Sun, and his ability to see through his rays; the Greeks thought that one saw by means of the light coming from the eye, rather than from light entering it.[18]

The Sun-god, like other gods, cares about his children and descendants and seeks to protect them. But that does not mean that Zeus or any other god approves of everything that she has done, or indeed that the Sun-god has done, because the Sun-god belongs to an earlier generation of gods. Zeus and his generation of gods care about Justice. When Zeus replaced Cronus as ruler of the gods, he made the goddess Justice (*Dikē*) sit at his right hand, and (unlike his grandfather Uranus and father Cronus) he attempted to give all the gods some share of his power. In dealing with the affairs of mortals, Zeus relies on mortals as well as gods to see that his will is accomplished. Jason committed an injustice,

Figure 6.1 Medea escaping the Sun-god's chariot with Erinyes flanking her on either side, with Jason looking on, and her dead sons lying on an altar, mourned by their tutor. Lucanian red-figure calyx crater, ca. 400 BC. Credit: Cleveland Museum of Art, Accession No.: 1991.1.

both when he took Medea on board his ship after she had killed her brother Apsyrtus, and when he broke his oath to protect her after she had saved his life.[19]

Without accepting full responsibility for what he has done, Jason recognizes that he is a victim of divine retribution. As he says to Medea as she looks down on him *ex machina* from the Sun-god's chariot, "the gods have sent an avenging deity (*alastor*) intended for you against me after you killed your brother when he was a guest in your house and boarded the fine ship Argo" (1333–5).[20] In the concluding lines of the drama, the chorus also acknowledges that Zeus was involved in what happened during the course of the action: "Zeus on Olympus is dispenser of many things, and the gods accomplish many things that we did not expect" (1415–6).[21]

Medea assisted Zeus in punishing Jason for breaking his vows to Medea and for the role he played in the murder of Apsyrtus. She can predict how Jason will die. But her final appearance *ex machina* in the Sun-god's chariot does not mean that she has achieved divine or even quasi-divine status, or that she will get away with the crimes that she has committed.[22] Jason claims that his sons will become avenging deities (*miastores*; 1371) that arise from the pollution (*miasma*) caused by the murder, and that an Erinys and murdering *Dikē* (Justice) will destroy her (1389–90). That is not just an idle threat.[23] Euripides' audiences believed in the existence of such deities.[24] In their depictions of Medea in the Sun's chariot, fourth-century vase painters portray winged figures hovering in the air above her as she departs from Corinth.[25] After she left Corinth, Medea did not settle down and live happily ever after. She fulfilled the prediction she made to Aegeus by bearing a son to him in Athens, Medus. But soon she was compelled to leave Athens along with Medus, because she tried to kill Theseus, whom Aegeus considered to be his own son and heir. Medus went with Medea to Persia and became the ancestor of the Medes, so through him Medea became the ancestress of the Greeks' traditional enemies.[26]

The gods remain offstage also in Euripides' *Hecuba*. The action of the drama takes place somewhere in the Thracian Chersonese, the peninsula that forms the west side of the Hellespont. The Greek fleet, now on the way home from Troy, has been stranded because of unfavorable winds. No god appears *ex machina*, or seems be listening to the prayers of Hecuba and the other Trojan women. No messenger comes to describe any miracle that happens offstage. Nonetheless, as in the *Trojan Women*, the audience learns in the prologue of the drama that the gods are aware of what is happening to Hecuba and her children.[27] The prologue is spoken by the shade or image (*eidōlon*) of a dead child. He comes before the audience as a god might appear, lifted by a device to the top of the stage building. From there he tells the audience that he is Polydorus, the youngest son of Priam and Hecuba. Because he was too young to fight in the war, he had been sent by his father Priam to stay with Priam's friend Polymestor, the king of Thrace. Along with his son Polydorus, Priam sent a large quantity of gold, so that if the Greeks won the war, Polydorus might have the means to live (6–15). But when Troy fell, Polymestor killed Polydorus and kept the gold. Not only did Polymestor kill a child entrusted to him for safekeeping, he did not respect the gods enough to give his victim proper burial; he threw the corpse into the sea. But the gods require mortals to treat the dead with respect, so that their souls may have an easy entry to the Lower World. The shade of Polydorus tells us that he has left his body and is hovering over his mother's head, as Patroclus does when he wishes Achilles to see him in a dream, "in all ways like him in form and aspect and voice, and wearing the same clothes" (*Il.* 23.65–7).[28] Patroclus' spirit tells Achilles that he too will soon die. Polydorus' shade also is able to make a prediction: on this day Hecuba will also need to bury another child, Polyxena, after she is sacrificed to the ghost of Achilles. Patroclus' spirit (*psychē*) asks the sleeping Achilles to bury his body, so that he can pass through the gates of Hades (*Il.* 23.71).[29] Polydorus says that he is hovering near the beach so his body will be washed up on the shore and discovered by one of Hecuba's slaves. "The gods

with power below," that is, Hades and Persephone, have granted
Polydorus this favor, so that his body will be given a tomb and fall
into his mother's hands (47–50).

Even if Polydorus did not explicitly say that the gods of the
dead intervened to make it possible for Polydorus to have a
proper burial, the ancient audience would have understood that
conjunction of these events was a result of something more
than coincidence. Polydorus' body has been drifting along the
shore for three days. Thanks to the intervention of Hades and
Persephone, his body will receive a proper burial. But this will be
the only kindness that the gods offer to Hecuba and her family. As
Polydorus tells Hecuba at the end of his speech, "in recompense
for your former prosperity a god is destroying you" (55–8). Before
she discovers that Polydorus is in fact dead, she learns from the
chorus that the ghost of Achilles has demanded the sacrifice of
her daughter Polyxena. When Odysseus enters to take Polyxena
away to die, Hecuba begs him to ask the Greek army to spare her.
Odysseus owes Hecuba a favor, because she saved his life when he
came to Troy in disguise. But he refuses to intervene on Polyxena's
behalf, citing what is essentially a legal technicality: he is obliged
to save Hecuba's life, not that of her daughter (301–2). As Homer
tells the story of Odysseus it was not Hecuba but Helen who
recognized Odysseus when he came to Troy. She had encountered
him in Sparta, when he was a guest at her wedding with Menelaus,
but did not reveal his identity to the Trojans, so that he was able
to return home and live to fight against them in the Trojan War
(*Od.* 4.244–56). Euripides includes Hecuba in the story, so that in
the midst of her present troubles Odysseus' refusal to help her will
seem all the more ungrateful and cruel.

Subsequent events serve to increase Hecuba's impression that
the gods have abandoned her. No sooner has Hecuba learned
from a messenger that her daughter Polyxena has died, than she

discovers that she has also lost her son Polydorus. The slave woman who went to fetch seawater to wash Polyxena's body returns instead with another dead body. At first Hecuba supposes that the new corpse might be that of her daughter Cassandra, but when she pulls back the cloth that covers the body, she sees that the dreams she had about Polydorus' death were true, and that he had been murdered by Priam's guest-friend Polymestor, who was supposed to have protected him (703–6). When Agamemnon comes to ask her to bury her daughter Polyxena so the fleet can leave, Hecuba asks Agamemnon to punish Polymestor for murdering her son Polydorus. When he does not respond to her request, she wishes that her arms, hands, hair, and feet all had a voice, "either through the agency of Daedalus or a god," as if becoming a moving statue might enable her to become more persuasive (836–40).[30] Her request for additional voices forcefully conveys her sense of isolation.[31] Finally, she appeals to a general morality: "A good man should lend a hand to justice and always do harm to evil doers, wherever they may be" (844).

Agamemnon acknowledges that Polymestor deserves to be punished for murdering the child he was supposed to protect and for stealing his money: "I take pity on your son and on your misfortune and your suppliant hand, and I wish for the sake of the gods and of justice that your impious friend pay you this penalty" (850–4). But he refuses to intervene on her behalf, because he is afraid of the army's reaction. It might appear that he was showing special favoritism for the mother of his concubine Cassandra. So Hecuba asks him to allow *her* to avenge her son's murder, and keep the army from taking any action against her (870–5). Agamemnon lets her send one of her slaves to invite Polymestor to come to see her, bringing his two sons along with him. Polymestor arrives, assuring her that Polydorus is alive and well; Hecuba in turn pretends to believe him, so that Polymestor will not be afraid to

send his guards away and enter her tent, where she says she will
tell him about treasures hidden in Troy. But once he is in the tent,
she and her women hold him down, kill his two sons before his
eyes, and then blind him: "he has paid the penalty for what he
did to me" (*dikēn de moi dedōke*; 1052–3). The blinded Polymestor
assures Agamemnon that he killed Polydorus in order to protect
Agamemnon, but Agamemnon rejects his argument and states that
Polymestor got what he deserved.

But Hecuba does not get away with the murder of Polymestor's
two innocent sons. Even though Agamemnon does not punish her,
Polymestor states that Dionysus prophesied to him at his oracular
shrine in Thrace that Hecuba would drown in the sea.[32] After
the Greeks set sail from the Chersonese, she will become "a dog
with firebrand glances" and climb up the ship's mast towards the
ship's yardarm. The site of her death and her tomb will be known
as the grave of the miserable dog (*cynossēma*) and a landmark for
sailors (1265–74).[33] Her "firebrand eyes" will be the torches that
warn sailors away from the promontory on which her tomb is
situated.[34]

The audience would have realized that this strange prophecy
was true, because Polymestor then utters another prophecy
that will soon prove to be all too accurate, that Agamemnon
and Cassandra will die when they get to Argos. Agamemnon
orders that Polymestor be abandoned on a desert island.[35] He
announces that the army will set sail for Greece, because the wind
is favorable: "May we have a safe journey and find that all is well
within our homes" (1291–2). But the audience knows that Greek
fleet will be scattered by a storm before they can reach the Greek
mainland, and that many lives will be lost. They also know that
when Agamemnon does reach the shore of Argos, Aegisthus and
Clytemnestra will be waiting to murder him, along with Hecuba's
daughter Cassandra.

All this action focuses our attention on the human characters in the drama. But nonetheless the audience can see that supernatural forces are present.[36] The gods of the world below sent the shade of Polydorus to tell both the audience and Hecuba that he had been murdered. Hecuba had a dream that told her that Achilles appeared above his tomb asking for the sacrifice of one of her daughters (92–7). Polymestor says that the god Dionysus told him that Hecuba will turn into "a dog with fiery glances" and drown in the sea. A god must be involved in some way, since only a divinity could perform such a sudden physical transformation. The nature of her metamorphosis reflects the character of her behavior.[37] Dogs are known for being kind to friends and hostile to enemies, an ethical stance of which most Greeks approved.[38] But they were also regarded as recklessly savage, prepared to attack indiscriminately and not hesitating to eat the bodies of the dead.[39] Polymestor's description of the metamorphosis makes it clear that Hecuba will not become an ordinary dog, but rather a mad dog. Her behavior will be destructive: she will climb up and jump from the masthead and fall into the sea (1263), displaying fiery glances (*pyrsa dergmata*; 1265). Irrational behavior and glinting eyes are symptoms of rabies (*lyssa*).[40] It is the term the dramatists use to describe any ruthless and indiscriminate madness, as when in Sophocles' *Ajax* Athena makes Ajax slaughter sheep and cattle, supposing in his delusion that he is killing his enemies, or when the goddess Lyssa compels Heracles to kill his wife and all of his children in Euripides' *Heracles*.[41] In the *Bacchae* the chorus of Asian bacchants calls upon Lyssa's dogs (*lyssas kynes*) to make the women of Thebes insane and to attack Pentheus, the "rabid" (*lyssōdēs*) man who is spying upon them.[42]

Although her plan to avenge her son Polydorus' death required on her part great fortitude and courage, Hecuba seems to realize that being transformed into a mad dog is an inglorious death, and a sign of divine disapproval, because she says that she does not care, since she has had her revenge (1274).[43] The transformation, which will occur "here" in the Chersonese (1270), will save her from spending the rest of her days as a slave in Odysseus' household; for her, as for Polyxena, death may be the preferable fate.[44] But it is also true that as a dog, Hecuba will not receive burial rites, much less a hero cult. If Hecuba had taken her revenge with the support of a god, her life might have had a less violent ending, though she would not have escaped some sort of punishment for taking part in a murder.[45] The story of Orestes makes it clear that mortals (and or their families) cannot escape responsibility for the blood they have shed, even when they are carrying out the orders of a god. Electra in Euripides' *Electra*, who helped hold the sword with which she and her brother Orestes murdered their mother (1224–6), is punished by exile from Argos and with the prospect of never seeing her brother Orestes again. Sophocles' Electra remains outside while her brother and Pylades enter the palace and kill Clytemnestra, but the audience knows that the family's troubles will not end there; as Aegisthus asks at the end of the drama, "Is this house compelled to see the present and future troubles of Pelops' family?" (*El.* 1497–8).[46] Euripides' drama *Hecuba* also ends before the whole of her life story has been told, with questions of timing and agency left unanswered.[47] Uncertainty about when and what and how mirrors the condition in which ordinary mortals find themselves, without the kind of precise resolution that only a *deus ex machina* would be able to offer.[48]

Since Zeus and his family of gods care about justice, it is striking that in both the *Medea* and the *Hecuba*, neither he nor any other god did anything to prevent innocent children from being murdered. The Sun-god did not rescue Medea's children. Dionysus does not warn Polymestor to leave his sons at home when he goes to visit Hecuba. Similarly in the *Heracles* Athena does not intervene to stop Heracles from killing his own children, although she appears in person in order to keep Heracles from murdering his stepfather Amphitryon. In the *Hecuba* Euripides makes it clear what Hecuba has lost by allowing the audience to see and hear from her children Polydorus and Polyxena.[49] Sympathy for their respective plights makes it possible to understand why Hecuba chose to punish Polymestor not only by blinding him, but also by murdering his two sons.

The *Hecuba* is just one of several dramas in which the gods demand that a young person be sacrificed. In the *Hecuba*, Polyxena was sacrificed to Achilles' ghost so the Greeks could have a favorable wind. In the *Erechtheus*, the gods demanded that Erechtheus sacrifice one of his daughters in order to save Athens. Presumably it is because humans place such a high value on their children that the gods require the sacrifice of a young person in order to secure a victory in battle.[50] Since human sacrifice was not practiced in their own times, the poets imagined that the rituals in which children were offered to the gods would follow the pattern of sacrifices of animals before battles.[51] Such sacrifices differ from ordinary animal sacrifices made to the gods, in that a seer determines that the sacrifice must be made, and the seer rather than a priest does the killing, using a sword instead of a knife to slit the throat of the victim, and the victims are not eaten. The victims must be young and physically perfect.[52] In Greek drama the gods never make requests for human sacrifices directly; generals preparing for battle learn about the need for human sacrifices from seers. The human sacrifices tend to be demanded by the chthonic deities, gods who have connections with the earth, or the killing of animals in contexts other than that of sacrifice, or the cults of the dead.[53] The imaginary human sacrifices were made in times of war to Artemis, who retained some of characteristics of the pre-Greek goddess known as the Mistress of Animals.[54]

In Aeschylus' *Agamemnon* Artemis demands that Agamemnon must sacrifice to her his daughter Iphigenia, in return for the innocent lives that will be lost as the result of the Greek attack on Troy (123–39). Agamemnon learned that he had to perform the sacrifice from the prophet Calchas, who had seen two eagles kill a pregnant hare, and understood that the goddess was angry and would send unfavorable winds that would keep the Greek army from sailing from Greece to Troy. Eventually Agamemnon obeyed the oracle and sacrificed Iphigenia "like a goat on the altar" (232). The chorus of old men of Argos is horrified that he was willing to kill his daughter in order to avenge the loss of Helen and to allow his ships to sail (218–27). As they describe it, Iphigenia was bound and gagged, so her only means of protest was to shoot from her eyes "arrows begging for pity" (240–1).

But Euripides in his dramas lets the victims of child sacrifice speak and demonstrate their courage. As in the *Hecuba*, the children in the *Heraclidae*, the *Iphigenia at Aulis*, and the *Phoenissae* all volunteer to die, either on behalf of their families and cities, or in order to avoid spending the rest of their lives as slaves. In all but one case the gods require the sacrifice of a virgin daughter. There is of course no way to know exactly why in these myths the gods require that fathers sacrifice their daughters rather than their sons, and why children must be sacrificed before they are married or even betrothed. Perhaps in the original versions of the stories, it may have been thought that the sacrifice of a child would provide a compensation for what hunters had taken away through the slaughter of wild animals.[55] But whatever the original purpose of the custom may have been, in his tragedies Euripides uses the demands for human sacrifices as occasions for the children to display extraordinary heroism, and for the characters in the drama to reflect on the devastating cost of war, even for the victors.[56] As we have seen, Erechtheus, the king of Athens, hesitated when he was told by the Delphic oracle that he would need to sacrifice one of his daughters in order to defeat the Eleusinians in battle, but his wife Praxithea urged him to make the sacrifice, on the grounds that allowing a daughter to be sacrificed on behalf of the state is equivalent to sending a son off to war. When their daughter's two sisters insist on joining her in dying, Athena sees to it that all three will be honored with a hero cult.[57]

In Euripides' drama the *Children of Heracles* (*Heraclidae*) all the prophets tell Theseus' son Demophon, the king of Athens, that "in order to rout the enemy and save the city" he must sacrifice a daughter born to a noble father to "the maiden (*korē*) of Demeter" (407–9), meaning her daughter Persephone, the queen of the Underworld; her name was so terrifying that Athenians preferred never to use it.[58] That the sacrificial victim should be "a maiden daughter born to a noble father" suggests that the gods want the sacrifice to be significant—a slave's child cannot be offered as a substitute.

The enemies the Athenians need to defeat are the Argives, who are attacking Athens because the Athenians have offered refuge to the children of Heracles. They had come to Athens under the protection of Heracles' nephew Iolaus, in an attempt to avoid being killed by Heracles' enemy Eurystheus, the king of Argos (Heracles himself had become a god). Demophon is reluctant to sacrifice his own daughter or a daughter of any of his citizens: "who is there who would want to think so mistakenly, so as to give from his own hands the dearest of his children?" (413–4). But one of Heracles' daughters volunteers to be sacrificed instead—as she states, she would be killed in any case if Eurystheus won, and no one would want to marry her if she let one of her brothers die on her behalf. So for her the most glorious course is to die on behalf of her family and of Athens. Iolaus tries to dissuade her, suggesting that she draw lots with her sisters. But she refuses to do so, because that would not provide an occasion for gratitude (*charis*; 548); to be effective a sacrificial animal must be willing to die. She asks Iolaus to stand with her during the ceremony, so that she can die in his arms. But he cannot bear to accompany her, even though he has seen death many times in the past while fighting alongside of Heracles. So she asks Demophon to let her die not in the arms of men, but in those of women, presumably so that she could be sure that her body would be treated with proper respect (565–6).[59]

That privilege was not available to Hecuba's daughter Polyxena before she was sacrificed to the ghost of Achilles, because she was a slave. Instead (as Euripides tells the story in the *Hecuba*), with remarkable courage Polyxena asked that she be released by the young men who were holding her, so she could face her death alone. Then she tore down her tunic as far as her waist and revealed her breasts, "as lovely as a statue's," courageously offering Neoptolemus the choice of striking his sword into her neck or her chest. To a modern audience the gesture might appear to have been intended to taunt her male audience by reminding them of her sexuality.[60] But in Greek culture the gesture of baring the breast was primarily intended to elicit pity.[61] Neoptolemus chooses to cut her throat, as was conventional in sacrifice, and Polyxena dies with dignity, "hiding what ought to be hidden from the eyes of males" (*Hec.* 570). The Greek soldiers treat her body with strict decorum, expressing their admiration by covering her with leaves, as if she were a male victor in the games (574).[62]

The gods keep their part of the bargain. In the *Hecuba* the sacrifice of Polyxena succeeds in bringing a favorable wind, and in the *Heraclidae*, after the sacrifice of Heracles' daughter, the Athenians defeat the Argives. A messenger describes a miracle (*thauma*) that occurred during the course of the battle (849–63). Iolaus insists on fighting, despite his advanced age, but prays to Heracles' father Zeus and Heracles' wife Hēbē (the goddess of youth) that he might become young again, just for that day. Two stars then appear and hide Iolaus' chariot in a cloud. As he emerges from the cloud he is young again, and able to capture Eurystheus and his chariot. The messenger believes that the two stars were Heracles and Hēbē. Iolaus and Heracles' son Hyllus put up the customary *tropaion*, a statue of Zeus commemorating the victory.[63] The Athenians want to return Eurystheus to the Argives. But Heracles' mother Alcmene insists that he be killed. Nonetheless, in gratitude to Athens for wishing to spare his life, Eurystheus promises to protect the city against Heracles' descendants in the future, and tells them to bury him near the temple of Athena Pallenis, but not to pour libations on his tomb (1040–1). He does not wish to be fed through sacrificial offerings, as customary in hero cults, because even in the shadowy existence allotted to heroes he wants to remain perpetually hostile to the children of Heracles.[64]

The text of the *Heraclidae* that has come down to us ends with Alcmena directing her servants to kill Eurystheus and to throw his body to the dogs. Eurystheus will have a hero cult, but Alcmena says nothing about any remembrance in cult or place names for Heracles' heroic daughter.[65] Only a *deus ex machina* would be able to provide such an overview, as Artemis does at the end of the *Hippolytus* and Athena at the end of the *Erechtheus*.[66] Later authors refer to the daughter by the name Macaria ("blessed one"), and say that the Athenians threw flowers and wreaths on her and buried her "magnificently."[67] Iolaus was said to have cut off Eurystheus' head and buried it in the village of Tricorynthus near Marathon, at the place known in the first century AD as Eurystheus' Head, below the wagon road near the spring of Macaria.[68] But the end of the drama as we now have it, like that of the *Hecuba* or Sophocles' *Electra*, keeps the emphasis on revenge and enmity.[69]

Euripides' drama *Iphigenia at Aulis* explores the moral dilemmas created by a god's demand for the sacrifice of a maiden. As in Aeschylus' *Agamemnon*, the prophet Calchas has told the Greek army that they would only be able to sail to Troy if Agamemnon sacrificed his daughter Iphigenia to Artemis (89–93).[70] Agamemnon was reluctant to comply, but his brother Menelaus persuaded him to "endure the dreadful act." So Agamemnon wrote his wife Clytemnestra to say he needed her to bring Iphigenia to Aulis so she could marry Achilles. He then had a change of heart and sent a second letter telling Clytemnestra not to bring her, but Menelaus intercepted the messenger, and Clytemnestra brought Iphigenia to the Greek camp. When Iphigenia discovers that her father is about to sacrifice her, she begs for mercy. But when the army demands that she be sacrificed, she suddenly changes her mind and asks for the opportunity to die with glory, on behalf of Greece: "it's better for one man to live than then a thousand women; if Artemis wants to take my body, shall I, a mortal stand in the way of a god?" (1394–6). Achilles offers to defend her if she changes her mind; her mother Clytemnestra tries to stop her, but Iphigenia forbids her to weep. She asks the young women in the chorus to sing a paean to Artemis. The chorus responds: "let us call upon Artemis, daughter of Zeus, queen of the gods, as if on good fortune. Lady, lady, who rejoice in human sacrifice, send the Greeks' army to the land of the Phrygians and the sad foundations of Troy, and grant that Agamemnon with spears shall place a most glorious crown on Greece and fame that will never be forgotten" (1521–31).

The original version of the drama may have ended with this prayer. The audience would have known that Iphigenia's willing death will allow the Greeks to sail for Troy, and that the goddess will keep her part of the bargain.[71] For Iphigenia, as for Macaria in the *Heraclidae*, there is no mention of special recognition or

a hero cult, but the army has the support from the gods that
it needs, and the audience knows that eventually the Greeks
will defeat the Trojans and recover Helen. But the text of the
drama that has come down to us contains yet another scene.
This epilogue offers a happier ending, which for many reasons
scholars believe was written after Euripides' death.[72] In the first
part of this additional scene (1532–78), a messenger enters to tell
Clytemnestra what happened after the Greeks started to perform
the sacrifice. He describes how Iphigenia willingly consents to be
led to the goddess' altar and be sacrificed, and asks that no Argive
soldier touch her. Like Polyxena in the *Hecuba*, she willingly offers
her neck to the knife, and Achilles offers a prayer to Artemis.
In the following lines, which appear to have been written by
another poet, possibly sometime during the early Christian era
(fourth to seventh century AD), a priest examines her neck for
a place to strike his sword, everyone hears the sword strike her,
but at that point the girl herself vanishes.[73] A dying doe is lying
on the ground, and the altar is covered with the doe's blood.[74]
The prophet Calchas explains that the goddess has substituted
the doe for the girl, so that her altar would not be defiled with
noble blood. The Greeks can set sail for Troy immediately. The
messenger says to Clytemnestra: "The girl has flown away to the
gods; stop grieving and give up your anger against your husband.
Mortals cannot predict what the gods will do. They save those
they love. This day has seen your child dead and alive" (1610–2).
Agamemnon then enters and assures Clytemnestra "on our
daughter's account we could be fortunate, for in truth she keeps
company with the gods" (1621–2).

 This account of the sacrifice in the *Iphigenia at Aulis* bears some
resemblance to Iphigenia's description in Euripides' *Iphigenia
among the Taurians*: "just as I was being held high over the altar
Artemis stole me away and in my place gave a deer to the Greeks.

She sent me through the bright air and brought me here to the land of the Taurians" (27–30). In that drama Iphigenia survives and lives to be able to return to Greece and spend the rest of her life as the priestess of Artemis at Brauron in Attica.[75] But the surviving text of the ending of the *Iphigenia at Aulis* says nothing about Iphigenia going to the Taurians and becoming a priestess of Artemis. Rather, the characters all state that Iphigenia is now "with the gods" (1608, 1614, 1622). Since to dwell with the gods one must become a god, they all appear to be saying that Artemis has made Iphigenia immortal.[76] This ending is even happier than what Athena offers at the end of *Iphigenia among the Taurians*, where she is promised a new home at Brauron as priestess of Artemis and a hero cult after her death.[77]

The human sacrifice Euripides describes in his drama *Phoenician Women* (*Phoenissae*) is even more terrifying, and its victim even more courageous than Polyxena in the *Hecuba* or Iphigenia in the *Iphigenia at Aulis*. The drama gets its name from the Phoenician women who form the chorus; they are temple servants of Apollo, who are present in Thebes at the time when Oedipus' son Polynices returns from exile to his homeland to take the kingship of Thebes away from his brother Eteocles. Polynices brings with him an army from Argos and six captains, who become known as the Seven against Thebes. Their attack and defeat take place in mythological time just before the action of Euripides' *Suppliants*, which describes how the Athenians assist the families of the defeated Argives in recovering and burying their dead. The principal characters in the drama are members of Oedipus' family, whose crimes against each other have brought Thebes to the brink of disaster. No gods appear onstage, but all the characters in the drama are aware of the role that they have played in determining the course of their lives. Jocasta observes that her husband Laius refused to heed Apollo's oracle at Delphi and begot the son who murdered him and married her; Oedipus in turn blinded himself when he discovered what he had done, and cursed his and Jocasta's sons Eteocles and Polynices because they then imprisoned him. As a result of their father's curse, the sons quarreled and Polynices has come with an army to attack Eteocles. Jocasta blames both the gods and her family for these troubles. When Polynices comes to see her, she says: "A curse on all these—whether it was the sword or Strife (*Eris*) or your father was responsible or if the power of the gods has been celebrating victory over the house of Oedipus—the sorrow of these evils has fallen on me" (350–4).[78] She tries to reason with her sons, but fails to reconcile them.

After Polynices leaves and prepares to attack the city, the chorus recalls how Cadmus came to the fields near the stream of Dirce, where Dionysus was born. The stream was guarded by a dragon, the son of Ares and the Earth. Cadmus killed it and was told by Athena to sow the dragon's teeth in the ground. The Earth, the dragon's mother, sent up a crop of armed men, some of whom Cadmus killed, soaking the Earth with their blood.[79] The chorus calls on Epaphus, the son of Zeus and Io, to help their descendants, and Persephone and her mother Demeter, whom they equate with Earth: "defend this land. Everything is easy for the gods" (688–9). None of these divinities appears to have heard the chorus' prayer, because the audience soon learns that Ares is still angry that Cadmus killed his son the dragon. In order to defend his city Eteocles seeks the advice of his mother's brother Creon about war strategy. He cannot ask the seer Tiresias, because he has quarreled with him. So he sends Creon's son Menoeceus to fetch Tiresias so the seer can tell Creon what he predicts about the battle. Tiresias is led in by his daughter; he has just returned to Thebes from Athens, where his prophecies allowed the Athenians to defeat the Eleusinians, and they awarded him a golden crown. When Creon asks him what the Thebans must do to save their city, Tiresias tells him that Eteocles and Polynices will kill each other, and that many men on both sides will die. Unless his advice is followed, Thebes will be defeated, but he is afraid to give the advice, and prepares to leave. When Creon insists that he speak, Tiresias wants Creon's son Menoeceus to leave, but Creon insists that he remain. So Menoeceus hears Tiresias declare that Creon must slaughter his son (*sphaksai*) Menoeceus as a sacrifice on behalf of the city. Creon refuses, but Tiresias explains that Menoeceus must die in the chamber where the snake that guards the spring of Dirce was born. Blood from a member of Creon's family is required, since he was a descendant on both sides of his family from the surviving men who were sown from the dragon's teeth.[80] Ares is still angry at Cadmus for killing the snake—even though Cadmus killed the snake because he needed to get water for a sacrifice (657–75).

Creon offers to die himself in place of his son, and orders Menoeceus to flee. The son agrees, but as soon as his father leaves, he tells the chorus that he wants to die to save his country. But instead of letting himself be sacrificed by his father or a seer, he is prepared to cut his own throat. He argues that it would be shameful if he were not willing to die, when soldiers are prepared to die without instructions from oracles or compulsion from the gods: "By Zeus who dwells in the stars and murderous Ares who settled the Sown Men who rose out of the ground as rulers of this land—yes, I shall go and stand on the high battlements and I shall sacrifice myself into the deep dark den of the snake, as the prophet explained, and set the city free. I have said what I have to say" (999–1012).[81] The chorus sings of the terrible history of Thebes and Oedipus, but concludes their song by expressing their admiration for the one who goes to his death on behalf of his fatherland, leaving lamentations for Creon, but "making the seven-gated enclosure of the land victorious" (1054–9). Euripides appears to have invented the story of Menoeceus especially for this

drama.[82] The inspiration for this invention may have come from
Euripides' own drama *Erechtheus*, in which one of Erechtheus'
daughters volunteers to die in order to save Athens. Tiresias says
that he has just returned from Athens, where he was able to save
that city by his prophecy, which would have included the need to
sacrifice one of Erechtheus' daughters.[83]

Creon comes back with his dead son in his arms, hoping to find
his sister Jocasta to wash the child's body. But Jocasta has left for
the battlefield along with her daughter Antigone in an attempt
to prevent her sons from killing each other. By the time they get
there Eteocles is dead and Polynices on the brink of death. After
he dies, Jocasta kills herself over their bodies. While the generals
argue over which of the two had won, the Thebans attack and
rout the Argives. In the text that we now have, the drama races
headlong into new disaster, offering no respite to the characters or
to the audience. It seems likely that this ending was substituted for
whatever Euripides wrote, in order to reconcile the outcome of
the drama with Sophocles' *Oedipus at Colonus* and *Antigone*.[84] Creon
demands that Oedipus go into exile and refuses to bury Polynices.
Antigone tells Oedipus that she will bury Polynices secretly
(1745), and then go with her father into exile. The audience is not
told if Antigone will be able to depart with Oedipus after burying
Polynices, or if will she be left to die in an underground chamber,
as she was in Sophocles' drama. But whoever wrote this ending
does not fail to acknowledge the power of the gods. Oedipus
says: "I am not so devoid of sense that I devised what I did to my
eyes and the lives of my sons without one of the gods" (1612–4).[85]
Antigone also does not expect any of the gods to help her. When
Oedipus asks her to come with him to Cithaeron to the untrodden
grove of the maenads, Antigone answers that she went there
with the holy *thiasos* led by Dionysus' mother Semele, "offering
a service to the gods that was unrequited" (1756–7). Oedipus

speaks the last lines of the drama, reflecting on his former glory: "but why should I lament this and grieve in vain. I must bear what the gods impose because I am a mortal" (1762–3).

Here the drama ends, leaving many questions unanswered. Why did Ares wait for four human generations before demanding a human sacrifice in recompense for the death of the snake that guarded the stream of Dirce? Why did the gods allow Oedipus to survive and murder his father and marry his mother, and then also cause the death of his two sons? Apollo, Ares, Athena, and Earth have all had a direct influence on the action of the drama, but neither they nor any other gods appear *ex machina* to answer these questions or to comment on the role which they or other gods have played in orchestrating the events the audience has just witnessed, or to offer the audience a sense of closure. Some modern critics have found the plot of the *Phoenissae* to be disappointing because of its lack of a definitive ending.[86] But an ancient audience did not necessarily require an ending that tied up all the loose ends of the plot. As Aristotle observed in the *Poetics*, it is not the whole story, but the action that the drama represents, that must have a beginning, middle, and an end.[87] The *Iliad* ends before the death of Achilles or the fall of Troy, but the audience and indeed the characters in the epic all know what is going to happen. The *Phoenissae* also has a thematic cohesion, and in antiquity it appears to have been one of Euripides' more popular dramas.[88] Speeches were parodied in contemporary comedy, and passages from it were quoted for many centuries.[89]

Along with the *Hecuba* and *Orestes*, the *Phoenissae* was one of the three Euripidean dramas that continued to be studied in the Byzantine era. No ancient source provides any explanation for the choice of these particular dramas. But of the many characters in the fast-moving plot of the *Phoenissae*, it is Menoeceus who is most often cited. Even though he makes only a relatively brief appearance in the drama, his name occurs frequently in orators' lists of heroic individuals who died on behalf of their country.[90] Plutarch compared him and Heracles' daughter to the Spartan general Leonidas, who died defending the pass at Thermopylae in the First Persian War.[91] Through remembrance, if in no other way, young Menoeceus' self-sacrifice had given him a kind of immortality.[92] For the Christians who taught the dramas in schools, as for the Church Fathers, the brutal human sacrifices could serve a different purpose, as powerful indictments of the cruel and immoral divinities of ancient Greek religion. Clement of Alexandria (150–215 AD), for example, used the practice of human sacrifice as a means of persuading his readers to reject the "inhumane and misanthropic gods" of traditional religion, and included in his long list the human sacrifices offered by the Taurians and Korē's demand for the sacrifice of the daughter of Erechtheus of Athens (*Prot.* 3.42.1).[93] But he was also aware of the heroism displayed by the victims; he observed that Polyxena, even though she did not die on behalf of her country, could nonetheless serve as a model of courage and modesty (*Strom.* 2.23).

Like Plutarch, Clement regarded sacrifice as a demand by a god for the life of a child for a particular purpose. But in the twentieth century scholars have tended to focus on the social (as opposed to the theological) purposes of sacrificial ritual, and its function within the community. As Helene Foley describes it, adapting the theories of the French sociologist Émile Durkheim (1858–1917), the celebration in drama of "violent mythical and theological traditions" reasserts the illusion created by their religion "by endowing it with the palpability of a physical and group experience."[94] The poets may not have wanted to acknowledge that their views of divinity were a human fiction, if only because the existing religious system supported their own work. Foley states that "of the three tragic poets, Euripides consistently comes

closest to such dismantling of the divine superstructure, while
simultaneously insisting on a restoration of ritual to a central place
in the politically and socially unstable worlds he creates."[95] In her
discussion of Euripides' *Phoenissae*, for example, Foley says that the
poet portrays human sacrifice as "a cruel and ideally unnecessary"
means of unifying the community, which could provide only a
"legendary and literary cure" for the dangerous political situation
in Athens in 410 BC, the approximate date of the drama's
performance. But at the same time she states that the poet seeks
to encourage his audience to continue to believe in the efficacy of
ritual: "when Euripides invents the human sacrifice of Menoeceus
to redirect his sick plot to the outcome prescribed by tradition,
he seems to make a marginal gesture of confidence in ritual and in
the poetry that incorporates this sacrificial cure."[96]

Such an understanding of the social purpose of ritual in drama
seems plausible, but only at some distance from the text.[97] Foley
states that sacrifice "defines a political community," in that "only
citizens participate in the act, and share, on pre-established
principles of distribution, its benefits." That interpretation might
have some relevance to the large sacrifices of cattle offered to
the gods in civic rituals, in which the slaughtered animals were
cooked, portions of fat and bones offered to the gods, and the
meat distributed to priests and celebrants and other participants.
But the human sacrifices portrayed in drama do not follow
that ritual pattern, because they are offered in times of war, on
behalf of an army rather than a community of citizens. There
is no community participation in war sacrifices because the
victims were not eaten.[98] Rather, the blood of the human victim
was allowed to fall on the ground, and the bodies of the victims
were then buried. In the dramas the focus is primarily on the
individual child who volunteers to be sacrificed, even though it
is a collective, an army or a city, that will be the beneficiary of

the victim's heroic action.[99] If the poet describes its effect on the collective, it is in order to allow its members to express their appreciation of the heroism displayed by the victim, as in the *Hecuba*, where the Greek soldiers cover Polyxena's body with leaves and branches, as if she were a victor in the games.[100]

If instead we look at what the poet says about the reasons why human sacrifices are required, it is always in order to appease a particular divinity. The gods' demands for human sacrifice (as interpreted by seers) are taken seriously because they have been made by a god or a hero. In the *Phoenissae* Menoeceus explicitly dies in order to pay Ares back for the death of his son the snake, who was killed by Menoeceus' ancestor Cadmus. Artemis demands the sacrifice of Iphigenia so the Greek ships can sail to Troy (*IT* 17–24; *IA* 90–2). In the *Hecuba* the ghost of Achilles wants human blood to be shed in order to gratify the Greeks who died in the Trojan War (132–40). In the *Heraclidae*, the sacrifice to Korē of the blood of a valuable young female victim, as in Euripides' *Erechtheus*, prevents the death of many young Athenian men. If Euripides allows his characters to complain about the gods and the cruelty of their demands, it does not necessarily follow that he or his audiences were prepared to regard their religion as an illusion. Debate and controversy are essential aspects of the nature of drama; they allow the poet to make sure the audience remains aware that even though a human sacrifice will bring immediate success in a particular venture, it will have a devastating effect on the family of the victim, and often cause them to harm the human agents of the sacrifice or someone else.

Even though it was thought that after the Trojan War the gods had withdrawn from intervening in human life, it was believed that the gods could occasionally be seen, and that they continued to communicate with mortals through dreams and prophecy.[101] Even though there were no eyewitness accounts of this or any other human sacrifice performed in the ancient Greek world, Greek writers believed that in times earlier than their own the gods had demanded human sacrifices. They knew that child sacrifice was practiced elsewhere in the Mediterranean, most notably by the Carthaginians. So the idea that the gods might demand human sacrifice was taken seriously even in historical times. In his *Life of Themistocles* (13.1–2) Plutarch relates how the Athenian seer Euphrantides told the Athenian general Themistocles that in order to defeat the Persians at Salamis he would need to sacrifice to Dionysus the Raw-Eater the Persian king Xerxes' three young nephews, whom the Greeks had captured. Themistocles was reluctant to comply, but the army demanded that he do so (as in the *Iphigenia at Aulis*). Plutarch's source for the story was the fourth-century historian Phaenias of Eresus, a pupil of Aristotle's (fr. 25 Wehrli = 1012 *FGrHist* 19). The story cannot be historical, since the cult of Dionysus Raw-Eater was not known in Attica at the time of the Battle of Salamis (480 BC), and the timing and place of the sacrifice given by Plutarch in his *Life of Aristides* (9.1) would have come after the battle as it is described by the fifth-century authors Aeschylus and Herodotus.[102] Neither Aeschylus (who might have been present) nor Herodotus says anything about it. But from his perspective six centuries after Salamis, Plutarch regarded it as credible enough to include in two of his *Lives*. Even if the story is not historical, in his account of Themistocles' sacrifice of Xerxes' nephews, Plutarch's emphasis, like that of the dramatists, is on the general's moral dilemma and the effectiveness of the sacrifice; he says nothing about the effect of the event on the religious beliefs of the rank and file of any of the armies.

Plutarch follows the same narrative pattern in his accounts of two other sacrifices. When Agesilaus II, the king of Sparta, was assembling his troops at Geraestus on the island of Euboea before undertaking an expedition to Persia in 396 BC, he went

with friends to Aulis for the night, because that was the site
where Agamemnon had assembled all the various contingents
from the cities of Greece before setting sail for Troy. Plutarch
did not need to point out to his original audience that Agesilaus
was acutely conscious of the historical parallel, and perhaps
believed that if he went to Aulis he also would be able to defeat
an Asian enemy.[103] While there Agesilaus was told by a voice in a
dream that since he was making the same kind of expedition as
Agamemnon "you should make the same sacrifice to the goddess as
Agamemnon made before he set sail." Agesilaus was not upset by
the dream, but told his friends that he would appease the goddess
by offering a sacrifice, "but not by imitating Agamemnon's lack of
sensibility." He told his seer to sacrifice a doe to the goddess, but
the Boeotians said the sacrifice violated their laws and took the
thigh-pieces away from the altar. Agesilaus sailed off with his army
but believed that the Boeotians' actions were a bad omen, and
that his plans would not be enacted and the expedition would not
achieve its goals (*Ages.* 5.4–6).[104]

Plutarch also describes how before the Battle of Leuctra (371
BC) the Theban general Pelopidas dreamt that the Leuctridae (three
sisters who were buried there after they killed themselves because
they had been raped by Spartans) demanded that he sacrifice a
chestnut-haired virgin. The seers told Pelopidas that he must
obey the message sent to him in his dream, citing the examples of
Menoeceus and Macaria, the sacrifice of the three young Persians
to Dionysus Raw-Eater before the Battle of Salamis, and the death
of the Spartan general Leonidas at Thermopylae (who knew that
he and his men would die, but nonetheless did not retreat). The
seers also pointed out that when Agesilaus refused to imitate
Agamemnon and sacrifice his own daughter at Aulis, his expedition
failed. Fortunately for Pelopidas, he was able to avoid sacrificing a
human virgin, because a beautiful chestnut-colored filly suddenly

galloped into the camp. Pelopidas sacrificed the young horse to the Leuctridae and won the battle (*Pelop.* 21–2). None of these narratives seems intended to discourage belief in the traditional gods, or in the accuracy of traditional methods of prophecy. If anything, the stories leave their audiences with the impression that no matter how offensive and gruesome the procedure, such sacrifices can achieve their purpose. Humans try to avoid human sacrifice, but realize nonetheless that the sacrifices work, unless the human beings (like Agesilaus) fail to do what the gods require.

The same can be said for the sacrifices portrayed in Euripides' dramas, though the poet makes his audiences aware of the terrible cost of the practice by allowing the young victims to speak for themselves and giving them an opportunity to display their extraordinary courage. Their parents and friends also try to find some way out, even if it means offering themselves instead of their children. But these same characters do not question whether or not the gods are entitled to demand human sacrifices, or claim that their demands are unjustified. It is also significant that none of the parents or friends of the victims asks a powerful god like Zeus, Athena, or Apollo to intervene on their behalf to stop Artemis, Ares, Persephone, or the ghost of Achilles from asking for the blood of a human victim. The mortals seem to know that cooperation and concerted effort are not what they can expect from Mt. Olympus. Foley nonetheless states that "Euripides, in his involvement with ritual, is simultaneously ironic, theologically iconoclastic, and intensely religious."[105] I would agree, if by "Euripides" she means not the individual poet but the characters in his dramas, who express their divergent views. Such conflict is required in drama, if only for purposes of entertainment. Few rituals could be more polarizing than a human sacrifice, which pits individual against state, and human concerns against the gods' constant desire for tribute and honor. Even though Euripides makes sure that his audiences will have no doubts about what it means to die on behalf of an army or a city, it does not follow from the fact that he does so that he believes or wants his audiences to suppose that the gods do not exist or that ritual perpetuates an illusion. If anything, the outcomes of the dramas would suggest that the theology of the traditional religion of Athens provides an accurate account of a world dominated by powers with which human beings have few effective means of communicating and over which they have little or no influence or control.

In the dramas we have considered in this chapter, the gods remain in the background but nonetheless determine what happens to all the mortal characters. Medea's divine grandfather the Sun-god rescues her by sending his chariot to take her from Corinth to Athens. In the *Hecuba* the gods allow Polydorus to be buried, but do nothing to rescue Polyxena or to help Hecuba, or to stop her from killing Polymestor's innocent children; she will be transformed into a dog and die without proper burial. The human sacrifices in the dramas achieve their immediate purpose, but do not right past wrongs or put an end to human suffering. Heracles' daughter dies heroically, but Athens will need to fight many more wars in the future. Agamemnon and the army are allowed to set sail for Troy, but the audience knows that when he returns home he will in turn be murdered by his wife Clytemnestra. In the *Phoenissae* Menoeceus dies heroically to save Thebes, but even though the war against the Seven is over, the Epigonoi, the sons of the Seven, will destroy Thebes in the next generation. And Oedipus' departure for Athens augurs that there will be a conflict between Thebes and Athens in the future, as indeed there was. If at the end of these dramas we wonder why the gods have allowed all these crimes to be committed, have let innocent people die, and do not seem to see that justice has not been done, we have begun to be aware of the nature of the world in which we live and die. We begin to understand that the gods are there for themselves and not for us, that we can only know what they choose to tell us, and that because we are fragile and short-lived we are likely to misinterpret what they allow us to hear. If as we leave the theater and think about what we have seen, we feel that all is not right in the world, isn't that just the point?

CONCLUSION

Gods who come to us when they are inclined to, and
not when we choose to call on them; gods who respond
to perceived slights with the greatest cruelty; gods who
demand that parents offer their children to them in sacrifice;
gods who destroy a city for the crimes of an individual; gods
who punish another god by harming their favorite human
beings—all these we have seen in the preceding chapters,
along with the most terrible human suffering, and on
occasion, a miraculous rescue, or a promise of good fortune
and support in the future. Such divinities have seemed
unworthy of worship, and certainly of belief, to all of us who
have been raised in a monotheistic tradition. And yet these
are the gods that appear in the dramas of Euripides, and of
the other dramatists whose work has survived the erosion of
the centuries. We know that the ancient Greeks continued to
worship them through the early centuries AD. But how can
we know that the dramatists themselves believed in them,
and did not seek, subversively at least, to suggest to the
audience that these gods had been misrepresented by earlier
poets, such as Homer and Hesiod? In the absence of any
contemporary information about audience response to the
dramas, either individual or collective, how can we know
what the people who watched the dramas thought about the
behavior of the gods they saw portrayed on the stage?

In an attempt to answer these questions without speculation, I shall suggest that we look again at the final lines of some of the dramas we have surveyed. Four of Euripides' dramas (*Alcestis, Andromache, Helen*, and *Bacchae*) end with a general description of divine action:

> Many are the forms of divinity; the gods bring many things to pass unexpectedly. And what people think will happen does not come to pass, but the god finds a means to bring about what we do not imagine. That is the outcome of this action.

The last several lines appear also at the end of the *Medea*, but with a different beginning: "Zeus on Olympus is dispenser of many things."[1] These lines about the gods apparently served as a kind of coda, marking the chorus's departure from the stage. But because the language of the coda seems repetitive and the sentiments that they express appear to lack distinction, most scholars believe the lines were added by later writers. Some have also argued that these coda lines do not seem equally well suited to the five dramas to which they were appended.[2] The lines have been thought to be disappointing for another reason as well: they express an outlook that remains foreign to monotheistic ways of thinking about divinity.[3] As Matthew Wright has observed: "If we were expecting something more profound than that—moral justification of what happened, or some sign that the gods care about human life—we will be grievously disappointed."[4] As Wright notes, the coda lines do not attempt to offer "an 'explanation' of all the suffering that has preceded them"; rather, he suggests, they "may be intended to highlight, in a grimly ironic way, the pitilessness of the play's outlook."[5]

Yet surely the notion that these lines are ironic derives not from the text of the drama, but from our own response to them.

The coda states explicitly and without any hedging that the gods do what they choose to do and that humans are only able to understand what has happened after the fact, by which time it may already be too late to prevent further suffering and loss. To an ancient audience, the coda would have described the relationship between gods and humankind with some precision. The wording is so general that it can be applied to any divinity, local or Olympian, the gods people encountered in their daily lives, or the gods of epic and tragedy. *Many are the forms of divinity*: gods can appear as themselves, or in disguise, like Dionysus in the *Bacchae*. *The gods bring many things to pass unexpectedly*. At the beginning of a drama none of its characters knows what is going to happen to them. Certainly Hippolytus, as Aphrodite observes, does not realize at the beginning of the drama that he will be dead before that very day has ended. In the *Alcestis* Admetus had no reason to suppose that his dead wife would be restored to him just a short time after she had died. In the *Bacchae* Pentheus was certain that he could get rid of the new cult that was disrupting the normal pattern of life in Thebes. When he went to spy on the women who had gone off to the mountains, he had no idea that the god whose existence he refused to believe in was leading him to his death. Even characters with prophetic powers, like Medea or Tiresias, know only part of what will happen. *What people* (like the ancient audience) *think will happen does not come to pass*, for instance, that the Sun-god would send his chariot to rescue Medea (a possibility that she never mentioned earlier in the drama), or that old Peleus would be able to rescue Andromache, and that Thetis would appear *ex machina* and make Peleus immortal. Who could have expected that Helen and Menelaus could manage successfully to trick the cruelly suspicious Theoclymenus into lending them a ship on which to escape? In every one of the five plays *the god finds a means to bring about what we do not imagine*.

The coda also reminds the audience of their mortal inability to comprehend or anticipate what the gods can do. The gods bring many things to pass *unexpectedly* (*aelptōs*); what we *think* would happen (*dokēthenta*) did not happen. Rather, a god finds a way to achieve something *we do not imagine* (*adokētōn*). Human inability to understand what the gods want or even what the gods try to tell them helps to determine the outcome of every drama. If Hippolytus and Pentheus had not supposed that it was up to them to decide which gods they chose to worship, they would not have died such violent deaths. Conversely, human intelligence can help the gods carry out their plans, as when Helen plots to deceive Theoclymenus, or Iphigenia devises a scheme to rescue Orestes so he and Pylades will not be sacrificed to Artemis in Tauris. But if a god had not found a way to rescue them, neither the *Helen* nor the *Iphigenia among the Taurians* would have had such relatively happy endings.

A few dramas (*Iphigenia among the Taurians* and *Orestes*, as well as *Hippolytus* and *Phoenician Women* in some manuscripts) end with a different coda, a prayer to the goddess Victory (*Nikē*), spoken by the chorus, asking for continued success in dramatic contests.[6] Barrett thought these lines could not have been written by Euripides because they were "illusion-destroying," presumably because they abruptly draw the audience away from the action of the drama back into the present world.[7] But like the other repeated coda, the prayer clearly attributes to a god (and not to the human judges) the power to enable the author of the drama to defeat his rivals. It would be a mistake to dismiss either of these codas as mere interpolations or unwelcome distractions. Even if Euripides did not write them himself, and they were added by a later writer, and even if their content seems to us to be undistinguished, whenever they were written was in a time far closer to Euripides' own day than that of the commentators on the manuscripts of his plays or that of any later critics, including ourselves.

Because of their relative antiquity the two codas can give us an idea of how poets (and presumably, their audiences) understood the role of divine action in Euripides' dramas and in the outcome of the dramatic competition. We could even say that the first coda about the role of the gods would not be out of place at the end of any of Euripides' dramas. The lines state that human knowledge is impaired not only through ignorance of the gods' plans, but also because of the mortals' conceits and their flawed judgments based on partial evidence. In the *Ion* Creusa is so certain that her son by Apollo is dead that she almost kills him when she does actually encounter him. Ion tells his mother to run from the apparition that proves to be Athena; he had no way of knowing that the goddess has come in order to make sure that he and his mother will know about the future, so they will understand why it is necessary to keep Xuthus from discovering that Ion is not his own son. Her intervention was needed, because if Xuthus were to realize that that Ion is not his own son, Ion would not be able to inherit the kingship. In the *Orestes*, Orestes would have murdered his cousin Hermione, if Apollo had not intervened to stop him, and ordered him to marry her instead. Athena appears at the end of the *Suppliants, Erechtheus*, and *Iphigenia among the Taurians*, in order to make sure that the mortal characters establish the cults that will ensure the future safety of her city.

In ending some of his dramas with general reflections about the nature of the gods and the limitations of human knowledge, Euripides appears to have been following established practice. Sophocles competed against Euripides in the dramatic contexts, and several of his dramas end with similar reflections about the nature of the gods and the limitations of human understanding. His drama *Women of Trachis* ends with the following lines: "Young

woman, do not be left behind in the house. You have seen terrible
new deaths, and also many sorrows never before experienced,
and of these there is not one that is not Zeus" (1275–8). The
deaths referred to in these lines include the suicide of Heracles'
second wife Deianeira, and of Heracles himself, who is dying in
agony from the poison embedded in a robe which his wife had
sent to him. The cause of this misery can be attributed to Zeus
because he is Heracles' father, and Heracles' actions were in turn
the cause of Deianeira's death and his own suffering. Heracles had
attacked the city of Oechalia because he had fallen in love with the
king's daughter Iole. When Deianeira had learned of this she had
sent Heracles a robe that she had anointed with the blood of the
centaur Nessus, whom Heracles had killed, and which she believed
would serve as a love charm to win back Heracles' affections.
But when she learned that the robe was tearing away Heracles'
skin, she killed herself. As Heracles was dying, he ordered his
son Hyllus to marry Iole, the woman who had indirectly caused
his mother's death. Without Zeus, there would have been no
Heracles, and none of these terrible events described in the drama
would have happened. The speaker of the drama's concluding lines
may be Hyllus, or the chorus of women of Trachis from whom
the play takes its title; both attributions appear in the surviving
manuscripts. In either case, the concluding lines reinforce what
Hyllus has just observed in the lines immediately preceding, as
his father Heracles was being carried out to be burned alive.
Hyllus had spoken about the gods who do nothing to stop human
suffering—the gods "who beget us and are called our fathers
look down on such misery. No one can view the future, but these
events are lamentable, and to the gods they are a reproach, and
they are harshest of all on the one who must endure this disaster,"
Heracles himself (1266–74). As P. E. Easterling observes, the
lines "deepen the irony" of the passage, not in the modern sense

of undercutting belief in the gods, but in the ancient sense of emphasizing human ignorance. No one onstage yet knows what the audience knows, which is that Heracles will become a god.[8]

The endings of two other plays by Sophocles also concentrate on human ignorance. At the end of the *Ajax*, the chorus of sailors from Salamis reflects on the terrible events of the drama: "Indeed it is possible for mortals to understand many things once they had seen them. Before they have seen them, no prophet can say what he will do in the future" (1418–20). In the drama, Athena drove Ajax insane, so that he killed flocks of cattle and sheep while he supposed that he was killing Agamemnon and Menelaus. When he recovered his sanity and learned what he had done, he killed himself. The chorus' comments are appropriate for a plot in which Ajax (while planning to die) pretends that he will try to go on living, though the same reflections about uncertainty could equally well be applied to other plays.[9] Similarly, some lines from Sophocles' lost drama *Tereus* may offer a reflection on the gruesome plot of that drama: "mortals must think mortal thoughts, because they know that there is no dispenser other than Zeus of what will happen in the future" (*TrGF* 4, F 590). Tereus had seduced his wife Procne's sister Philomela, and then cut out her tongue so she could not report what he had done. But Philomela wove an account of what happened into a tapestry, and in a Medea-like revenge Procne killed their son Itys, cut him in pieces, and then served him to his father for dinner.[10]

At the end of the *Oedipus Tyrannus* the chorus reflects on Oedipus' rise and fall, and deduces from it that mortals must wait till someone dies before they can call him fortunate:

> Dwellers in our homeland Thebes, look, this is Oedipus, who solved the famous riddle and was the most powerful man. Who among the citizens did not look on his fortune with envy? What a

great wave of dreadful misfortune he has come upon. So mortals
should watch for that final day before they call someone happy,
until he has crossed the boundary of life without suffering sorrow
(1524–30).

The lines restate what the chorus said about Oedipus earlier in
the drama: "when I look on your fate (*daimōn*), I can call nothing
in mortal life happy" (1194–6). Herodotus also puts a similar
sentiment into the mouth of the Athenian lawgiver Solon, when
the Lydian king Croesus asked him who in the world surpassed all
others in happiness (1.30.4).[11] Most modern commentators have
considered the lines at the end of the *Oedipus* to be spurious.[12] But
even if they were not composed by Sophocles himself, like the
coda to the five Euripidean dramas, they comment on the limits of
human knowledge, even though they say nothing specific about the
role of the gods.

Although the concluding lines of these tragedies by Sophocles in
many respects offer an even bleaker outlook than the coda about
the action of the gods at the end of Euripides' five plays, no one
has tried to argue that in writing them or the concluding lines
about Zeus in the *Women of Trachis* Sophocles meant to encourage
his audiences to reflect on the immorality of the gods, or that he
was using them to suggest to his audiences that they should reject
traditional belief in favor of more caring and responsible deities.
No one appears to have been inclined to suggest that Sophocles
had any doubts about traditional religious beliefs or practices, if
only because Aristophanes does not seem to have accused him
of corrupting the youth or of not believing in the gods in whom
the city believed. On the contrary, Sophocles' biographer judged
him to have been "more pious than anyone else" (*TrGF* 4, T 1.12).
Sophocles was said to have been the priest of a hero Halon (*TrGF*
4, T 1.11) and to have built a shrine to Heracles Informer because

he had had a dream in which Heracles told him where to find a golden crown that had been stolen from the Acropolis (*TrGF* 4, T 1.12). According to other sources, Sophocles received in his house the cult statue of the god Asclepius (*TrGF* 4, T 67, 68).[13] But his piety apparently did not stop him from representing the actions of the gods and the nature of human life in much the same ways as did his contemporary Euripides.

It is in large part because of the nature of these gods that the genre of drama came into being in Greece, and not (for example) in ancient Israel. There would have been no reason to write tragedies, if the ancient Greeks had believed that their gods cared for humankind and were concerned about their suffering, or if they had supposed that the gods were willing to make their intentions clear, or were prepared to endow more than a few human beings with partial clairvoyance. In the absence of canonical religious texts, covenants, and revelations, miscommunication and lack of understanding were inevitable. The action in all ancient Greek dramas is propelled forward by human uncertainty about the wishes and plans of the gods, and in all dramas the audience's attention is held by sporadic and gradual revelations. But in most cases understanding, even if it comes in time to prevent death and disaster, does not bring lasting happiness, and the gods offer no comfort, with the possible exception of Castor, who was a mortal once, and knows what mortal life is like.[14] Even when the action ends on a positive note, when the principal characters are rescued and promised a reasonably secure future, the gods never tell the mortals all that they know. The gods rarely take any notice of the suffering their indifference has caused. Many dramas end with regret and lamentation, with the surviving characters uncertain about what the future may hold for them. Ends are not tied up neatly, as they might be at the conclusion of a novel by Dickens. There is no promise of future redemption. Sympathy and support must come from other mortals; Heracles thinks of Amphitryon, not Zeus, as his father. In his misery, guilt, and isolation Heracles is not rescued by Zeus, but by his mortal friend Theseus.

The remote and indifferent Zeus in the dramas of Sophocles and Euripides is the same god as the Zeus in Aeschylus' *Suppliants* and *Agamemnon*. In Aeschylus' *Suppliants*, the daughters of Danaus think that Zeus will be disposed to help them because they are descended from him through their ancestress Io (86–103, 590–9).[15] But in the *Danaids*, the last play of the trilogy of which the *Suppliants* was a part, only one god comes to help one of them, and that is not Zeus, but Aphrodite (*TrGF* 3, F 44). In the *Agamemnon*, the chorus of old men calls on Zeus because he is the god who rules with the assistance of Justice (*Dikē*), but at the end of the trilogy it is not Zeus but his daughter Athena who intervenes to save Orestes and the city of Athens. Zeus is portrayed as a cruel tyrant in the *Prometheus Bound*, a drama attributed to Aeschylus but quite possibly by another author. In that drama Zeus punishes his father's brother Prometheus for disobeying him by having him chained to a rock in the Caucasus Mountains. The mortal maiden Io wanders in, in a state of delirium. When she refused Zeus' advances, he turned her into a cow, so that he could approach her in the form of a bull, thus keeping his wife Hera from seeing what he was doing. But Hera then saw to it that Io was pursued by the herdsman Argos, who had a hundred eyes and never slept, so Zeus could not come to her again without Hera's knowledge. Zeus' son Hermes killed Argos, but Argos' ghost in the form of a gadfly kept on pursuing and stinging Io, as she wandered from her home in the Peloponnesus until she came to the Nile. Only after this long and arduous journey did Zeus release her from her suffering, so that could give birth to Zeus' son.

In the *Rhesus*, a play that was attributed to Euripides, but probably was written by a later writer, Zeus does not protect his descendants.[16] The chorus of Trojan soldiers prays in vain for Apollo to come to help them (he had been on the Trojan side throughout the war). When the Thracian king Rhesus arrives with his army; both the chorus and Hector believe that Zeus is on their side (319–20, 341–59). But soon Zeus' daughter Athena appears *ex machina* to help the Greeks. She pretends to be Aphrodite in order to give the Trojan prince Paris misleading advice, and as a result the Greeks are able to kill Rhesus and his men. At the end of the drama Rhesus' grieving mother comes to take away his body. She is a goddess, one of the Muses, the nine daughters of Zeus; she bore Rhesus to the Thracian river Strymon. Even though the Muse is his daughter, Zeus does not take her suffering into account, and his more powerful daughter Athena actively works to bring about the defeat of the Trojan army, as in the *Iliad*.

If we judge the behavior of gods by what they actually do, and not by what mortal characters suppose that gods ought to do, the gods in Euripides' dramas are recognizably the same beings that appear in the dramas of the other poets whose works have come down to us. Plato excluded Euripides along with the other dramatists from his proposed ideal state. Apparently he did not think that Euripides shared with Socrates the notion that the gods were never the cause of harm for mortals (*Resp.* 379c–80c). As we have seen, from a mortal point of view, Euripides' gods can do considerable harm and behave with the greatest cruelty. The dramas describe gods who only occasionally involve themselves in human life, sometimes as lovers or parents or particular friends, but more often as implacable enemies.[17] We can only guess why Euripides appears to have paid more attention to divine action than the other poets appear to have done, but I would like to offer a possible answer. The gods of Greek drama look down upon human activities as distant spectators. The poets call attention to the gods' ability to distance themselves from the disasters (or even happier outcomes) that they have witnessed, like Artemis at the end of Euripides' *Hippolytus*. In this respect, though not in others, the gods bear some resemblance to the human audience listening to the recitation of an epic poem or watching the performance of a drama in the theater.

After seeing the outcome of a particular drama, the human audience can get up and return to their own homes, putting a distance between themselves and the suffering of the heroes that the poets have described. This affinity between audience and the gods is strictly limited and temporary, but it gives the audience a fleeting opportunity to look down upon human action as a god might see it, without the usual mist of partial understanding that clouds mortal eyes. Unlike the characters and the chorus, the audience has a clear view of everything that is happening on the stage, and a better opportunity than any of the characters involved to grasp the meaning of the dramatic action.[18] The audience can see the gods and hear what they say before the action begins. They can learn about their intentions from oracles, they can become aware of the precise timing that signifies that the gods are directing the outcome of the action that they are witnessing. The opportunity to have some limited access to such knowledge is an integral aspect of a religion that encouraged its adherents to question in order to believe. Far from undermining the religion of his peers, Euripides, by means of his vivid depictions of the gods, equaled and in some cases surpassed his contemporaries in his ability to describe one of ancient Greek religion's more important and admirable aspects, the attempt to define and understand what it means to be human.

NOTES

Introduction

1 Harvey 1973, 769.

2 The theme of service is carried out in the windows of the nave of the chapel, which portray "The Love of God in Christ," "The Call to Service," and "The Life of Service"; Glasscock 1975, 305.

3 See esp. Korpel 1990, 621–6.

4 See also [Hesiod] *Cat.* fr. 1.6–7 M-W.

5 Aristophanes describes humans as "creations of mud" (*Birds* 685–7), using some of the same language as [Aesch.], *PV* 547–50. A similar story is attributed to the sophist Protagoras by Plato (*Prt.* 320d). See esp. Dunbar 1995, 429–30.

6 The term Erinys is often translated as "Fury" (Latin *Furia*), which in modern English conveys the notion of anger; rather, they are goddesses of retribution.

7 See esp. Sourvinou-Inwood 2003, 291–2.

8 Hornblower 2008, III 294. Even if Euripides did not have Melos specifically in mind when he wrote the Trojan Women, the drama's relevance to the Athenians' conduct in war would have been

recognized, especially if it were performed shortly after the Athenians' conquest of that island.

9   Kovacs 1997, 162–76; Parker 1997, 149: "Troy is a symbol of the grim truth that even a city—any city—could be mortal."

10   The Athenians also enslaved the women and children and killed some of the men of Torone in summer 422 (Thuc. 5.3.2–4). In retrospect, these events appeared discreditable to fourth-century writers; see Gomme, Andrewes, and Dover 1970, IV 191. In the case of the revolt of the city of Mytilene in 427, even though the Athenian Assembly was persuaded not to kill all the men, they still put one thousand men to death and confiscated all the land belonging to the city (Thuc. 3.50).

11   Mastronarde 2010, 181.

12   For a brief appreciation, see Solomon 2001, 264–5.

13   At the beginning of the *Aeneid*, Virgil describes how Hera's Roman counterpart Juno pursues the last surviving Trojans "because of the wrong done to her when her beauty was rejected" (*spretaeque iniuria formae*; I. 27). Juno's anger at Paris extends also to the blameless Aeneas and his comrades, simply because Aeneas was the son of Venus (the Roman Aphrodite), and (like Paris) he was a Trojan.

14   The story was told in Euripides' (now-lost) drama *Alexandros, TrGF* 5.1, test.iii (hypothesis); see Scodel 1980, 76–9; it is alluded to in Eur. *And.*, 293–300 and several other dramas, see esp. Collard, Cropp, and Gibert 2004, 43–4.

15   The same pattern of an oracle disobeyed and then fulfilled occurs in Herodotus' account of how Cyrus became king of Persia (Hdt. 1.106–30).

16   On the date of the stone reconstruction of the theater of Dionysus, see Papastamati-von Moock 2014, 23–5.

17   See Pickard-Cambridge 1968, 99–100. Green and Handley 1995, 67–8; Papastamati-von Moock 2014, 63.

18   On the meaning of *hamartia*, see esp. Lucas 1968, 299–307; Bremer 1969, 60–3; Belfiore 1992, 166–70.

19   *TrGF* 4, T 53a = *TrGF* 5.1, T 71a, translation by Kovacs 1994a, 57. The remark (and other pithy quotations attributed to Sophocles) may have originated in comedy (cf. the dialogue between Aeschylus and Euripides in Ar., *Frogs* 1053–7; see also Lefkowitz 2012, 82 and 181 n. 20). When quoted by other authors, the remark is interpreted

to contrast the two poets' ethics: "when asked why he wrote about people's good habits, and Euripides about their bad ones, he said, "I write about people as they ought to be and Euripides as they are" (*TrGF* 4, T 53b = *TrGF* 5.1, T 71b; cf. also *TrGF* 4, T 172 [Sophocles wrote about good women, Euripides bad]).

20 Compare Walton 2009, 116 ("the gods in his plays are a dramatic device"), 86–7 on the prologue to the *Trojan Women* ("Poseidon 'appears' to open the play").

21 Griffin 1980, 189. For recent support of this approach, cf. Riedweg 1990a, 129; 1990b, 93; Wright 2005, 383.

Chapter 1

1 On the sources of Euripides' biography, see Lefkowitz 2012, 87–97.

2 Lefkowitz 2012, 1–5, 128–31; Kivilo 2010, 201–24.

3 For the etymology of *alētheia*, see Beekes 2010, 60–1 on *a-lēthēs*.

4 Only the concluding sentence of this treatise survives in its entirety.

5 On the formation of Euripides' biography, see esp. Lefkowitz 2012, 87–103.

6 On terms for atheism, see Fahr 1969, 15–7, 164–7; Winiarczyk 2011, 163 n. 246. Atheism and impiety (*dyssebeia*) are closely related (see, e.g., Hippocrates, *On the Sacred Disease* [1.74]), but an accusation for one did not necessarily bring an accusation for the other; see Winiarczyk 1984, 182–3.

7 See esp. Versnel 2011, 139–41, and 139 n. 426 with bibliography.

8 See esp. Parker 2002, 129.

9 Scholars have assumed that the lines (which were quoted out of context) were spoken by Bellerophon (see Riedweg 1990a, 130 and 1990b, 46–50), but Dixon (2014, 493–506) suggests that they were spoken not by Bellerophon but by Stheneboea (who had fallen in love with him even though she was married to Proetus). When Bellerophon refused her advances, Stheneboea told her husband that Bellerophon had tried to rape her. Later Bellerophon became hateful to the gods after he tried to ride to Mt. Olympus on the winged horse Pegasus, supposing that he would be rewarded for his piety.

10 Dover 1993, 16: "Evidently the fact that, after that outburst, Hippolytus kept his oath was immaterial. What mattered was that the thought could be entertained, formulated, and pronounced before an audience to some of whom it might seem like a bright idea."

11 "Who knows if living is that which is called being dead, and living is dying? . . . Among mortals those who see the light are sick but the dead are in no way sick and have no troubles" (*Phrixus TrGF* 5.2, F 833), and the similar question, "who knows if living is being dead, and if being dead is living down below?" *TrGF* 5.2, F 638, from Euripides' lost *Polyidus*.

12 See Wildberg 2008, 25.

13 Cf. also Callias, fr. 15 K-A, *PCG* IV 46 (*TrGF* 5.1, T 51a); Lefkowitz 2012, 90.

14 Perhaps the "woman" in Teleclides' lost comedy (fr. 41 K-A, *PCG* VII, 683) was Euripides dressed up in women's clothes; see Wildberg 2008, 34 n. 13.

15 Satyrus' interlocutor may have been referring to *TrGF* 5.1, F 325, though Kannicht (ad loc.) thinks it was another passage, now lost (F 326).

16 The passage is quoted by Diogenes Laertius (2.44), who adds that the fourth-century historian Philochorus knew that the chronology was wrong (*FGrHist* 328 F 221). Palamedes was a Prometheus-like figure who aided the Greeks at Troy with his inventions of writing and board games, and organizational skills, but who was falsely accused and murdered by Odysseus and Diomedes; see Collard-Cropp 2008, 46–7.

17 The quotation about virtue is attributed to the *Auge* in Diogenes' text; *TGrF* 5.1, p. 335. Its relativistic content seems appropriate for the *Auge*, a play to which Aristophanes' Aeschylus alludes when he blames Euripides for portraying women giving birth in shrines (*Ran.* 1077), which was shocking because of the pollution from the bloodshed of childbirth; see Hall 2006, 69–71. It is conceivable that Euripides could have used the line in both the *Electra* and the *Auge*, since it appears to be proverbial; see Denniston 1939, 94–5. *Hel.* 780 = *Phoen.* 972 is another example of repetition between plays; Mastronarde 1994, 423.

18 According to Homer, Aeolus married his six daughters to his six sons (*Od.* 10.5–7).

19 The line from the *Aeolus* was also used to make fun of Euripides in
a clever story by the third-century BC comic poet Machon (407–10
Gow): the courtesan Laïs asks Euripides why he wrote the line "get
lost, doer of shameful deeds" (*aischropoios*, 1346), and the poet replies,
"aren't you an *aischropoios?*" Laïs promptly answers him with the famous
line from the *Aeolus*: "is something shameful, if it doesn't seem so to
those who practice it?" The *Medea* had been produced in 431 BC, but by
the time the *Frogs* was produced in 405, the word *aischropoios* could also
denote obscene behavior. An ancient commentator (schol. Eur., *Med.*
1346, II p. 211 Schwartz) claims that Euripides had been "ejected from
the theater" because he used the word (obscenity was not permitted in
tragedy).

20 See esp. Curd 2007, 87, 101, 194–205; also Cleve 1949, 156–9;
Kirk-Raven-Schofield 1983, 362–5.

21 On the language of this passage see esp. Scodel 1980, 93–5;
Mastronarde 2010, 173. The verb "I address you in prayer"
(*proseuchomai*) is not common either in literature or in inscriptions;
Pulleyn 1997, 218–20. The prayer is also unusual in that Hecuba makes
no particular request; Aubriot 1991, 233 n. 118.

22 See esp. list of parallels in Norden 1956, 145–6 n. 3; and on
incertitude in prayer as an admission of human ignorance, Lee 1976,
224; Aubriot 2005, 486–9; cf. also below, ch.2 on Aesch., *Ag.* 160–6.

23 Janko 1992, 363; cf. also [Aesch.], *Prom.* 68; Griffith 1983, 102 and
Griffith 1978, 133 n. 77. The author of the Hippocratic treatise
on "Airs" says air (*aēr*) is the *gēs ochēma*, quoting Hecuba's prayer
(Diogenes of Apollonia 64 C 2 D-C = Hippoc., *de Flat.* 3). More
accurately, the author of the Hippocratic treatise (and Scodel 1980,
94) should have identified it with *aithēr*; see Diggle 1981, 106; Yunis
1988, 85–6.

24 Cf. also *TrGF* 5.2, F 919 ("also the head of the gods, the *aithēr* that
embraces the earth"), *TrGF* 5.2, F 877 ("*aithēr* that men call Zeus"),
and *TrGF* 5.2, F 1004. See Matthiessen 1968, 699–700; Barlow 1981,
209 suggests that the association between Zeus and *aithēr* may refer
to Anaxagoras, who also called Earth and Zeus' *aithēr* the parents
of the world and everything in it (*TrGF* 5.1, F 839N = Anaxagoras
59A112 DK; see also *TrGF* 5.1, F 182a, F 330; *TrGF* 5.2, F 1004).

But Anaxagoras was not the first thinker to make the connection;
Aeschylus had said "Zeus is *aithēr*, Zeus is earth, Zeus is heaven,
Zeus is everything beyond all these" (*TrGF* 3, F 70). When Euripides'
characters talk about *aithēr* or Zeus as the parent of all things, they
always use conventional anthropomorphic terminology. Aristophanes
enjoyed making fun of these ideas, parodying Euripides' "I swear by
aithēr, Zeus' 'habitation'" (*TrGF* 5.1, F 487) in *Thesm.* 272, and calling
the *aithēr* "Zeus' little house" (*dōmation*) in the *Frogs* (100, 311). The
philosopher-poet Empedocles also speaks of "the roofed home (*domoi*)
of aegis-holding Zeus" (31B142 DK).

25 To the idea of Zeus having a seat upon earth (*epi gēs echōn hedran*)
Scodel 1980, 94 n. 33 compares Poseidon's characteristic epithet
gaiēochos, used by Aeschylus of Zeus (*Supp. 816*) and by Sophocles of
Artemis (*OT* 160).

26 On *Alc.* 962–3, see esp. L. Parker 2007, 245–6: "the personages of
tragedy intellectually, as well as physically wear modern dress."

27 Chapouthier 1954, 216–8; Riedweg, 1990b, 51–3; Matthiessen 2004,
57–8. See also the discussion of the *Trojan Women* in the Introduction.

28 Kirk-Raven-Schofield 1983, 380–2. Diogenes of Apollonia, a
contemporary of Anaxagoras, was the first to say that the air (*aēr*) gives
life and intelligence to men and beasts (64 B4 DK = fr. 8 in Laks 1982,
39–41); the air gives intelligence to all humans, and all of them are
governed by it and it controls everything, and if the text as emended
is correct, the air seemed to him "to be a god" (64 B5 DK = fr. 9 Laks
1982, see esp. pp. 49–51).

29 In fact the idea of Earth and Air having equal shares goes back to
Hesiod, *Theog.* 126–7; on the passage, see esp. Finglass 2007, 123–4.

30 The line "in each of us our mind is god" (*TrGF* 5.2, F 1018) was also
attributed to Menander (*Monostich.* 588 Jaekel).

31 See Wilamowitz 1875, 163–4; Scodel 1980, 94–5 and 95 n. 36.

32 The anecdote (which may go back to the third-century BC Stoic
Chrysippus) is preserved by Galen (*de plac. Hipp. et Plat.* iv. 7.6 = CMG
V.4 p.282 De Lacy = Dale 1954, xxxvii). Diels-Kranz 1956, II 14 (*re*
59A33) suggests that Anaxagoras' words may be reflected also in *Alc.*
903–10, when the chorus speak of a relative who lost an only child.
But their words, like Theseus' in *TrGF* 5.2, F 964, are standard forms of
consolation; see Dale 1954, 117.

33 By the Hellenistic period *metarsios* had the same meaning as *meteōros*, and Anaxagoras was known for his *meteōrologia*, see (e.g.) Plato, *Phaedr.* 269 E = 5 9A15; Dover 1988, 146; for example, doctrines about the heavens are called *logoi peri tōn metarsiōn* by Plut., *Per.* 32.1. Cf. how the second-century BC grammarian Crates of Mallus in Cilicia (fr. 89 Broggiato) conjectured on the basis of a description of the stars in *Rhes.* 528–31 that Euripides did *not* know about observing what was in the air (*ten peri tōn metarsiōn theorian*) because he was a young man when he wrote the *Rhesus* (schol. *Rhes.* 528, II 340 Schwartz); apparently he had reason to believe (victor lists?) that Euripides was the author of that drama; see Ritchie 1964, 18–9; Broggiato 2001, 247. But most modern scholars believe that the drama was written by an unknown author, possibly in the fourth century; see esp. Liapis 2014, 93–112.

34 Dale 1954, *ad loc.*, described the gloss as a naive reaction to the prominent initial *egō*. See also L. Parker 2007, 245–6: "The idea that this is a personal statement by the poet appears in the scholia, and has continued to reappear even into the twentieth century. But it can be ignored."

35 On *Orestes* 282–5, see esp. West 1987, 252.

36 Barrett 1964, 272; Griffith 1983, 101–2.

37 Archelaus was listed as one of Euripides' teachers because he used Anaxagorean words like *nous, aer,* and *mydros* in his discourses on physics (60 A 11, 12, 15, 17 DK). According to Socrates' contemporary Ion of Chios, Archelaus was a friend of the young Socrates and went with him to Samos (*FrGHist* 392 F9 = fr. *111 Leurini). According to Aristoxenus (fr. 52a Wehrli = Diog. Laert. 2.19, fr. 52b = Suda, Sigma 829), Socrates was Archelaus' boyfriend (60 A 3 DK); but in biography influence can be represented as eroticism, especially for purposes of slander.

38 Anaxagoras was said to have been known as "Mind" (*nous*) to his contemporaries (59A15 DK), and was caricatured by the third-century BC satirical writer Timon as "the mighty hero Mind, because it was his Mind that belted everything tightly together that had previously been in disorder" (Timon of Phlius, fr. 798 *Supp.Hell.*). *Synesphēkōsen*, literally, gave everything a waist like a wasp's, is the kind of bizarre term that comic poets liked to use; Clayman 2009, 100–1. The notion of a boarding school presided over by a teacher who embodied his

own ideas could have been inspired by a scene in a comedy analogous
to Aristophanes' portrayal of an imaginary "Thinkery" (*phrontistērion*)
presided over by Socrates in the *Clouds*.

39 Anaxagoras is said to have believed that the source of the Nile
was melted snow from the mountains in Ethiopia (59A42.15–7,
A91.8 DK).

40 The idea about the melted snow was so familiar in Athens that
Herodotus mentioned it without attributing it to any particular
philosopher (2.22.1; also see the other references cited by Radt in
TrGF 3, F 300, pp. 391–3; Lloyd 1976, II 101–2; Schorn 2004, 169).
Euripides also offers the same explanation of the Nile's origins in the
prologue of the *Helen* (1–3). Aristotle's pupil Theophrastus included it
in his *Book on the Nile*, but rejected that explanation in favor of "rains
caused by etesian winds driving clouds against mountains in Ethiopia;"
Sharples 1998, vol. 3.1, 197–8. The true sources (Lake Victoria and
various feeder rivers) were not discovered until the nineteenth century.

41 All the characters in Anaxagoras' trial were famous, which in itself
could suggest a comic setting: Thucydides the son of Melesias brought
charges against Anaxagoras for Medism as well as for impiety (Diog.
Laert. 2.12 = 13 = Satyrus F 16 Schorn), and was defended by Pericles
(Sotion, fr. 3 Werli), but the only contemporary parallel for the charges
of Medism (long after the Persian Wars) comes from comedy
(Ar., *Eq.* 478, *Pax* 107–8). Plutarch appears to have relied on comedies
(or Atthides based on comedy) for his account of Pericles' intellectual
development (*Per.* 4); e. g., he was a pupil of the musicologist
Damon (37A 4 DK = Plato Comicus, fr. 207 K-A, *PCG* VII 523) and
the philosopher Zeno (Timon, fr. 819 *Supp. Hell.*). The comic poet
Hermippus was the source of Plutarch's account of Cleon's attack on
Pericles (*Per.* 33.8 = fr. 47 K-A, *PCG* V, 582) and of Aspasia's trial for
impiety (*Per.* 32.1 = T 2 K-A, *PCG* V 561).

42 Diogenes reports that Protagoras read his book either at Euripides'
house, or at the home of an otherwise unknown Megaclides or at the
Lyceum with Archagoras as his reader (Diog. Laert. 9.54 = 80A1
DK = *TrGF* 5.1, T 40). His accuser was either Pythodorus, one of the
four hundred, or Euathlus, according to Aristotle (fr. 67 Rose).

43 As Dover has shown (1988, 143–4; 1985, 21), the idea of earlier
book-burning was inferred by Cicero from Timon's *Silloi* (779 *Supp. Hell.*).

44 Lloyd-Jones 1983, 130–1.

45 Dover 1988, 142–3.

46 On the connection of shipwreck with impiety, see Eur., *El.* 1355, *HF* 1225; Antiphon 5.82; see Edwards and Usher 1985, 117.

47 On the *Augē*, see above n. 17, and on the incest in the *Aeolus*, see above n. 19).

48 Dodds (1960, 104–5) thought that *Ba.* 274–85 might reflect the thinking of Prodicus (84 B 5 DK); because Tiresias argues that the gods Demeter and Dionysus are great because of what they represent (bread, wine). But *PHerc.* 1428 fr. 19 shows that Prodicus was unequivocally atheistic; Henrichs 1975, 110 n. 64; 1984, 145 n. 24. On the other hand, Galinsky (1972, 101–3) implies that Euripides' portrayal of a principled and ethical Heracles may have helped to inspire Prodicus' famous story about Heracles at the crossroads, making a choice between virtue and vice.

49 Cf. Pl., *Leg.* 890a, about how the young are thought to be particularly vulnerable to metaphysical speculation, which leads them not to respect the city's gods.

50 Homer does not say what Tantalus did to deserve his fate, but perhaps it has something to do with what he was saying; Euripides in the *Orestes* has Electra say that Tantalus was punished because of his "unbridled tongue" (10); Willink 1983, 31–2.

51 Dover 1988, 147–8; Willink 1983, 28.

52 Dover 1988, 148–51.

53 See the speeches by the fifth-century orators Andocides (1) and Lysias (6, 7); Harrison 1968, 104 n. 3; MacDowell 1962, 13–5.

54 Dover 1988, 144.

55 Hyperides fr. 168, 9 Jensen (tr. Burtt 1954, 598–9).

56 Aristophanes uses Hippolytus' line about his mind foreswearing the oath in *Thesm.* 274–6 as well as *Frogs* 101, 1471; see Lefkowitz 2012, 94. The other examples in the same section of the *Rhetoric* also come from literary sources, Sophocles' *Teucer* (TrGF 4, F 215–6/1416b1) and *Il.* 10.242–5/1416b11.

57 See Dover 1988, 150; Schorn 2004, 283–4.

58 On Hygiaenon's process against Euripides, see Jacoby 1959, 32 n. 19; Schwarze 1971, 110–3; Schorn 2004, 283; Lefkowitz 2012, 94.

59 Dover 1988, 154–7.

60 A commentator on the Aristotle passage cites allusions to the Mysteries in Aeschylus' (now lost) *Toxotides, Hieraiae, Sisyphus, Iphigenia,* and *Oedipus* (*TrGF* 3, T 93b). Aeschylus was acquitted in his Areopagus trial because of his deeds at Marathon, where he was wounded and his brother Cynegirus (or Ameinias; *TrGF* 3, T 84) lost his hands.

61 Lefkowitz 1984, 144–7.

62 According to Cicero (Sen. 7.22), the drama Sophocles was composing when he was on trial for senility was the *Oedipus at Colonus*; see Jebb 1900, xxxix–xlii; Lefkowitz 2012, 82–3. Aristotle may be referring to the same trial in the chapter of the *Rhetoric* in which he mentions Euripides' trial: Sophocles said that he was trembling not as his accuser said, so as to seem old, but because he couldn't help it; he did not want to be eighty years old (1416a15).

63 Dover 1988, 136.

64 See Lefkowitz 2012, 93–5.

65 The phrase "which he himself had raised" is itself an echo of the passage in the *Iliad*, where Priam predicts that he will be torn to pieces "by the dogs I raised as table- and watch-dogs" (*Il.* 22.69); Seaford 1996, 179.

66 Although Satyrus and the Euripides Vita say that the dogs attacked Euripides in a grove near the city (*TrGF* 5.1, T 1, II; Satyrus F 6 fr. 39 col. xxi), in another account the attack took place in a Macedonian village called Bormiskos (*TrGF* 5.1, T 126 = Steph. Byz., B 125 [I, 360–1 Billerbeck]).

67 Scullion 2003, 389–400; Lefkowitz 2012, 92–5.

68 On this fragment as evidence for suspicion of "natural philosophers," see Parker 1996, 209; Schorn 2004, 216–8.

69 Lefkowitz 2012, 95.

Chapter 2

1 On the interpretation of this line see esp. Bond 1981, 285.

2 The vase painting in Figure 2.1 portrays a variant version of the murders, in which Heracles throws his children along with his household possessions into a bonfire; see Taplin 2007, 143–5; *LIMC* IV.1, 1988, 835, no. 1684, s.v. Herakles.

3   Cf. also Xenophanes 21A 32.23–4 D-K; he also observed that humans portrayed gods as the mirror image of themselves (21B 15–6 D-K); see esp. Bond 1981, 399–400. It is certainly possible (as Bond suggests on p. 400) that these lines "may well represent Euripides' own considered view," and that "the miserable tales of poets" might thus include this very drama, but then why are there no such complaints about lies told by poets in other dramas which feature destructive actions by the gods, such as the *Hippolytus* and the *Bacchae*?

4   On reciprocity in Greek religion, see esp. Parker 1998, 105–25.

5   See Burnyeat 2002, 141; McPherran 2002, 175.

6   Conacher 1998, 18–9; Egli 2003, 122–35, lists similar statements in other Euripidean dramas.

7   See above ch. 1, n. 21 on the language of Hecuba's prayer.

8   On the meaning of *tychē* (1393), see Bond 1981, 409; Lloyd-Jones 1983, 162; to their refs. add *IT* 475–8, 865–7 with Cropp 2000, 37–8; Soph., *Phil.* 1316–8, 1326; Giannopoulou 1999–2000, 261, 269.

9   Parker 1998, 114.

10 Although Pausanias (9.11.2) does not mention the account in Euripides' drama, he does observe that Stesichorus (fr. 283 Finglass = *PMGF* 230) and Panyassis (fr. 1) told the story of the killing of the children, but that the Thebans added the story about Athena saving Amphitryon by hurling the stone; Bond 1981, 320; Papadopoulou 2005, 71–4, 126; Fowler 2013, 269–71; Davies-Finglass 2014, 570–1.

11 The only parody of a passage (1094–7) from the *Heracles* that we know of has nothing to do with the gods; see Bond 1981, 344–5.

12 For other examples of characters expressing traditional beliefs about the gods, see, e.g. the examples collected by Nestle 1901, 51–65.

13 Fraenkel 1950, II 99–100; Lloyd-Jones 1956, 61 (= 1990a, 251). See also above ch. 1, n. 21 on Hecuba's prayer's allegedly "Anaxagorean" terminology: "whoever you are, most difficult to estimate, necessity of nature or the *mind* of humankind" (885–6).

14 The resemblance was first noticed by Nestle; see Rösler 1970, 13 n. 33. But there is no reason to suppose that there is a direct connection; see Lloyd-Jones 1983, 85–6. Aeschylus' description of Zeus' power is not a "rather abstracted omnipotence" of Xenophanes and Heraclitus (Smith 1980, 14); the poet has not forgotten about

the existence of the other gods. In the very next stanza the chorus speaks of Zeus' triumph over his father Cronus, without mentioning Cronus by name, because an ancient audience would immediately have understood that they were referring to the story of Zeus' accession to power in Hesiod's *Theogony* (492–500). The chorus is praying to Zeus because he is the most powerful of the gods, and the god who sees that wrongdoers (such as the violent Cronus) are punished (Lloyd-Jones 1990a, 251). Significantly, when Plato in Book 10 of the *Republic* seeks to exclude the poets from his ideal state, he does not make an exception of Aeschylus, or suppose that Aeschylus' stage gods were the kind of beneficent deities of whom Socrates might have approved (Lloyd-Jones 1990a, 257).

15 Mortals consistently react to a god's epiphany with terror; see esp. the comprehensive list of parallels in Richardson 1974, 208–9. When seducing mortals, Zeus appears in disguise, like other gods. But Hera (in disguise) tricked Semele into asking Zeus to appear to her with thunder and lightning, which killed her (Ovid, *Met.* 3.259–315; Ps. Apollod. 3.4.3).

16 Aristophanes (fr. 694 K-A, *PCG* III.2, 356) is cited by Satyrus (F 6 fr. 39. ix Schorn) as "evidence" that Euripides was an isolated figure, disliked by the Athenians, who composed his works in a cave in Salamis.

17 But cf. the passage from a lost drama involving Heracles cited by one of Satyrus' interlocutors that expresses traditional views about the gods (*TrGF* 5.2, F 913), discussed above.

18 See Collard and Cropp 2008a, 577 n. 1 (though the line seems to me to express uncertainty rather than skepticism; cf. questions about how to address Zeus, ch. 1, n. 21). On the formation of the anecdote, see Pickard-Cambridge 1968, 274; Dover 1976, 45: "the story smells of Satyrus." Luppe 1983, 55–6, observes that the anecdote had its origin in comedy; another possibility would be that the more controversial line belonged to Euripides' drama *Melanippe Captive*. Cf. also Kannicht, *TrGF* 5.1, p. 530.

19 For example, in *Frogs* 1471 and 1475 Aristophanes has Dionysus allude to Euripides' lines about Hippolytus' mind not taking the oath (*Hipp.* 612), and Macareus' "is something shameful, if it doesn't seem so" (*Aeolus, TrGF* 5.1, F 19); see above, ch. 1, n. 56.

20   Burnett (1971, 166) also claims that Amphitryon is being punished
      for blasphemy; see, e.g., 164 n. 11 "Note the irony of his repeated
      matēn at 339 and 340 . . . the poet reminds the audience that he has
      taken his connection with Zeus 'in vain' in the same sense that one can
      take the name of the Lord 'in vain', i.e., without giving it its proper
      sacred meaning." But there is no equivalent to the third commandment
      (Exodus 20:7) in ancient Greek religion. See also Bond 1981, xix.
21   Pseudo-Justin (*de Monarchia* 2) attributes the same lines to the
      fourth-century comic poet Philemon.
22   For other Euripidean passages where Zeus is identified with *aithēr*,
      see *TrGF* 5.2, F 839, 877, 941; Matthiessen 1968, 699–700, and
      above, ch. 1.
23   There are also seven passages about "God," all from lost plays except
      for a few lines from a speech in the *Suppliants*, where Adrastus states
      that mortals depend on Zeus' will (734–6).
24   Turner 1981, 92.
25   On Verrall's approach to Euripides, see esp. Wright 2005, 342–9; also
      Jenkyns 1980, 109; Michelini 1987, 11–9, Mikalson 1991, 225.
26   Verrall 1905, 135, 191.
27   Verrall 1905, 136 (in italics).
28   Verrall 1905, 156–60; he had read (see p. v) Wilamowitz 1895 [1959],
      III 130–1 (on *HF* 566); see Bond 1981, xix, 206–7. Grube 1941, 252
      was also persuaded by Verrall's argument.
29   Verrall 1905, 142.
30   Verrall, 1905, 167.
31   Lloyd-Jones 1991, 142.
32   Verrall 1895, 138.
33   Verrall 1905, 192.
34   Verrall 1905, 102.
35   Fraenkel 1950, III 719.
36   On the similarities between the Nurse's and Theseus' arguments, see
      Barrett 1964, 243. Cf. Soph., *Ant.* 823–38, where the chorus states
      that Antigone, because she is a mortal, ought not to compare herself to
      Niobe, who "is a goddess and descended from gods."
37   In 1932 J. U. Powell referred to Verrall's work as "brilliant";
      Lehnus 2012, 272. Gilbert Murray approved of "the ingenious but

disingenuous and unscholarly Verrall (whom Headlam had rightly criticized)," but Wilamowitz' work on the text helped to counteract his influence; Lloyd-Jones 1982, xxiv.

38 According to the second-century traveler Pausanias, people in Hermione said that Heracles brought the "dog of Hades" up from a chasm near the city (2.35.10). See also Bond 1981, 219.

39 See Bond 1981, 408.

40 Verrall 1905, 193–4. That Heracles refers to Cerberus as the "miserable (*athlios*) dog," might seem to offer support for Verrall's interpretation, but most scholars believe that the adjective was inserted in the text as the result of a copyist's inadvertent mistake. The original text probably read "savage" (*agrios*); see Bond 1981, 408.

41 Cerberus was immortal, the offspring of two immortal monsters, Typhaon and Echidna. When not giving his genealogy, Hesiod refers to him not by name, but as the "dreadful dog before the gate" (*Theog.* 769); on euphemistic references to Hades and its inhabitants, see Richardson 1974, 145.

42 Nestle 1901, iii–iv refers to Verrall 1895; see also Schlesier 1985, 8–9 n. 6; Michelini 1987, 16 n. 64; Mikalson 1991, 8–9.

43 Nestle 1901, 102, 107.

44 Nestle 1901, 108.

45 Nestle 1901, 147.

46 Nestle 1901, 103–4.

47 Ancient doctors regarded rabies (*lyssa*, Chantraine 1983–4, II 651; Beekes 2010, 879–80) in humans as temporary and curable, e.g., by potions made with alyssum (Arist., *Hist. An.* 640a4–8; Gal., *de Simp. Med.* 1.11.823). The disease was thought to be caused by dog bite, or in literature and art, by deities associated with dogs, such as the Erinyes or Lyssa herself (see *LIMC* VI.1 (1992), 322–9, s.v. Lyssa). The Asian Bacchants describe Pentheus, delusional and dressed in women's clothes, as "rabid" (*lyssōdēs*; Eur., *Bacch.* 981). See also ch. 6, n. 40 on Hecuba's metamorphosis into a dog.

48 Norwood 1920, 325.

49 Norwood 1920, 231–5.

50 On this passage, see esp. François 1957, 117–8, 119 (and on tragedy in general, 94–150). The terms "gods" (*theoi*), "the god" (*ho theos*),

"god" (*theos*), "divinity" (*daimōn*), and "the divine" (*to theion*) are used interchangeably by Euripides and the other dramatists, particularly in cases where the poet chooses not to specify a particular divinity; Herodotus (Euripides' contemporary) also appears to use the terms *ho theos* ("the god") and *to theion* ("the divinity") interchangeably; Harrison 2000, 168–81; Lachenaud 2003, 66. See also Mikalson 2003, 139: ". . . the use of these terms in describing divine events not obviously tied to a specific sanctuary or ritual sequence is characteristically Greek."

51 Norwood 1920, 231.

52 See also Matthiessen 2004, 61: "Mir scheint eher, dass er sich Illusionen darüber macht, in welcher Welt und unter welchen Göttern er leben muss."

53 Greenwood 1953, 87.

54 Vellacott 1975, 22.

55 Rose 1953, 62; see also Golden 1961, 164 n. 17.

56 Grube 1970, 47; cf. also Lloyd-Jones 1991, 142, "[the Victorians] did not see that early Greek religion has a strong monotheistic element."

57 See, e.g., Hesiod's so-called "hymn to Zeus" in the proem to Hesiod's *Works and Days* (1–10).

58 Foley 1985, 164–7.

59 See also Lawrence (1998, 139): "What was previously our sense of Hera's injustice is now felt less specifically as powerlessness in the face of a mysterious, impersonal, and possibly random universe."

60 See above, n. 8.

61 Michelini 1987, 275.

62 Yunis 1988, 171; also Halleran 1986, 180; and Lawrence 1998, 146: "Heracles' new secularity is supported by a religious insight that forces upon at least the more intellectually capable members of the audience a theological challenge for which the play has in its own way carefully and progressively prepared for them."

63 Egli 2003, 255.

64 Hall 2010, 267.

65 Papadopoulou 2005, 127; Swift 2010, 155.

66 On the purpose of the portrayal of human suffering in this drama, see also Sourvinou-Inwood 2003, 376–7.

67 See esp. Chalk 1962, 15, who when commenting on Zeus' role as Heracles' father observes that "Olympian gods lack all human qualities." As Parker (1998, 124) observes, "the fact that mortals often prayed to 'dear Hermes' or 'dear Nymphs' and sometimes even to 'dear Zeus' does not refute the claim that it would be odd for anyone to say that he loved Zeus." The term suggests a respectful familiarity, and can be used along with terms like *anax* ("ruler") and *kyrios* ("lord"); Versnel 2011, 137.

68 On Socrates' *daimonion*, see esp. Bussanich 2006, 206–9.

69 Dodds (1960, 189) characterized these lines as "sceptical and bitter," but see Mastronarde 2010, 169: "These lines portray a yearning for something that the represented world of the play denies (and that, this representation implies, the real world denies)."

70 See esp. Kullmann 1992, 334; Papadopoulou 2005, 128.

71 Konstan 1999, 83.

Chapter 3

1 The descendants of Titan gods whom Heracles kills include the Nemean Lion (*HF* 59–60; Hes., *Theog.* 327), the Lernean Hydra (*HF* 419–21; *Theog.* 313), and Geryoneus (*HF* 423–4; *Theog.* 387).

2 On the identity of the chorus of the Persians, see Garvie 2009, 50.

3 On the alliance between Athens and Argos, see below n. 13. In the prologue to the *Eumenides* (9–14) Aeschylus has the Pythia, the priestess of Apollo at Delphi, say that Apollo came to Athens rather than landing in Boeotia before he came to Delphi (as in *Hymn. Hom.* 223 and Pind., fr. 298), and Athena in her first speech pointedly claims Sigeum (a fortress near Troy) as an Athenian possession (397–402; the Athenians had recently taken it from the Persians). Finglass 2011, 204; Sommerstein 1989, 81–2, 151–2.

4 On Athenian annexation of the myths of Salamis, see Kowalzig 2006, 88–91; Finglass 2011, 203–4. Sophocles represents Ajax as being honored as a hero at Troy, where he was buried; Finglass 2011, 46–50. But he was also honored as a hero on Salamis (Pausanias 1.35.3–4), and in Athens (Kearns 1989, 141–2; Henrichs 1993, 175–6 n. 40).

5 Amphiaraus, the sixth Argive captain, was swallowed up by the earth. The seventh captain, Polynices, was buried in Thebes by his sister Antigone.

6 For example, the last speeches in the *Iliad* are eulogies for Hector delivered by his mother Hecuba, his wife Andromache, and his sister-in-law Helen.

7 Cf. Creon in Sophocles' *Antigone*, who refuses to allow Polynices to be buried, and insists that Polynices' sister Antigone be put to death for having disobeyed his orders; before the drama ends, not only Antigone but Creon's last surviving son and Creon's his wife have killed themselves.

8 Kearns 2012, 174–5: "the oath—itself usually involving a sacrifice—was a way of calling both gods and the human community to witness the truth or good faith of a declaration or undertaking, and the one who swore the oath called down curses on himself and his family in the event of his swearing falsely."

9 Any such inscription that may have been on display at Delphi would have been created many centuries later, in retroactive confirmation of existing agreements or treaties. See Jacoby, *FGrHist* IIIb Suppl. II 351 n. 23; Scullion 1999–2000, 220.

10 Smith 1967, 166 suggests that Euripides had the *Oresteia* in mind when he wrote Athena's speech, but does not explain why he describes it as "an institution with sacred sanction as the product of the experiences of the play but without Aeschylus' faith in its efficacy." How can we know what either poet thought?

11 On the date of the *Suppliants*, see Morwood 2007, 26–8.

12 Cf. Dem. 23.67–8; Paus. 3.20.9, 4.15.8, 5.24.9. The Seven attackers of Thebes sacrifice a bull, pour its blood into a shield, and touch the blood with their hands (Aesch., *Sept.* 43–4); in Xenophon's *Anabasis* (2.2.9), the Greeks dip a sword into the blood of a sacrificed bull. See esp. Henderson 1987, 91 on Aristophanes, *Lys.* 186; Stengel 1924, 317–21; Burkert 1983, 36; Burkert 1985, 251–2.

13 On treaties between Athens and Argos, see Zuntz 1955, 71–2. Thucydides (4.47) reproduces the full text of the 420 BC treaty between Athens and Argos, fragments of which also survive (*IG* I³ 83);

on the details of the treaty, see Hornblower 2008, 109–20; for a
picture of the inscription, see Strassler 1996, 331.

14 Egli 2003, 94–7; see also Burkert 1985, 320.

15 On fifth-century notions of the *aithēr*, see above, pp. 36–7. also Eur.,
Hel. 1013–6.

16 *CEG* 10 = *IG*³ 1179; see Morwood 2007, 186; Collard and Cropp
2008a, 396 n. 14. Egli 2003, 99 lists examples of the same thought
on two fourth-century grave inscriptions, *CEG* 535 and *SEG* 38
(1988) 440.

17 Egli 2003, 104.

18 On "winged" phrases as conventional metaphors for death, see Collard
1975, 401; Morwood 2007, 232.

19 Greenwood 1953, 119.

20 Greenwood 1953, 113.

21 Gamble 1970, 404–5.

22 Zuntz 1955, 78, 81.

23 Mendelsohn 2002, 220; he also claimed that in Athena's command that
the knife used in the sacrifice "must be cast into the recesses of earth,"
may lie a reference to the ritual of casting the *thesmoi* into the earth
(not to be retrieved) in Demeter's festival of the Thesmophoria. But
Athena tells Theseus to hide or bury (*kryptein*) the knife, so that it may
be found again near the pyres of the Seven (1206–7), a ritual action
with an entirely different purpose.

24 Mendelsohn 2002, 221, 222.

25 Mendelsohn 2002, 223.

26 The festival is not named in the text, but Euripides may have had in
mind the Eleusinian festival of Proērosia; see Bowie 1997, 53.

27 Morwood 2007, 164.

28 Mendelsohn 2002, 219.

29 Tragedies tend to avoid direct reference to current events (see esp.
Griffin 1998, 57), but if the *Suppliants* had such relevance, it would
have been to the Theban refusal to bury the Athenian dead after their
unsuccessful attempt to recapture Delium in November 424 BC, as
(e.g.) suggested by Bowie 1997, 45–56; but see Morwood 2007,
30: "Euripides would seem to be distancing the particular historical
reference."

30 On the date of the *Erechtheus*, Sonnino 2010, 27–34; Collard, Cropp, and Lee 1995, 155; for more about the problems of establishing an exact date, Cropp and Fick 1985, 79–80; Parker 1987, 212 n. 64.

31 In the *Ion*, Creusa says that because she was a baby she alone was saved when her father sacrificed her sisters (277–80).

32 In the *Suppliants* (1139–41) the mothers of the dead seven Argive captains tell their grandchildren "the sky (*aithēr*) holds them now, melted in the fire's ash. With wings they have reached Hades." See Calame 2011, 14, and above n. 15.

33 The title "god" (*theos*) suggests that they have immortality; e.g., Pindar calls Heracles *herōs theos* (*Nem.* 3.23) but like most heroes the Hyacinthides are to be based in a specific location on earth, not on Olympus. In effect, they have been rebranded (Cropp 2014) as the daughters of a Spartan named Hyacinthus who lived in Athens when Minos of Crete was besieging the city (Apollod. iii.15.8; Sonnino 90–110, 119–24). The name Hyacinthus is connected with several different places in Greece (Mellink 1943, 57–9) and was probably a survival from pre-Greek religion (the word has affinities with Hebrew words meaning violet purple or dark blue; Mussies 1999, 434).

34 On the sacrificial rituals, see Ekroth 2002, 172–4, and on the religious function of such cults, see Parker 2005, 399, 446 n. 111.

35 Like Heracles' daughter, who volunteers to be sacrificed in Eur., *Heraclidae* (see below, ch. 6), the names of Erechtheus' daughters do not seem to be mentioned in this drama. The names and even number of the girls vary in different traditions; see O'Connor-Visser 1987, 167–9, and Sonnino's helpful chart of the various traditions and sources (2010, 439).

36 *Sphendoniai* seems to have been a known place name (Bekker 1814–21, I 202; Suda, Pi 668, s.v. Parthenoi). But the evidence that connects the Hyacinthides with the Hill of the Nymphs is circumstantial; see Kearns 1989, 102, 201; Sonnino 2010, 104–10. Calame 2011, 14 n. 40. There is a hill in that area with ancient inscriptions to the Nymphs (Wycherly 1978, 188; Henrichs 1983, 98 n. 54).

37 In specifying that Erechtheus is to be buried in the middle of the city, Athena indicates that the location of his grave is in a different place from where his daughters will be buried (i.e., not in the city center).

The Hill of the Nymphs, with which the Erechtheids/Hyacinthides were identified in historical times (see n. 36), seems to have been located to the west of the Acropolis. According to the second-century AD sophist Favorinus of Arles, one daughter was buried near the temple of Athena Polias, information that may have come from a part of the text of the *Erechtheus* that is now lost or from another version of the myth; see esp. Sonnino 20110, 109. Connelly (2014, 232–5) suggests that all three daughters were buried near or underneath the Parthenon, but there seems to be no support for that claim in any surviving fragment of the *Erechtheus*; see Cropp 2014.

38 Collard, Cropp, and Lee 1995, 193.

39 The connection may have been made by means of the sound-alike (but false) etymology *Hyakinthides/Hyades*, in the way that Euripides has Athena state that Artemis' epithet *tauropolos* commemorates her time in Tauris (*IT* 1454, 1456–7).

40 Collard, Cropp, and Lee 1995, 193–4; Parker 2005, 143 n. 29.

41 Herodotus mentions that the Taurians sacrificed shipwrecked sailors to a maiden goddess called Iphigenia (4.103.1–2). The story that a mortal maiden Iphigenia was taken there by Artemis before she could be sacrificed by her father Agamemnon was told in the now-lost epic *Cypria*, Argumentum 41–9, Bernabé 1996, 41 (translation in West 2003, 75, Argumentum ¶8); Kyriakou 2006, 20.

42 Some critics have found this last-minute appearance of a *deus ex machina* to be artificial; but such dramatic interventions are characteristic of divine behavior in a universe where gods do not often coordinate their activities with one another, see esp. Mastronarde 2010, 165.

43 Presumably they will be put on the same ship with Iphigenia and Orestes; see Kovacs 2000, 19–23.

44 On the sacrificial procedure described in this passage, see esp. Bremmer 2013b, 88–91.

45 The town known as Halae Araphenides (as opposed to the town Halae Aixonides on the west coast of Attica) was about five miles north of Brauron.

46 On the connotations of *tauropolos*, see esp. Finglass 2011, 175–6. In historical times the Tauropolia was an all-night festival at Halae celebrated by both men and women; Menander, *Epitrepontes* 451; see Gomme and Sandbach 1973, 330; and esp. Furley 2009, 174–5.

47 The Greek word for the process was *etymologein*, "saying the word's true meaning." See esp. Dodds 1970, 116–7, and for many examples of the practice, Kranz 1933, 287–9; Platnauer 1938, 62–3.

48 On the purpose of the ritual, see Cropp 2000, 263.

49 The third-century BC poet Euphorion refers to a cenotaph of Iphigenia at Brauron (*CA* fr. 91), but that may have been inspired by Athena's speech in this drama. It is also surprising that this cult is limited to the families of women who died in childbirth. For other testimonia, see van Groningen 1977, 160–2. Pausanias (1.33.1) reports that when Iphigenia fled from Tauris, she brought the statue of Artemis to Brauron and afterwards took it to Argos, a story that in part appears to have been inspired by the plot of the *IT*. Scullion (1999–2000, 229) argues that the cult never existed as Euripides describes it, but there is no way to be certain, given the fragmentary nature of our sources.

50 The belief was that the goddess who brought the disease could also cure it; Lloyd-Jones 1990a, 321. For translated examples of inscriptions recording offering of women's robes to Artemis, see Lefkowitz and Fant 2005, nos. 402–3, p. 284; more information in Lloyd-Jones 1990a, 319 n. 46, and Cropp 2000, 263–4.

51 On the association in myth between Artemis and women who died untimely deaths, see Larsen 1995, 118.

52 See esp. Scullion 1999–2000, 230–3; Kyriakou 2006, 23–5, 27–30; Cropp 2007, 40–2. Cf. also Orestes' praise for the court of the Areopagus and the unusual kindness shown to him by the Athenians during his trial (945–60).

53 Egli 2003, 127–8.

54 Burnett 1971, 69.

55 Burnett 1971, 68.

56 See above, pp. 90.

57 Vellacott 1975, 21–2.

58 Dunn 1996, 63.

59 Dunn 2000, 27.

60 Dunn 2000, 16.

61 On the ancient evidence for Sophocles' piety, see Lefkowitz 2012, 82.

62 In the other versions of the story Oedipus may have known that his wife was also his mother, and continues to rule in Thebes "after the

gods made the facts known to men" (e.g., *Od.* 11.271–6), but in Sophocles' drama *Oedipus Tyrannus* he only learns who his wife is long after their children have been born; he then blinds himself, and his wife's brother Creon takes over as king.

63 On locating Oedipus' grave in Thebes and Athens, see Richardson 1993, 243; Kowalzig 2006, 84. According to another tradition he was buried at a town called Keos in Boeotia but then when some residents of the town were affected by misfortunes his remains were moved to Eteonos (a town on the north side of Mt. Cithaeron) and buried secretly in the sanctuary of Demeter (schol. Soph., *OC* 91 = Lysimachus 382 *FGrHist* F 2); see Robert 1915, 1–2.

64 Euripides in his (now-lost) *Oedipus* may have had Oedipus come to Athens at the end of his life, because he invokes the "Acropolis of the land of Cecrops" and "the outspread *aithēr*" (*TrGF* 5.1, F 554b); Collard, Cropp, and Gibert 2004, 110, 132.

65 See esp. Kowalzig 2006, 83.

66 On Eurystheus' grave (*Heraclid.* 1032), see below n. 69. On Oedipus' grave, Mikalson 1991, 41; Griffin 1998, 52 n. 49; Scullion 1999–2000, 231; Ekroth 2002, 261–2. But as Currie (2012, 339) observes, the lack of evidence for a cult of Oedipus near Athens does not necessarily prove that it did not exist, since there are other examples of secret graves in hero cults.

67 At Colonus Pausanias saw a *herōon* of the heroes Pirithous, Theseus, Oedipus, and Adrastus, almost certainly of a much later date. See Frazer 1898, II 366–7. In historical times cities or even groups of citizens could establish hero cults; Currie 2005, 5 n. 22.

68 E.g., the tombs of Arcesilaus/Battus and other rulers of the Greek colony of Cyrene (Pind., *Pyth.* 5.94–104); on the location of hero cults in general, see Burkert 1985, 205.

69 Wilkins 1993, 189. Strabo was told that Eurystheus was buried northeast of Athens in the district of Marathon; his body was buried Gargettus and his head near the town of Tricorynthus "near the spring Macaria below the wagon road" (8.6.19 = 377). According to Lucian his grave was near the temple of Heracles (*Deor. Conc.*7).

70 Aelius Aristides, *In Response to Plato in Defense of the Four* 172; see Jebb 1900, xxix–xxx.

71 On Dunn's failure to understand the religious importance of the aetiologies in the *IT*, see esp. Sourvinou-Inwood 2003, 419–20; Kyriakou 2006, 25–6.

72 The idea that Helen never went to Troy was said to have been invented by the sixth-century poet Stesichorus (fr. 90–1 Finglass = *PMGF* fr. 192–3); see the helpful discussion in Allan 2010, 18–22.

73 Kyriakou 2006, 452.

Chapter 4

1 On Apollo's oracles at Delphi, see Parker 1985, 300–2. When an earlier generation of gods was in charge, humankind received true information in dreams, but in order to keep dreams from competing with Apollo and his oracle at Delphi, Zeus no longer allowed the dreams to convey information to mortals clearly (IT 1276–83; see Cropp 2000, 252).

2 On the etymology of Loxias, see Beekes 2010, 871. The messenger in Lycophron's *Alexandra* refers to his obscure speech as *loxos* (1466), which the ancient commentators (II, p. 397 Scheer) glossed as "enigmatic (*ainigmatodēs*), hence also secretive (*mystikos*), hence also Loxias."

3 In Euripides' later dramas the style of the standard recitative meter (iambic trimeter) becomes more relaxed, allowing two short syllables to be substituted more frequently for a long syllable, and a greater variety of rhythmic effects; see Cropp 2000, 60–1; Cropp and Fick, 1985, 1–4.

4 In Aesch., *Eum.* 725, Apollo explains that he was doing a kindness in return for the respect Admetus showed to him (*ton sebonta euergetein*). Admetus also behaves in a dutiful manner when Heracles arrives unannounced, offering him hospitality in return for the hospitality Heracles had shown him in the past (559–60); that reciprocity was proverbial, and one of the traditional "Sayings of Admetus," was "learn who your friends are and love them" (Praxilla, 749 = Carm. Pop. 897 *PMG*); Scodel 1979, 51–62, esp. 59. According to what seems to have been a later tradition, Apollo was the young Admetus' lover (Call. *Hymn* 2.49); see Williams 1978, 49–50.

5   Cf. the terrifying arrival of Apollo at the beginning of the *Iliad*, when
    the god comes to attack the Greek army: "he came from the peaks
    of Olympus, angry in his heart, with his bow on his shoulder and the
    enclosing quiver; as he moved, the arrows on his shoulder clattered in
    his anger, and he came like the night" (1.44–7).

6   See esp. L. Parker 2007, 50, who compares this scene with Apollo's
    dialogue with the Erinyes in Aesch., *Eum.* 179–234; other versions of
    their genealogy exist (see esp. Finglass 2007, 132), but all put them in
    the generation of gods defeated by Zeus.

7   Hermes says "Loxias has shepherded [Ion's] fortune, although it seems
    as if he has forgotten" (67–8). When Xuthus comes he will give him his
    own child and will tell him that he was begotten by him, where "him"
    (*keinou*, literally "that one") could mean either Xuthus or Apollo; see
    Neitzel 1988, 275.

8   See also Wassermann 1940, 600.

9   On the purpose of Euripides' revision of the traditional genealogy,
    see Wasserman 1940, 594–5; Conacher 1959, 24–6; West 1985, 57;
    Lee 1997, 318; Cole 2008, 313–5. Dunn argues that the purpose of
    Athena's narrative was designed to call attention to the ways in which
    Euripides had altered the traditional historical record, and to make
    the audience aware of their "complicity in these fabrications" (Dunn
    2000, 27). But that is to assume that the genealogy presented in earlier
    epic had a canonical authority that mythological narratives were never
    required to possess. In practice, narratives about the remote past could
    be reshaped at any time by different poets. In any case, the date of the
    Hesiodic *Catalogue of Women* is unknown; the format is so loose that
    the original version could have easily been added onto in the seventh
    (Janko 1982, 200, 247 n. 37) and sixth (West 1985, 130–7) centuries;
    see Rutherford 2011, 152–4.

10 E.g., esp. *Od.* 11.236–54, where Poseidon tells Tyro that she will
    bear glorious children, and tells her to care for them and raise them;
    Lefkowitz 2007, 58.

11 See esp. Wassermann 1940, 589; Lefkowitz 2007, 61–3. Pindar
    describes Apollo behaving with similar lack of empathy towards the
    mortal women on whom he fathers children—e.g., Evadne (*Ol.*
    6.35–71; see Farrington 1991, 123), Coronis (*Pyth.* 3, 8–46), Cyrene

(*Pyth.* 9, 17–75)—though as in the *Ion* he protects the sons that are born to him, Asclepius and Aristaeus.

12 See also Mastronarde 2010, 166–7.

13 Burnett 1971, 127–8.

14 On Verrall's interpretation of divine action in Euripides' dramas, see above, ch. 2; on his treatment of the *Ion*, see also Spira 1960, 34; and on ironic treatments of this play in general, see Lee 1997, 32.

15 Norwood 1920, 238–9.

16 Conacher 1959, 31, 33.

17 Willetts 1959, 78; 1973, 209.

18 On Ion's speech see Spira 1960, 73, and esp. Lee 1997, 205: "why should the poet mount an attack on the god which the play itself shows to be in error?"

19 Cf. Kindt 2007, who calls attention to the contrast between the characters' suffering and the drama's happy ending, and insists that the ending must be illusory: "Not only does the drama allow an ironic reading of Apollo and his oracles: even in the end, after Athena's intervention and the final words of Ion, who now embraces his new identity, a feeling of unease remains."

20 Aeschylus may have been following the sixth-century poet Stesichorus in giving Clytemnestra an important role in the murder of Agamemnon; see Davies-Finglass 2014, 488–91. In the *Odyssey* Nestor praises Orestes for avenging his father's death, but alludes to Clytemnestra's death only in passing, when he says that Orestes "gave a feast for the Argives at the tomb of his hateful mother and cowardly Aegisthus" (3.309–10, though these lines may be a post-Homeric addition; see Heubeck, West, and Hainsworth 1988, 180–1). The story that Orestes and Pylades killed Clytemnestra was first told in the epic (now-lost) *Nostoi* ("Returns," Arg. 5; cf. [Hes.] *Cat.* fr. 23a. 27–30 M-W; Davies-Finglass 2014, 484).

21 In Figure 4.1 (*LIMC* VII 1, 1994, 72, no. 22, s.v. Orestes) Apollo defends Orestes from an Erinys, with Athena looking on; in other vase paintings Apollo is accompanied by his sister Artemis; see Prag 1985, 49–50.

22 This scene was so well known that Aristophanes in the *Frogs* (303; see n. 31), could make fun of it without specifying who wrote it

or what drama it came from. When he sees that the Erinyes have departed, Orestes says he now sees calmness (*galēn'*, neuter plural of the adjective *galēnos-ē-on*) emerging from the waves (279). According to Aristophanes, the actor Hagelochus accented the final syllable of the word "calmness" (*galēn'*) so that Orestes sounded as if he were saying that he was seeing a weasel (*galēn*) emerging from the waves, transforming the line into a statement that was both ludicrous and unlucky, since a weasel crossing one's path was considered to be a bad omen (Dover 1993, 231).

23 See esp. Willink 1986, 154–5; "A striking line appealing at once to 'piety' . . . and to human helplessness under divine despotism."

24 On Apollo's epiphany, see also Mastronarde 2010, 185.

25 See also West 1987, 292; Willink 1986, 355.

26 See esp. Spira 1960, 138–45, who compares Apollo's role in the Orestes to that of Heracles, who appears *ex machina* at the end of Sophocles' *Philoctetes*. Zeitlin 1980, 71 appears to have misunderstood the point of Euripides' revision of Aeschylus' account of the court, because she viewed the idea of gods serving as justices in a negative light: "the god in a regressive nullification of the Eumenidean achievement has taken away from mortals the right and power to judge these difficult issues and has given it to the gods who have the freedom (and perhaps the license) to make their own choices at will." But in the *Eumenides* also it was a god (Athena), and not a mortal, who cast the deciding vote to acquit Orestes.

27 See esp. Burkert 2007, 107–10; Hall 1990, 266–71; Hall 2010, 287.

28 During the Persian Wars some Athenians had imagined that they saw Theseus attacking the Medes at the battle of Marathon in 490 BC (Plut., *Thes.* 35), and that Boreas, the god of the North Wind, had helped the Athenians defeat the Persians at Artemisium in 480 BC (Hdt. 7.189). Also in that same year Castor and Polydeuces were believed to have appeared to help the Greeks at Salamis (Hdt. 8.122). For details and other instances, see esp. Pritchett 1979, 19–27.

29 See esp. Gould 1985, 22–4: "Divinity, it seems, speaks to man but in a language that he cannot understand, a language where words are no more than ambiguous signs and do not mean what they seem to say, and where, characteristically, they are replaced by signs." On Apollo's

gesture as portrayed in the pedimental sculpture at Olympia, see also Tersini 1987, 150–2; *LIMC* II.1, 1984, 293, no. 914, s.v. Apollon. In a few instances divine speech was said to be different from mortal speech, e.g., the idea that a predatory bird (unidentifiable, according to Dunbar 1995, 609–10) is called *chalkis* by the gods and *kymindis* by mortals, *Il*. 14.290; see esp. Janko 1992, 196–7. For other examples of names said to be used only by gods, see Kirk 1985, 94–5.

30 For the anecdote about Socrates and *Or.* 1–3, see Cic., *Tusc. Disp.* 4.63 = *TrGF* 5.1, T 47b. Pickard-Cambridge 1968, 274; Hall 1990, 263.

31 West 1987, 28; Arnott 1983, 13. The *Orestes* was performed in Athens in 340 BC (*TrGF* 1, p. 26 = *IG* II² b2320 = Pickard-Cambridge 1968, 109) and also again in the third century (*TrGF* 1, p. 41). The scene in the first part of the drama where Orestes is lying on a bed and Electra is looking after him was depicted in wall-painting in a room of a house in Ephesus, along with other paintings illustrating scenes from Menander's *Sicyonius* and Euripides' *Iphigenia in Aulis*; Strocka 1973, 366, 371–2. Fragments of music for lines 338–42 (the only extant music for any Greek drama) are preserved on a papyrus dating to ca. 200 BC (see West 1987, 203–4). Dionysius of Halicarnassus (*Comp.* 63) discusses the relationship between accentuation and music in the *kommos* between Electra and the chorus *Or.* 139–41; West 1987, 191; West 1992, 198.

32 According to the ancient commentator on Ar., *Ran.* 303, the joke about Hagelochus mispronouncing Orestes' line about calm after the waves (Eur., *Or.* 279; see above, n. 22) was still being quoted in comedies in the fourth century by the poets Strattis (frs. 1, 63 K-A, *PCG* VII 624, 652) and Sannyrion (fr. 8 K-A, *PCG* VII 588); see Arnott 1983, 13 n. 4; Bond 1986, 132. Virgil had the *Orestes* in mind in *Aen*. 2.567–76 and 4.471–3). The author of *Christus Patiens* drew on the texts of both *Orestes* and *Bacchae*. See Hall 2010, 285.

33 Kovacs 1994b, 37. The ten plays are *Hecuba, Orestes, Trojan Women, Hippolytus, Medea, Andromache, Alcestis, Rhesus* (which is almost certainly not by Euripides), *Trojan Women*, and *Bacchae*. All the other extant plays, including the *Heracles* and the *Ion*, come from a single manuscript that contains plays beginning with the letters epsilon, eta, iota, and kappa.

34   Pack 1965, 42–3. On the popularity of the *Orestes*, see also Nervegna 2014, 162.
35   So, e.g., Willink 1986, 130. In Aeschylus' *Choephoroe* Orestes can see the Erinyes coming, even though they are visible to no one else, but there may have been practical reasons for not trying to put them on the stage (1048–62).
36   Kovacs 2002a, 281–3.
37   See esp. Kovacs 2002, 281–3.
38   In addition to the passages discussed below, see also Porter 1994, 254–80.
39   Arrowsmith 1958, 190.
40   Burnett 1971, 222.
41   Burnett 1971, 212.
42   Vellacott 1975, 79–80.
43   The Phrygian says that that Pylades seemed to him to look like Hector or Ajax, whom he had seen in action during the siege of Troy (*Or.* 1479–81). He also compares Orestes and Pylades to Bacchant women (though without their ritual fennel stalks) attacking a mountain cub (1492–3); does that mean that Dionysus also intervenes?
44   Vellacott 1975, 81.
45   Euben 1986, 249.
46   Knox 1985, 332.
47   Roberts 1988, 192.
48   Dunn 1996, 171.
49   Seidensticker 1996, 392.
50   See also Steidle 1968, 112; Porter 1994, 188.
51   Mastronarde 2010, 194.
52   See esp. Mastronarde 2010, 195.
53   See esp. Lloyd-Jones 1983, 4.
54   Zeus takes his time in administering justice, sometimes punishing instead of the wrongdoer his children or later descendants (Solon, fr. 13.25–32).
55   See also Mastronarde 2010, 199.
56   On the reasons why Laius received the oracle, see esp. Lloyd-Jones 2005, 18–35.
57   See esp. Kovacs 2009, 357–68.

58 See also the discussion of Castor's epiphanies in ch. 5. Castor was the son of Leda and Tyndareus, but his twin brother Polydeuces was the son of Leda and Zeus. As the fifth-century poet Pindar tells the story (*Nem.* 10.73–90), when Castor was on the verge of death, Polydeuces asked his father Zeus to let him die with him; Zeus offered Polydeuces a choice: to become a god himself and let Castor die, or be a god half the time and live the other half beneath the earth (as a hero); Polydeuces chose the latter, and Castor came back to life.

Chapter 5

1 The idea that the various gods are members of a family derives from epic and seems not to have figured so much in actual worship as it does in literature, because originally the gods appear to have been worshiped independently of one another, and locality mattered more than their relationship to other gods in song and story.

2 According to Hesiod, Aphrodite was born from the severed testicles of Zeus' grandfather Uranus, and thus technically was Zeus' aunt (Hes., *Theog.* 191–206; *Hymn. Hom.* 6). But Homer portrays Aphrodite as the daughter of Zeus and Dione (*Il.* 5.312, 370–1, and also *Hymn. Hom.* 5.81, 191). Euripides followed the Homeric tradition that Aphrodite is the daughter of Zeus in his lost drama *Theseus*, where Athena *ex machina* states that mortals should try to avoid passionate love (*TrGF* 5.1, F 388.5).

3 She is called Aphrodite Cypris at the beginning of the *Homeric Hymn to Aphrodite* (*Hymn. Hom.* 5.1–2); on uses of the name in epic, see Faulkner 2008, 75.

4 On the translation of this passage, see esp. Barrett 1964, 160–1. No remains of the temple of Aphrodite near the tomb of Hippolytus on the Acropolis have been found, but the site "[Aphrod]ite near Hippolytus" or "in [the precinct of] Hippoly . . ." is mentioned in inscriptions set up around the time that Euripides' drama was performed (*IG* I³ 383 233–4; 369.66). Pausanias saw a "[funerary] monument for Hippolytus" (*mnēma*; 1.22.1); Kearns 1989, 173; Kowalzig 2006, 92.

5   Euripides has Athena use the same phrase to caution mortals against
     Aphrodite in the *Theseus* (see n. 2).

6   See also Gregory 1991, 55–9.

7   Mastronarde 2010, 172.

8   As Parker (1997, 158) observes, these lines "could be a kind of motto
     for the whole of tragedy."

9   A lovely fragrance is a sign of divinity, as in *Hymn. Hom.* 2.277, Aesch.,
     PV 115. For a complete list of examples, see Richardson 1974, 252.

10   If the poet had anyone specific in mind, it was probably Aphrodite's
     lover Adonis, who was killed during a boar hunt; see Barrett
     1964, 112.

11   Paus. 2.32.1–4; a third-century BC inscription (*IG* 4.754) refers to
     a gymnasium of Hippolytus; Barrett 1964, 3–6; Kowalzig 2006, 92.
     The second-century AD author Lucian claims that in his day at Troezen
     young men as well as young women dedicated a lock of their hair to
     Hippolytus, comparing that custom to dedications of hair by both
     young men and women to the goddess known to Greeks as the Assyrian
     Hera in Hierapolis (Bambuke) in Syria, as he himself also did as a young
     man (*de Dea Syria* 60); Lightfoot 2003, 534–6.

12   In avoiding the pollution of death, Euripides represents Artemis as
     following the procedures of her cult: "Birth or death within a temple is
     sacrilege; the sacred island of Delos [Artemis' birthplace] must be free
     from all taint of the processes of mortality" (Parker 1983, 33–4, 37);
     see also Burkert 1985, 201–3.

13   Barrett 1964, 414. Barrett observes that Hippolytus' speech is not
     meant as a rebuke. But certainly he expresses regret; Allan 2000, 241.

14   Kowalzig 2006, 93–4.

15   See above, n. 4.

16   Foley 1985, 22.

17   Dunn 1996, 97.

18   Girls offered locks of their hair before marriage (Pollux 3.38),
     e.g., to Eucleia in Boeotia and Locris (Plut., *Aristides* 20.6), to
     Iphinoe in Megara (Paus. 1.43.4), and to Athena on the acropolis
     of Argos (Stat. *Theb.* 2.253–6). Both girls and boys offered locks of
     their hair to the Hyperborean maidens who died on Delos (Hdt.
     4.34.1–2). In the Hellenistic era young men offered hair clippings

to Apollo at Delphi, to mark the transition to the status of *ephebe* (e.g., Euphorion *HE* 1801–4; Rhianus *HE* 3242–5; Antipater of Thessalonica *GP* 632–8; Plut., *Thes.* 5); see Fraser 1898, II 280–1, with references to analogous practices in other cultures, and Burkert 1983, 63 n. 20.

19 Scullion 1999–2000, 225.

20 Foley 1985, 22.

21 On the oath that the Athenians demand from the Argives, see above, pp. 79–80.

22 Zeus killed Apollo's son Asclepius for bringing the dead back to life, Eur., *Alc.* 127.

23 On the cult of Adonis, see Deubner 1932, 220–2; Burkert 1979; 105–11; Parker 2005, 284, n. 59. The cult came to the cities of Eastern Greece from the worship of Ishtar and the vegetation god Tammuz in Syria (e.g., to the island of Lesbos, Sappho 140a); Page 1955, 127. On the similarities between the stories of goddesses and handsome young men, see Burkert 1979, 111–8.

24 Mettinger 2001, 113–48, esp. 116–24, on Adonis in Greece.

25 Ekroth 2002, 139 n. 47.

26 Mikalson 1991, 41–2; See also Swift 2010, 278–9.

27 Cf. how Antigone mourns that she is dying "unwept, without a friend, unmarried" (Soph., *Ant.* 876–7); for examples of epitaphs lamenting a maiden's death before marriage, see *CEG* 1.184, 2.732; *GVI* 115, 949, 988, 1400, 1483. There is nothing in this context that suggests that maidens are honoring Hippolytus because they are "confronting the difficult transition to marriage," itself a form of symbolic death, as Foley argues (1985, 87), or that the ritual facilitates the transition from the phase of virginity to that of heterosexuality (Nagy 2013, 561).

28 See also Faulkner 2008, 233–4.

29 For Ovid's version of the story, see *Met.* 3.253–315.

30 Apollo took the infant Asclepius from the womb of his dead mother (Pind., *Pyth.* 3.73–4), but because he was not born again from a god, Asclepius remained mortal.

31 See above, pp. 79–80.

32 Euripides' portrayal of Pentheus appears to have been influenced by Aeschylus' characterization of Lycurgus in his *Edonians* (*TrGF* 3, F 59.),

the first play of his tetralogy *Lycurgeia*. Polyphrasmon, the son of Aeschylus' rival Phrynichus, also produced a *Lycurgeia* in 467 BC, the same year that Aeschylus produced the *Seven against Thebes* (*TrGF* 1, p.7). See Sommerstein 2008, 60–5.

33 Mastronarde 2010, 173.

34 The name dithyramb was interpreted to refer to the god's double (as if "di-" were a prefix) birth; Dodds 1960, 143. On the thigh as a source of nourishment, see Onians 1954, 183 n. 1.

35 In this context Dionysus' exclamation "*ã*" (810), which breaks the pattern of the meter, must mean something like "stop!"; see Dodds 1960, 175.

36 The red-figured vase painting in Figure 5.1 (*LIMC* VII.1, 312, 1984, no. 43, s.v. Pentheus), which depicts the maenads with pieces of Pentheus' body, antedates the production of the *Bacchae* and may have been inspired by Aeschylus' *Pentheus* (now lost). See esp. Shapiro 1994, 172–5: "It is a celebration of the god Dionysos and his cult, as is Euripides' play, on a vessel made for the enjoyment of Dionysos' gift of wine."

37 The story that Cadmus and Harmonia were transformed into snakes is connected to (and possibly a compensation for) Cadmus' killing of the serpent of Ares (Harmonia's father); his grandson Pentheus is the son of Echion, one of the men who were sown from the teeth of the snake; see Ogden 2013, 181–2; see ch. 5, n. 80.

38 See esp. Dodds 1960, 238.

39 The statement also seems shocking because it allows him to evade personal responsibility, even though he held Cadmus and Agave accountable for their actions; Mastronarde 2010, 189.

40 Cf. March 1989, 65; also Kovacs 1987, 77–8.

41 March 1989, 64.

42 For the story of Lycurgus see the beginning of the discussion of the *Bacchae*. Aeschylus (*Eum.* 25–6) has the Pythia say that Dionysus established his cult on Delphi from the time when "he commanded his army of Bacchants and wove a death for Pentheus, like a hare," presumably on Mt. Cithaeron, as he described the scene in his (lost) drama *Xantriae, TrGF* 4, F 172b); March 1989, 37, 50–2; Shapiro 1994, 176.

43 The details of the messenger's description of the scene in the temple are realistic; see Ekroth 2002, 43–4.

44 Euripides may have invented this account of Neoptolemus' death; according to most other authors (e.g., Pindar, *Nem*. 7.40–2), Neoptolemus was killed in an argument over distribution of the meat from his sacrifices to Apollo; see Lloyd 1994, 2–3; Allan 2000, 25–30.

45 Inserting line 1254 after 1235 (with Diggle and Lloyd, following Jackson) makes this point more clearly than the transmitted text; see Lloyd 1994, 162.

46 According to Pindar, Neoptolemus' tomb was beside the well-built house of the god (*Nem*. 7.46); on its location at Delphi and accompanying rituals, see esp. Currie 2005, 296–301.

47 Segal 1996, 160; see esp. Allan 2000, 238.

48 Kovacs 1980, 80 argues that Apollo's action has a healing effect, but both Peleus' and Andromache's descendants might have been able to remain and prosper in Phthia, if Apollo had prevented Neoptolemus' murder.

49 Allan 2000, 266.

50 Cf. Stevens 1971, 242, who said that the function of Thetis' intervention is to "tie up loose ends," and "these matters have been arranged on a human plane."

51 Polydeuces asked his father Zeus (and Zeus agreed) to make Castor immortal, although he (like Clytemnestra) was the son of the mortal Tyndareus; see ch. 4 n. 58.

52 See esp. Cropp 1988, xxxi; also Spira 1960, 112 n. 41.

53 Mastronarde 2010, 190.

54 On the Kēres, see Cropp 2013, 234, 239–40.

55 *Enopai*, here translated "demands," literally "cries," is pejorative in tone, as it is in *Ion* 882 when Creusa speaks of the shrill tone of Apollo's lyre ("furiously insulting"); Denniston 1939, 209; Lee 1997, 260.

56 Denniston 1939, 210.

57 Allan 2008, 196.

58 On this passage, see esp. Wright 2005, 371: "This is a frank statement, not of disbelief, but of ignorance: the chorus is admitting defeat."

59 The chorus of Spartan women supposes that Helen has offended the Great Mother (or Demeter) by not honoring her with sacrifices (1353–7), but no other mention is made of this issue in the drama; see Burian 2007, 274–5. The suggestion that the goddess is offended because of Helen's refusal to marry (Allan 2008, 306–7) does not seem to suit the context.

60 The text is corrupt, but appears nonetheless to convey its general sense; Allan 2008, 345. On Castor's intervention, see also above, pp. 126–7.

61 Dunn 1996, 135–42; Cropp 1997; Burian 2007, 290–1.

62 Roberts 1988, 192 n. 39.

63 So also in Euripides' lost drama *Antiope* (*TrGF* 5.1, F 223), Hermes appears suddenly to stop Amphion and Zethus from killing Lycus, the husband of Dirce, whom they had already killed because she had persecuted their mother Antiope. Hermes confirms that they are the sons of Zeus, and tells them about the honors they will receive in the future: they will build a new Thebes with seven gates, easily, because the stones and the trees will follow Amphion when he plays his lyre.

64 See also Wright 2005, 361–2.

65 Divine epiphanies are not infrequent; see Porter 1994, 281 and notes 116–7.

66 See esp. Harrison 2000, 17, quoting Parker 1996, 209–10: "A wide variety of opinions about the gods could be comfortably accommodated, in a religion that lacked dogma and revelation."

Chapter 6

1 In addition to the plays discussed in the previous chapters (*Antiope, Erechtheus, Hypsipyle, Archelaus*), gods appeared in *Phaethon, Rhadymanthys*, both Phrixus plays, *Alcmene, Andromeda, Theseus, Ino, Melanippe the Wise*, and *Meleager*; see Porter 1994, 281 n. 116; Lefkowitz 2003b, 103 n. 2.

2 In Troezen, Aegeus seduces Pittheus' daughter Aethra, and becomes the putative father of Theseus; but Theseus' real father is Poseidon.

3 The lyric poet Pindar also portrays Medea as a prophet in *Pyth*. 4.11–6. Unusual perspicacity is characteristic of divine ancestry. In the *Iliad*, Helen, the daughter of Zeus, recognizes Aphrodite even when the

goddess appears to her disguised as an old slave-woman from Sparta (*Il.* 3.396–7). Achilles, the son of the sea-goddess Thetis, realizes that a god must have brought Priam safely through the Greek lines to ask Achilles to let him take Hector's body back to Troy (*Il.* 24.563–7).

4 In Corinthian tradition, Medea was a goddess (Pind., *Pyth.* 4.11, with Braswell 1988, 76; also Hes., *Theog.* 992). But she also had a tomb in Thesprotia (West 1966, 429). In this drama she lacks the authority and power to be "assuming the power of deity" (*pace* McClure 1999, 392).

5 On Aphrodite in the Hippolytus, see also above, ch. 5, and Blundell 1989, 65 on the parallels between Aphrodite's behavior in the *Hippolytus* and Athena's attitude in Sophocles' *Ajax*.

6 Women in Greek tragedy are prepared to avenge themselves if they have no male relatives to defend them, as is also the case in Sophocles' *Electra*, when Electra is led to believe that Orestes is dead, and in Euripides' *Hecuba* (discussed below); see esp. Foley 2001, 161–4.

7 Mastronarde 2002, 294. Buttrey (1958, 1–17) explained the pivotal importance of the Aegeus scene, but believed it to be "unmotivated" (15) because he did not suppose the gods had been involved in it. Dunkle (1969, 107), without taking into account the possibility of divine action, understood the Aegeus scene's importance as a microcosm of the human action in the drama both because of its emphasis on childlessness, and because it "mirrors the self-interested opportunism and chaotic irrationality which dominate the play."

8 Kovacs 1987b, 268–9; Kovacs 1993, 67; Mastronarde 2002, 387; Mastronarde 2010, 200. Some scholars have considered the last lines of the Medea to be spurious, because they are repeated (with a different first line) in the *Alcestis, Andromache, Helen*, and *Bacchae*, but see esp. Rees 1961, 176–81; Roberts 1987, 51–64, and the conclusion to this book.

9 Kovacs 1993, 58–9; Mastronarde 2002, 282–3. Hesiod advises men to marry, so that they do not arrive at "deadly old age without a companion" (*Theog.* 605), meaning a son (West 1966, 334). Euripides may have invented the idea of making Medea kill the children; according to another tradition, the children were murdered by the Corinthians; see n. 12. On why she makes that decision, at

considerable cost to herself, and why the audience still can retrain some sympathy for her, see esp. Gill 1996, 154–74.

10 On the *topos* of parental love for children, see Golden 1990, 89–97, Mastronarde 1994, 250.

11 On this passage see Wildberg 1999–2000, 241, and Wildberg 2002, 51–2.

12 Euripides here may be alluding to the tradition that the children were murdered by the Corinthians; Mastronarde 2002, 50–3, 340–1.

13 In the fourth-century depictions of the myth on vase paintings, Medea appears in a chariot drawn by winged dragons (i.e., not the chariot the Sun uses every day to travel from East to West across the sky; see *LIMC* VI. 2 (1992) 198–9, s.v. Medeia, nos. 36–9; Mastronarde 2002, 377–8).

14 In 406 and 954 Medea refers to Helios as her ancestor, and swears by him in 746, and also in 764, where she boasts that she now has a refuge in Athens, but does not reveal that she will use his aid in getting there.

15 On Medea's need for supernatural transportation, see Worthington 1990, 504–5; Lawrence 1997, 53–4; Taplin 2007, 114.

16 Cf. Lawrence (2013, 306): "In the Medea, as regularly in Euripidean tragedy, there is little or no sense of divine immanence, for all that Medea calls on Zeus . . . The divine associations of her 'epiphany' then are purely symbolic." But in denouncing the use of devices such as the Sun-god's chariot, Aristotle is not criticizing traditional religion (which he tolerates) but actions that do not appear to derive directly from the plot. Such irrational actions also include the operations of *tychē* ("happenstance"). *Tychē* should not be understood as a random force. Rather *tychē* and "the gods" may be "alternative and equivalent ways of accounting for the operation within human life of factors which cannot be explained in entirely human terms"; Halliwell 1986, 230–1.

17 See Shapiro 1994, 179; Taplin 2007, 123 and Pl. 35; *LIMC* VI.1, 1992, 391–2, no. 36, s.v. Medeia. Figure 6.1 (Cleveland 1991.1) depicts the plot rather than the last scene of Euripides' *Medea*; actual performances are rarely represented on vase paintings (see Small 2005, 103–8).

18 Richardson 1974, 173.

19 Medea calls Themis, Artemis (16), and Zeus (332, 516) to witness her sufferings, and the chorus reminds her (155–8, 168–70) that the gods

ought to be prepared to punish Jason because humans swear by Zeus when they bind themselves to stand by their oaths. See esp. Kovacs 1993, 51–2.

20 See Allan 2002, 379; and Parker 1983, 315 on how both Jason and Medea deny responsibility for the crimes they have committed. An *alastor* also arises from the brutal treatment by Eteocles and Polynices of their father Oedipus (e.g., Eur., *Phoen.* 1556); see Mastronarde 1994, 583; 2010, 201. An *alastor* can be an avenging spirit (*daimon*) itself or a human being who acts as its instrument; see esp. Fraenkel 1962, III 711–2; Gomme-Sandbach 1973, 527; on its etymology, see Chantraine 1983, 54–5; Beekes 2010, 61.

21 Cf. Sophocles' description of Zeus as *tamias* in his *Tereus*: "no one other than Zeus is the dispenser of what will happen in the future" (*TrGF* 4, F 590), and see n. 8.

22 Lawrence 1997, 54–5; Cowherd 1983, 135. Cf. Foley (2001, 261), who says that "the story of her revenge takes on a pattern typical of divine rather than human action," and speaks of her "as a semi-divine fury," and a few pages later (267) speaks of "Medea's final transformation into an amoral deity."

23 Mastronarde 2002, 379. Orestes serves as a *miastor* for the murder of Agamemnon (Soph., *El.* 603); see esp. Parker 1983, 104–43, esp. 109 n. 15, 120–1; Finglass 2007, 278.

24 Parker 1983, 315; Allan 2002, 97–9.

25 See esp. illustrations and discussions in Taplin 2007, 117–23.

26 No one seems to have described how Medea died, but according to the poets Ibycus (*PMG* 291) and Simonides (*PMG* 588) she went to the Elysian Fields, where she married Achilles—entry there was based on connections rather than merit; e.g., Menelaus goes to the Elysian Fields not because of his achievements, but because he is the son-in-law of Zeus (*Od.* 4.563–5; Eur., *Hel.* 1676–7). In the fifth century the Elysian Fields had been identified with the White Island at the mouth of the Black Sea, which is where his father Peleus will go to visit Achilles in Eur., *And.* 1260; see Lloyd 1994, 163–4.

27 On the prologue of the *Trojan Women*, see the Introduction.

28 The soul of Patroclus stands over Achilles' head, asking that he be buried (*Il.* 23.65–74).

29 The spirit of Elpenor makes the same type of request to Odysseus in *Od*.11.72–8.

30 Daedalus (like a god) was believed to have been able to animate statues so realistically that people thought they were alive (the ancient commentator on this passage cites *TrGF* 5.1, F 372); see Stieber 2011, 412–3; Bremmer 2013a, 11.

31 Cf. how Electra wishes that her hand, tongue, mind, head, and the dead Agamemnon could join her in sending a message to Orestes (Eur., *El.* 333–5, though the lines may not be genuine; see Cropp 1988, 121). On such appeals to inanimate objects in general, Fraenkel 1962, II 24 (on Aesch., *Ag.* 37); also Gregory 1999, 144–5. Characters in Homer speaking in isolation address their heart (*thymos*); see esp. Pelliccia 1995, 121–3, 139–50.

32 On Dionysus' oracular shrine in Thrace (*Rhes.* 972–3), see esp. Boteva 1997, 293–7. Matthiessen 2010, 45–6; Dodds 1960, 108–9; Liapis 2012, 326.

33 Hecuba does not have a tomb but only a sign or marker (*sēma*); on its location, see Collard 1991, 198. Euripides in his drama *Alexandros* had Cassandra predict that she would become "a dog, a favorite of Hecate the light-bearer" (*TrGF* 5.1, F 62h). Dogs were associated both with Hecate (see esp. Gow 1965, II 38; *LIMC* VI.1, p.995 6a–b) and the Erinyes; like them, Hecate is associated with dogs and snakes (Ogden 2013, 254–9). The first-century AD rhetorician Dio Chrysostom (*Or.* 33.59) says "the poets say that the Erinyes turned Hecuba into a dog, a final ill on top of all the others" (*PMG* 965), quoting a fragment of an unknown poet who said that her endless barking (a characteristic of dogs that Semonides of Amorgos complains of, fr. 7.15–8W; see Lloyd-Jones 1975, 67) can be heard as far away as Mt. Ida or Tenedos. Foley (2001, 299 n. 76), however, argues that the metamorphosis was meant to silence her.

34 See esp. Burnett 1994, 160; but even though the *cynossēma* thus serves a useful purpose, it seems like wishful thinking to suppose (161, followed by Foley 2015, 60) that "it marks the place where men must change as they move from wild justice toward a tamer kind."

35 The idea of abandonment on a desert island may have been inspired by Aegisthus' treatment of Agamemnon's bard in *Od*. 3.270–1; see

also Gregory 1999, 196. Such isolation is a form of execution that technically does not incur blood guilt for the executioners, because they do not directly cause their victim's death; cf. Soph. *Ant.* 889–90.

36 See also Matthiessen 2010, 45–7.

37 On various interpretations of Hecuba's metamorphosis, see esp. Forbes Irving 1990, 207–10; Foley 2001, 297 n. 72.

38 Kovacs 1987a, 108–9 and n. 68. For approval of kindness to friends and attacking enemies, even deviously see Pindar, *Pyth* 2.84–5, *Nem.* 8.38–9; Plato, *Resp.* 376a–b. In war, men attack enemies like wolves (*lykoi; Il.* 4.471; see Most 116, n. 98).

39 See Nussbaum 2001, 414–5.

40 On the etymology of *lyssa*, see above ch. 2 n. 47. Forbes-Irving rightly observes that Hecuba becomes "no ordinary dog," but being "irrational" (*ekphrōn*) and fiery eyes are indications of rabies, rather than a sign that that she has become a "ghostly" or a supernatural being. Hecuba also becomes a "dog with flashing eyes" (*charopan kyna*) which bellows so loudly (*chalkeon phengomenas*) that it can be heard for miles around in the fragment of lyric quoted above, n. 34 (*PMG* 965). *Lyssa* produces howling and menacing eyes like a bull's in human beings affected by the disease, according to the second-century BC poet Nicander (*Alex.* 222–4). The face of a person who is bitten by a rabid dog "has a sharp glare (*drimu blepon*) and is full of anger," according to the sixth-century AD medical writer Aëtius (6.24). Zeitlin (1996, 185–6) connects Hecuba's fiery gaze with the many references to light throughout the drama and Sirius the Dog Star, giving the transformation a curiously positive meaning.

41 It was essentially proverbial that gods destroy mortals by first causing them to make errors in judgment, e.g., Agamemnon apologizing to Achilles for taking away his prize, "I was deluded, since Zeus took away my wits" (*Il.* 19.137), and esp. Soph., *Ant.* 622–5: "in wisdom someone brought to light the famous saying, 'evil seems good to him whose mind the god is leading toward destruction (*atē*).'"The scholia on that line quote an unknown tragic poet: "when a god bestows evil on a man, he first harms his mind" (*TrGF* 2, F 455). The fourth-century BC statesman Lycurgus said in a speech (*In Leocr.* 92) that he considered some lines from another unknown tragic poet to be like "a statement

by an oracle" (*chrēsmos*): "when the gods' anger harms someone, first
of all, it takes clear perception from his mind, then it turns it to worse
thinking, so that he has no understanding of what he is doing wrong"
(*TrGF* 2, F 296). See esp. Jebb 1900, 119–20, 255–6. See also the
discussion of *hamartia* in the Introduction.

42   Soph., *Aj*. 452; Eur., *HF* 843–72; Eur., *Bacch*. 977. Dodds' note (1960,
199) on the *Bacchae* passage is (I think) misleading, Lyssa's dogs are not
"hell-hounds," but explicitly rabid; their goal is to drive the women of
Thebes crazy (*anoistrēsate*); see esp. Seaford 1996, 228.

43   Sourvinou-Inwood 2003, 343. But cf. Kovacs 1987, 108–12; Mossman
1995, 195–201; Gregory 1999, xxxiii–v; and Matthiessen 2002, 112,
all of whom take a more positive view of the metamorphosis.

44   Mossman 1995, 200; Nussbaum 2001, 417. This view of the ending of
the tragedy is characteristic of recent criticism; see esp. Heath (1987,
253), who argues that the sixteenth-century understanding of the
drama is closer to that of the original audience, where the vengeance
taken by the defenseless is understood to be completely justified and
the action of the drama complete (230, 260).

45   As in the Old Testament, only a god can kill with impunity (e.g.,
Deuteronomy 32:35); hence Paul's advice "Beloved, never avenge
yourselves, but leave it to the wrath of God" (Romans 12:19).

46   See Roberts 1988, 185–6; Finglass 2007, 526–8, 543.

47   On such "open" endings, see below n. 87.

48   Mossman 1995, 201; see also Mastronarde 2010, 202–3.

49   On the importance of children in the *Hecuba*, see esp. Nussbaum
2001, 397–9.

50   In Euripides' *Diktys*, a drama that was part of the same tetralogy as the
Medea and performed on the same day, someone says that "there is
one law (*nomos*) common to all humans—with the gods' agreement,
as I clearly state—and to all animals: they love the offspring that they
bear. In everything else we follow different laws from one another"
(*TrGF* 5.1, F 346). At another point in the same drama, someone also
says "I think that a father's dearest possessions are his children, and
children's dearest possessions are their parents; I say that no one else is
a more rightful ally" (*TrGF* 5.1, F 345).

51   Lloyd-Jones 1990b, 309–10; Mastronarde 2010, 206; Henrichs 2013,
123–4, 132–3.

52 Henrichs 1981, 213–4; Bremmer 2013b, 88–91; on the choice of the
victim, see esp. Bonnechere 2010, 50–3.

53 O'Connor-Visser 1987, 191.

54 Lloyd-Jones 1990b, 324–8. The Mistress of Animals (*Potnia Therōn*), to
judge from visual representations, came to Greece from the Near East
sometime in the second millennium BC and was identified with several
different Greek goddesses, including Artemis, Hera, and the Mother
(*Mēter*); see Roller 1999, 47, 127, 135–6.

55 Burkert 1983, 62–6; Lloyd-Jones 1990b, 128–30.

56 See also Lefkowitz 2007, 93–4.

57 See above, pp. 87–88.

58 The gods of the dead also require sacrifice: Death drinks the clotted
blood of his victims (*Alc.* 845,851); Parker 2007, 220–1. Allan
(2001, 166) suggests that in the *Heraclidae* Kore is an appropriate
recipient of the sacrifice because she too was deprived of marriage and
childbearing.

59 Wilkins 1993, 123.

60 E.g. Loraux 1987, 60, and for other examples, see Gregory 1999, 113.
Bremmer observes (2007, 65) that "we cannot but remain puzzled by
the fact that Greek civilization was so keen especially to put maidens on
the stage." One answer may be that their complete vulnerability makes
them ideal representatives of the human condition.

61 On the significance of the gesture in this context, see esp. Mossman
1995, 157–63; Lefkowitz 2007, 207. Mothers used the gesture
to remind their sons to obey them, e.g., Hecuba in an attempt to
persuade Hector not to fight against Achilles, *Il.* 22.80; Clytemnestra
in Aeschylus' *Choephoroe* 896–8, which causes Orestes to hesitate, in
the only example of breast-baring on the stage; Garvie 1986, 292.
Clytemnestra's gesture is mentioned in Eur. *El.* 1206–7 (on which see
esp. Denniston 1939, 199), *Or.* 527, 566–8 "women . . . seeking pity
with their breasts." In Eur., *Phoen.* 1568 Jocasta employs the gesture
in a vain attempt to stop her sons Eteocles and Polynices from killing
each other; cf. the pleas to respect one's mother in *AP* 9.126–7 and
Euphorion, fr. 92 Powell = 96 Groningen. On the gesture as a sign
of innocence, see Mylonopoulos 2013, 61. Later writers inferred
from the text of an oration by the fourth-century orator Hyperides
(Ath.13.590d–e = Hyperides fr. 171 Jensen; Hermippus fr. 68a

246 | Notes to pages 176–177

I Wehrli = Hermippus 1026 *FGrHist* F46) that he defended his mistress
Phryne the courtesan by tearing off her clothes to expose her breasts;
the sight made the jurors afraid to condemn a priestess of Aphrodite
and yielded "to pity" instead of sentencing her to death; see Cooper
1995, 303–18, and *FGrHist* IV A.3, 388–9. Only in the case of Helen,
the most beautiful woman in the world, was the gesture have been said
to have an erotic effect; instead of killing her, Peleus claims, Menelaus
threw away his sword and kissed her (Eur., *And.* 629–30).

62 On the custom of throwing leaves (*phyllobolia*; schol. *Hec.* 573,
    I p. 53–4 Schwartz) on a victor or on anyone who had accomplished
    an extraordinary feat, see Gregory 1999, 114–5, and esp. Braswell
    1998, 327–8 on Pindar, *Pyth.* 4.240, with many examples. I do not see
    any reason to suppose that in this context the throwing of leaves is "an
    abreaction of aggressive feelings" (cf. Burkert 1985, 76).

63 On the custom of setting up statues to Zeus, the lord of victory, see
    Pritchett 1971, II 252–8; Burkert 1985, 267.

64 Allan 2001, 218–9. The beneficent daughters of Erechtheus are
    treated differently: at the end of the *Erechtheus* Athena told Praxithea
    and the Athenians not to pour wine on the fire accompanying the
    sacrifice to the heroic daughters of Erechtheus, but to offer honey and
    water instead (*TrGF* 5.1, F 370.83–5); on wineless offerings, see esp.
    Henrichs 1983, 87–100.

65 Wilkins 1993, 193.

66 There is a lacuna here, at least of a few lines; Wilkins 1993, 193; Allan
    2001, 222–3.

67 The information about Athenian honors for Macaria is provided as a
    somewhat contrived explanation for the proverb "go to Macaria" (*ball'
    es Makarian*), schol. Ar. *Eq.* 1151a II–IV p. 246 Koster; schol. [Pl.],
    Hipp. Maj. 293a, p. 176 Greene. The phrase was a euphemism for "go to
    Hades," analogous to the phrase *ball' es korakas* ("go to the crows," i.e.,
    "go to hell," as in Ar., *Thesm.* 1079); see Austin-Olson 2004, 324. The
    phrase may have been inspired by the description of the Greek soldiers
    throwing leaves on Polyxena (*Hec.* 571–80, discussed above); Wilkins
    1993, xvi, xxii n. 77. Pausanias' version of the story sets the scene
    of the sacrifice a generation earlier, during the reign of Theseus, and
    has Macaria cut her own throat (*aposphaxasa heautên*; 1.32.6); on the
    different versions, see O'Connor-Visser 1987, 36–8.

68 Strabo 377 = 8.6.19, and also Stephanus of Byzantium (s.v. Gargettus), but there is no independent evidence of a hero cult; Kearns 1989, 164; see above ch. 3 n. 68.

69 See esp. Allan 2001, 32–4.

70 In the text of the *IA* as we have it, the reason why Artemis demands the sacrifice is not specified. In the *IT* Iphigenia says it was because Agamemnon had vowed to offer the goddess the most beautiful thing the year produced, which happened to be Iphigenia (20–4). According to the earliest extant source, Stasinus' epic *Cypria* ¶8 (West 2003, 74), it was because Agamemnon boasted that he was a better hunter than Artemis (schol. Eur. *Or.* 658, I p. 165 Schwartz); in Soph., *El.* 566–9 Electra's version of the story makes her father somewhat less culpable: he angered the goddess by accidently startling and then shooting a stag in the goddess' sacred grove and boasting about it; see Finglass 2007, 267–9.

71 Kovacs 2003, 100.

72 See esp. the detailed analysis of the exodus of the *Iphigenia at Aulis* by Page 1934, 192–204.

73 On the authorship of the ending of these sections of the messenger's speech, see esp. West 1981, 73–6. In any case, having a priest preside at a sacrifice before a battle is an anachronism; see above, n. 52.

74 Aelian (*NA* 7.39) attributes to Euripides a few lines from a speech by Artemis describing how she will place a deer in their hands, "which they can slaughter and proclaim that they are slaughtering Iphigenia" (*TrGF* 5.2, F857), but the lines may come from an inauthentic substitute ending to Euripides' play; Kovacs 2002, 161. See also O'Connor-Visser 1987, 133–4.

75 See above, pp. 90–2.

76 The idea that Iphigenia was made immortal and called Hecate may ultimately derive from Stesichorus (fr. 218 Finglass = 222a fr. 32 *PMGF*); see Davies-Finglass 2014, 178–9, with bibliography. In the sixth-century BC Hesiodic *Catalogue of Women* (fr. 23a.17–26 M-W) she is called Iphimede (on whom see also Cropp 2000, 44) and becomes Artemis Einodia, i.e., Hecate (on whom see Soph., *TrGF* 4 F 535; Kannicht 1969, II 170–1; Richardson 1974, 294–5; Johnston 1999, 142, 241 n. 118). On the variations in the names and number of Agamemnon's daughters, see esp. Hainsworth 1993, 77.

77 See above, pp. 90–2.

78 Craik (1988, 191) identifies *to daimonion* as Dionysus, because of his association with revels (*kōmoi*). But usually *to daimonion* refers not to a particular divinity, but to the general power of the gods, as in Eur., *Bacch.* 894–6 and *TrGF* 5.1, F 152; see Dodds 1960, 189; Mastronarde 1994, 249. The idea seems to be that the power of the gods has celebrated (*katekōmase*) its defeat of the house of Oedipus, as if it had won a victory in the games.

79 On the serpent of Ares, see Mastronarde 1994, 239–40, and esp. Ogden 2013, 48–54. The serpent guarded Ares' daughter Harmonia, whom Cadmus married after serving Ares for eight years.

80 On the surviving Sown Men (Spartoi) see Ogden 2013, 181–2. But we have no precise information about the genealogies of Creon's parents; perhaps this requirement, like the story of Menoeceus' sacrifice itself, was invented by Euripides; see Mastronarde 1994, 417.

81 Menoeceus' argument is similar to that of Praxithea in the *Erechtheus* (see ch. 3), who says that since she would have sent her son to war, she will permit her daughter to be sacrificed (*TrGF* 5.1, F 360, 22–37); Sourvinou-Inwood 2003, 381.

82 There is no reference to the sacrifice of Menoeceus in Aeschylus' *Seven against Thebes*; see O'Connor-Visser 1987, 85–6.

83 Mastronarde 1994, 28–9. Menoeceus cannot have been the same person as Creon's son Megareus, who was one of the Theban captains (Aesch., *Sept.* 474–9) and died in the battle against Argos (Soph., *Ant.* 1303).

84 See esp. Mastronarde 1994, 591–4.

85 Sourvinou-Inwood (2003, 383) interprets Oedipus' statement to mean that he is "denying all responsibility for his actions," but if that were so he would not say "I killed, I begot, I married," etc. It is rather that since the god did not stop him from doing these things; the responsibility is shared.

86 Foley describes the plot as "sick" (1985, 146; see below n. 96). Sourvinou-Inwood 2003, 386 observes: "The problematization is very light; for the religious dimension of the issue is not pursued, and the issue is not resolved; Antigone does not bury the body within the

tragedy, and the audience would have made no assumptions about what would happen afterwards."

87 "A tragedy is a representation of a complete and whole action that has a beginning, middle, and an end" (Ar., *Poet.* 1450b23–6); Else 1957: "This definition amounts to a declaration of independence—and therewith also responsibility—for the poet. The dramatist is not required to begin at the 'beginning of the story,' i.e. with Oedipus' birth and exposition, nor to end with his death. He is bound by an inner necessity, which it is his job to perceive and follow, not by tradition or biology." See also Heath 1987, 103.

88 On the coherence of the plot of the *Phoenissae*, see esp. Craik 1988, 44; Mastronarde 1994, 3–4.

89 See esp. Cribiore 2001, 242–3; Papadopoulou 2008, 106–9.

90 According to Cicero, *Tusc.* 1.116, the standard examples were Erechtheus, Codrus, Menoeceus, Iphigenia at Aulus, Harmodius and Aristogiton, Leonidas, and Epaminondas. See also Cribiore 2001, 247–8.

91 Cf. also the story of Thrasybulus, who foresees that he will die in battle, but nonetheless goes into battle because it will bring victory (Xen., *Hell.* 2.4.18–9); Parker 2013, 151.

92 Plut., *Pelop.* 21.2, with Hughes 1991, 117, and *Per.* 8.6 (Stesimbrotus, 107 *FGrHist* F 9, IIB 518).

93 Hughes 1991, 118–22.

94 Foley 1985, 23.

95 Foley 1985, 59.

96 Foley 1985, 134, 146.

97 On some of the problems involved in interpreting the meaning of ritual in drama, see also Wright 2005, 355–7.

98 See above, n. 52.

99 See also O'Connor-Visser 1987, 203.

100 See above, n. 62.

101 On the myths of the Iron Age and the decline of human morality, see (e.g.) Lefkowitz 2003a, 27–38, 35.

102 On the story of the human sacrifices before the battle of Salamis, see esp. Henrichs 1981, 208–24; Hughes 1991, 111–5; Marr 1998, 105–6; Henrichs 2013, 132–3.

103 Herodotus also regards the expedition to Troy as an early example of
    the hostility between the Greeks and the Asians (1.4.1). Alexander the
    Great went to Elaious before crossing the Hellespont to Troy in order
    to offer a sacrifice to the hero Protesilaus (the first Greek to be killed
    in the Trojan War), in the hope that his own expedition would be more
    successful (Arrian 1.11.4).
104 On the story of Agesilaus at Aulis, see esp. Shipley 1997, 124–8.
105 Foley, 1985, 64.

Conclusion

1 On the last lines of the *Medea*, see above, ch. 6, n. 21.
2 See (e.g.) Barrett 1964, 417–8. On similar criticism by other scholars,
   see Roberts 1987, 51–5.
3 But cf. esp. Rees (1961, 181): "if his comment is naive, it is none the
   less true for all that; it is a moral which finds a way straight to the
   human heart and awakens a quick and poignant response even in these
   sophisticated days, as the briefest glance at popular entertainment will
   show. Athenian Drama, despite its religious background—unless one
   would rather say because of it—was above all popular entertainment
   of the most enlightened kind; the audience was composed not of
   metaphysicians, as some editors seem to imagine, but of ordinary
   people, who never fail to find a grim satisfaction in the tragic
   commonplaces of human existence—birth, love, and death, and the
   unpredictability of the ways of God with men."
4 Wright 2003, 381.
5 Wright 2003, 382.
6 E.g., Barrett 1964, 417–8, but cf. Roberts 1987, 63.
7 Barrett 1964, 418. On Barrett's dismissive treatment of this and other
   "tail-pieces," see Calder 1965, 281.
8 Easterling 1982, 231–2, who assigns the lines to the chorus and
   compares them to other such allusions to the events outside of the
   drama in Sophocles' other plays, e.g., the future troubles of the
   house of Atreus (*El.* 1498), (a warning to Neoptolemus to respect
   the gods) *Phil.* 1440–4, and (Antigone asks Theseus to be sent to
   Thebes to intervene in her brothers' quarrel) *O.C.*1769–72. Davies

1991, 266–7 assigns the lines to Hyllus, and sees in them a kind of "sublimity," similar to what the chorus of old men says in Aeschylus' *Agamemnon*: "what happens to mortals without Zeus? Which of these events has not been accomplished by the god?" (1485–8). On the identity of the speaker, Lloyd-Jones and Wilson 1990, 177–8; 1997, 102.

9   On Athena in the *Ajax*, see above ch. 4, and on the drama's last lines, see Lloyd-Jones and Wilson 1990, 41; Finglass 2011, 524–5.

10 In the traditional narrative, Tereus in turn tried to kill the two sisters, the gods changed them all into birds. On the ending of the *Tereus*, see Pearson 1963, 232–3.

11 On Herodotus' story of Solon and Croesus, see Asheri 2007, 97–8. On similar ideas in Herodotus and Sophocles, see Lefkowitz 2012, 80 and 180 n. 12.

12 For a careful discussion of why the coda to the *OT* should be considered spurious, see esp. Finglass 2009, 59 n. 50. Dawe (1982, 247) rejected the lines as "demented balbutience"; but Arkins (1988, 555–8) shows why the lines are entirely appropriate to their context; see also Jebb 1893, 198–9; Roberts 1987, 57–8; and Lloyd-Jones and Wilson 1990, 113–4.

13 On anecdotes about Sophocles' piety, see Lefkowitz 2012, 84–5.

14 On Castor see also above, pp. 126–7, 158.

15 Critics continue to suppose that Aeschylus himself was expressing his own beliefs through the mouths of his choruses. But if the choruses of his dramas expect that the god will do what they wish him to do or what they think may be right, it does not necessarily follow that the god will in fact carry out their wishes, or that the poet shares the expectations that he puts into the mouths of his characters.

16 On the identity of the author of the *Rhesus*, see above ch. 1, n. 33.

17 See also Wright 2005, 382–4.

18 For a brief account of why the chorus should not be understood as representing the poet, see Goldhill 1986, 267–70.

BIBLIOGRAPHY

Allan, W. 2000. *The Andromache and Euripidean Tragedy*. Oxford.

———. 2001. *Euripides: The Children of Heracles*. Warminster.

———. 2002. *Euripides: Medea*. London.

———. 2004. "Religious Syncretism: The New Gods in Greek Tragedy," *HSCP* 102: 113–55.

———. 2008. *Euripides: Helen*. Cambridge.

Arkins, B. 1988. "The Final Lines of Sophocles, *King Oedipus* (1524–30)," *CQ* 38: 555–8.

Arnott, W. G. 1983. "Tension, Frustration and Surprise: A Study of Theatrical Techniques in Some Scenes of Euripides' *Orestes*," *Antichthon* 17: 13–28.

Arrowsmith, W., 1959. "Introduction to the *Orestes*," in *The Complete Greek Tragedies*, ed. D. Grene and R. Lattimore: IV, 186–91. Chicago.

Asheri, D., A. Lloyd, and A. Corcella. 2007. *A Commentary on Herodotus Books I–IV*. Oxford.

Attridge, H. 1985. "Fragments of Pseudo-Greek Poets," in *The Old Testament Pseudepigrapha*, ed. H. Charlesworth, 821–30. New York.

Aubriot-Sévin, D. 1991. *Prière et conceptions religieuses en Grèce ancienne jusqu'à la fin du Ve siècle av. J.-C.* Lyon.

Aubriot, D. 2005. "L'Invocation au(x) dieu(x) dans la prière grecque: Contraine, persuasion, ou théologie?" in *Nommer les Dieux: Théonymes, épithètes, épiclèses, dans l'Antiquité*, ed. N. Belyache, Pierre Brulé, et al., 473–90. Rennes.

Austin, C., and S. D. Olson. 2004. *Aristophanes: Thesmophoriazusae*. Oxford.

Avezzù, G. 1982. *Alcidamante: Orazioni e Frammenti*, Bolletino dell'istituto di filologia greca, Suppl. 6. Rome.

Barlow, S. 1986. *Euripides: Trojan Women*. Warminster.

Barnes, J. 1982. *The Presocratic Philosophers* [Ed. 2]. London.

Barrett, W. S. 1964. *Euripides: Hippolytus*. Oxford.

Beekes, R. 2010. *Etymological Dictionary of Greek*. Leiden.

Bekker, I. 1814–21. *Anecdota Graeca*. Berlin.

Belfiore, E. S. 1992. *Tragic Pleasures: Aristotle on Plot and Emotion*. Princeton.

Bernabé, A. 1996. *Poeti Epici Graeci*, vol. 1. Stuttgart.

Billerbeck, M., ed. 2006. *Stephani Byzantii Ethnica*, vol. 1, Alpha-Gamma. Berlin.

Bond, G. 1981. *Euripides: Heracles*. Oxford.

Bonnechere, P. 2013. "Victime humaine et absolue perfection dans la mentalité grecque," in *Sacrifices humaines / Human Sacrifice*, ed. P. Bonnechere and R. Gagné, 21–60. Liège.

Boteva. D. 1997. "Saint Athanase d'Etropolé, Sabazios et l'oracle de Dionysos," *Dialogues d'histoire ancienne* 23.1: 287–98.

Bowie, A. M. 1997. "Tragic Filters for History," in *Greek Tragedy and the Historian*, ed. C. Pelling, 39–62. Oxford.

Braswell, B. K. 1998. *A Commentary on the Fourth Pythian Ode of Pindar*. Berlin.

Bremer, J. M. 1969. *Hamartia: Tragic Error in the Poetics of Aristotle and in Greek Tragedy*. Amsterdam.

Bremmer, J. N. 2007. "Myth and Ritual in Greek and Roman Sacrifice: Lykaon, Polyxena and the Case of the Rhodian Criminal," in *The Strange World of Human Sacrifice*, ed. J. N. Bremmer, 56–79. Leuven.

———. 2013a. "The Agency of Greek and Roman Statues," *Opuscula* 6: 7–21.

———. 2013b. "Human Sacrifice in Euripides *Iphigenia in Tauris*: Greek and Barbarian," in *Sacrifices humaines / Human Sacrifice*, ed. P. Bonnechere and R. Gagné, 87–100. Liège.

Broggiato, M. 2001. *Cratete di Mallo: I frammenti*. Rome.

Burian, P. 2007. *Euripides: Helen*. Oxford.

Burkert, W. 1983. *Homo Necans*, tr. P. Bing. Berkeley.

———. 1985. *Greek Religion*, tr. J. Raffan. Oxford.

———. 2007 [1974]. "Die Absurdität der Gewalt und das Ende der Tragödie: Euripides' Orestes," *Kleine Schriften* VII: *Tragica et Historica*, 97–110. Göttingen.

Burnett, A. 1971. *Catastrophe Survived*. Oxford.

———. 1994. "Hekabe the Dog," *Arethusa* 27: 151–64.

Burnyeat, M. 2002. "The Impiety of Socrates," in *The Trial and Execution of Socrates*, ed. T. C. Brickhouse and N. D. Smith, 133–45. New York.

Burtt, J. 1954. *Minor Attic Orators*, vol. 2. Cambridge. MA.

Bussanich, J. 2006. "Socrates and Religious Experience," in *A Companion to Socrates*, ed. S. Ahbel-Rappe and R. Kamtekar, 200–13. Malden/Oxford.

Buttrey, T. V. 1958. "Accident and Design in Euripides' Medea," *AJP* 79: 1–17.

Calame, C. 2011. "Myth and Performance on the Athenian Stage: Praxithea, Erectheus, Their Daughters, and the Etiology of Authochthony," *CP* 106: 1–19.

Calder, III, W. M. Euripides: "Hippolytus" by W. S. Barrett, *CP* 60, 277–81.

Chalk, H. H. O. 1962. "*Aretē* and *Bia* in Euripides' Heracles," *JHS* 82: 7–18.

Chantraine, P. 1983. *Dictionnaire étymologique de la langue grecque*. Paris.

Chapouthier, F. 1954. "Euripide et l'accueil du divin," in *La Notion du divin depuis Homère jusqu'à Platon: Sept exposés et discussions par H. J. Rose*, Entretiens Hardt 1, 205–25. Vandoeuvres-Genève.

Clayman, D. L. 2009. *Timon of Phlious*. Berlin.

Cleve, F. M. 1949. *The Philosophy of Anaxagoras*. New York.

Cole, S. 2008. "Annotated Innovation in Euripides' *Ion*," *CQ* 58: 313–5.

Collard, C. 1975. *Euripides: Supplices*. Groningen.

Collard, C., M. J. Cropp, and K. H. Lee. 1995. *Euripides: Selected Fragmentary Plays*, vol. 1. Warminster.

Collard, C., M. J. Cropp, and J. Gibert. 2004. *Euripides: Selected Fragmentary Plays*, vol. 2. Oxford.

Collard, C., and M. J. Cropp. 2008a. *Euripides: Fragments, Aegeus-Meleager*. Cambridge, MA.

———. 2008b. *Euripides: Fragments, Oedipus-Chrysippus, Other Fragments*. Cambridge, MA.

Conacher, D. J. 1959. "The Paradox of Euripides' Ion," *TAPA* 90: 20–39.

———. 1998. *Euripides and the Sophists*. London.

Connelly, J. B. 2014. *The Parthenon Enigma*. New York.

Cooper, C. 1995. "Hyperides and the Trial of Phryne," *Phoenix* 49: 303–18.

Cowherd, C. E. 1983. "The Ending of the *Medea*," *CW* 76: 129–25.

Craik, E. 1988. *Euripides: Phoenician Women*. Warminster.

Cribiore, R. 2001. "Euripides' *Phoenissae* in Hellenistic and Roman Education," in *Education in Greek and Roman Antiquity*, ed. Y. L. Too, 241–59. Leiden.

Cropp, M. J., and G. Fick. 1985. *Resolutions and Chronology in Euripides: The Fragmentary Tragedies* (BICS Supplement 43). London.

———. 1997. Review of Francis M. Dunn, *Tragedy's End, BMCR* 97.8.21.

———. 2000. *Euripides: Iphigenia in Tauris*. Warminster.

———. 2013. *Euripides: Electra*, Ed. 2. Oxford.

———. 2014. "Cropp on Queyrel on Connelly," *BMCR* 2014.10.45.

Curd, P. 2007. *Anaxagoras of Clazomenae. Fragments and Testimonia*. Toronto.

Currie, B. 2005. *Pindar and the Cult of Heroes*. Oxford.

———. 2012. "Sophocles and Hero Cult," in *A Companion to Sophocles*, ed. K. Ormand, 331–48. Malden/Oxford.

Dale, A. M. 1954. *Euripides: Alcestis*. Oxford.

Davies, M., and P. J. Finglass. 2014. *Stesichorus: The Poems*. Cambridge.

Dawe, R. D. 1982. *Sophocles: Oedipus Rex*. Cambridge.

Denniston, J. D. 1939. *Euripides: Electra*. Oxford.

Deubner, L. 1932. *Attische Feste*. Berlin.

Diels, H., and W. Kranz, eds. 1954. *Die Fragmente der Vorsokratiker*. Berlin.

Diggle, J. 1981. "Review of Scodel 1980," *CR* 31: 106–7.

Dixon, D. W. 2014. "Reconsidering Euripides' *Bellerophon*," *CQ* 64: 493–506.

Dodds, E. R. 1960. *Euripides: Bacchae*, Ed. 2. Oxford.

Dover, K. J. 1988. "The Freedom of the Intellectual in Greek Society," in *The Greeks and Their Legacy*, vol. 2, 135–58. Oxford. (=*Talanta* 7, 24–54).

———. 1993. *Aristophanes: Frogs*. Oxford.

Drachmann, A. B. 1922. *Atheism in Pagan Society*, London.

Dunbar, N. 1995. *Aristophanes: Birds*. Oxford.

Dunkle, J. R. 1969. "The Aegeus Scene and the Theme of Euripides' *Medea*," *TAPA* 100: 97–107.

Dunn, F. M. 1996. *Tragedy's End: Closure and Innovation in Euripidean Drama*. New York.

———. 2000. "Euripidean Aetiologies," *Classical Bulletin* 76.1: 3–27.

Edwards, M., and S. Usher. 1985. *Greek Orators I: Antiphon and Lysias*. Warminster/Chicago.

Egli, F. 2003. *Euripides in Kontext Zeitgenössischer Intellektueller Strömungen*. Munich.

Ekroth, G. 2002. *The Sacrificial Rituals of Greek Hero-Cults in the Archaic and Early Hellenistic Period*. Liège.

Else, G. F. 1957. *Aristotle's Poetics: The Argument*. Cambridge, MA.

Euben, J. P. 1986. "Myths and the Origins of Cities: Reflections on the Autochthony Theme in Euripides' *Ion*," in J. P. Euben, ed. *Greek Tragedy and Political Theory*, 222–51. Berkeley.

Fahr, W. 1969. *Theous Nomizein*. Hildesheim.

Farrington, A. 1991. "GNŌTHI SAUTON: Social Self-Knowledge in Euripides' *Ion*," *RhM* 134: 120–36.

Faulkner, A. 2008. *The Homeric Hymn to Aphrodite*. Oxford.

Finglass, P. J. 2007. *Sophocles: Electra*. Cambridge.

———. 2009. "The Ending of Sophocles' *Oedipus Rex*," *Philologus* 153: 42–62.

———. 2011. *Sophocles: Ajax*. Cambridge.

Foley, H. P. 1985. *Ritual Irony: Poetry and Sacrifice in Euripides*. Ithaca.

———. 2001. *Female Acts in Greek Tragedy*. Princeton.

———. 2015. *Euripides: Hecuba*. London.

Forbes Irving, P. M. C. 1990. *Metamorphosis in Greek Myth*. Oxford.

Fowler, R. L. 2013. *Early Greek Mythography*, vol. 2. Oxford.

Fraenkel, E. 1950. *Aeschylus: Agamemnon*. Oxford.

François, G. 1957. *Le polythéisme et l'emploi au singulier des mots theos, daimōn*. Paris.

Frazer, J. G. 1898. *Pausanias' Description of Greece*. London.

Furley, W. D. 2009. *Menander: Epitrepontes* (*BICS* Suppl. 106). London.

Galinsky, G. K. 1972. *The Herakles Theme*. Totowa, NJ.

Gamble, R. D. 1970. "Euripides' 'Suppliant Women': Decision and Ambivalence," *Hermes* 98: 385–405.

Garvie, A. F. 1986. *Aeschylus: Choephori*. Oxford.

———. 2009. *Aeschylus: Persae*. Oxford.

Giannopoulou, V. 1999–2000. "Divine Agency and *Tyche* in Euripides' *Ion*," *ICS* 24–5: 257–71.

Gill, C. 1996. *Personality in Greek Epic, Tragedy, and Philosophy*. Oxford.

Golden, M. 1990. *Children and Childhood in Classical Athens*. Baltimore.

Goldhill, S. 1986. *Reading Greek Tragedy*. Cambridge.

Gomme, A. W., A. Andrewes, and K. J. Dover. 1970. *A Historical Commentary on Thucydides*. Oxford.

Gomme, A. W., and F. H. Sandbach. 1973. *Menander: A Commentary*. Oxford.

Gould, J. 1985. "On Making Sense of Greek Religion," in *Greek Religion and Society*, ed. P. E. Easterling and J. V. Muir, 1–33. Cambridge. (= *Myth, Ritual, Memory and Exchange*. Oxford [2001] 203–34).

Gow, A. S. F. 1950. *Theocritus*. Cambridge.

———. 1965. *Machon*. Cambridge.

———. 1965. *The Greek Anthology: Hellenistic Epigrams*. Cambridge.

———. 1968. *The Greek Anthology: The Garland of Philip*. Cambridge.

Greene, W. C. 1938. *Scholia Platonica*. APA Monographs 8. Haverford.

Greenwood, L. H. G. 1953. *Aspects of Euripidean Tragedy*. Cambridge.

Gregory, J. 1991. *Euripides and the Instruction of the Athenians*. Ann Arbor.

Griffin, J. 1980. *Homer on Life and Death*. Oxford.

———. 1998. "The Social Function of Attic Tragedy," *CQ* 48: 39–61.

Griffith, M. 1978. "Aeschylus, Sicily, and Prometheus Bound," *Dionysiaca (Festschrift D. L. Page)*. Cambridge: 105–39.

———. 1983. *Aeschylus: Prometheus Bound*. Cambridge.

Grube, G. M. A. 1941 [1961]. *The Drama of Euripides*. London.

———. 1970. "Zeus in Aeschylus," *AJP* 91: 43–55.

Hainsworth, B. 1993. *The Iliad: A Commentary*, vol. 3, books 9–12. Cambridge.

Hall, E. 1990. "Political and Cosmic Turbulence in Euripides' Orestes," in *Tragedy, Comedy and the Polis*, ed. A. Sommerstein et al., 263–85. Bari.

———. 2006. *The Theatrical Cast of Athens*. Oxford.

———. 2010. *Greek Tragedy*. Oxford.

Halleran, M. 1986: "Rhetoric, Irony, and the Ending of Euripides' *Heracles*," *CA* 5: 171–81.

Halliwell, S. 1986. *Aristotle's Poetics*. London.

Hansen, P. A. 1983, 1989. *Carmina Epigraphica Graeca*, vols. 1–2. Berlin.

Harrison, A. R. W. 1968. *The Law of Athens*. Oxford.

Harrison, T. 2000. *Divinity and History*. Oxford.

Heath, M. 1987. *The Poetics of Greek Tragedy*. Stanford.

———. 2003. "'Iure principem locum tenet': Hecuba,'" in *Euripides*, ed. J. Mossman, 218–60. Oxford Readings in Classical Studies. Oxford (=*BICS* 34 [1987] 40–68).

Henderson, J. 1987. *Aristophanes: Lysistrata*. Oxford.

Henrichs, A. 1975. "Democritus and Prodicus on Religion," *HSCP* 79: 93–123.

———. 1981. "Human Sacrifice in Greek Religion: Three Case Studies," in *Le Sacrifice dans l'Antiquité* (*Entretiens Hardt* 27): 195–242.

———. 1983. "The 'Sobriety' of Oedipus: Sophocles *OC* 100 Misunderstood," *HSCP* 87: 87–100.

———. 1984. "The Sophists and Hellenistic Religion," *HSCP* 88: 139–58.

———. 1993. "The Tomb of Aias and the Prospect of Hero Cult in Sophokles," *Classical Antiquity* 12: 165–80.

———. 2013. "Ritualisation de la violence dans le sacrifice grec," in *Sacrifices humains/Human Sacrifice*, ed. P. Bonnechere and R. Gagné, 119–44. Liège.

Heubeck, A., S. West, and B. Hainsworth. 1988. *A Commentary on Homer's Odyssey*, vol. 1. Oxford.

Hornblower, S. 2008. *A Commentary on Thucydides*, vol. 3. Oxford.

Hughes, D. D. 1991. *Human Sacrifice in Ancient Greece*. New York.

Janko, R. 1982. *Homer, Hesiod, and the Hymns*. Cambridge.

———. 1992. *A Commentary on the Iliad*, vol. 4: books 13–16. Cambridge.

Jebb, R. C. 1893. *Sophocles: The Plays and Fragments, Part I, The Oedipus Tyrannus*, Ed. 3. Cambridge.

———. 1900. *Sophocles: The Plays and Fragments, Part II, The Oedipus at Colonus*, Ed. 3. Cambridge.

Jensen, C. 1963. *Hyperides: Orationes Sex cum Ceterarum Fragmentis*. Stuttgart.

Johnston, S. I. 1999. *Restless Dead*. Berkeley.

Kannicht, R. 1969. *Euripides: Helena*. Heidelberg.

Kearns, E. 1989. *The Heroes of Attica* (*BICS* Suppl. 57). London.

———. 2012. *Ancient Greek Religion: A Sourcebook*. London.

Kindt, J. 2007. "Apollo's Oracle in Euripides' *Ion*: Ambiguous Identities in Fifth-Century Athens," *Ancient Narrative* 6 (Annual 2007). Available from www.ancientnarrative.com.

———. 2012. *Rethinking Greek Religion*. Cambridge.

Kirk, G. S. 1985. *The Iliad: A Commentary*, vol. 1: books 1–4. Cambridge.

Kirk, G. S., J. E. Raven, and M. Schofield. 1983. *The Presocratic Philosophers* (Ed. 2). Cambridge.

Kivilo, M. 2010. *Early Greek Poets' Lives*. Leiden.

Knox, B. M. W. 1985. "Euripides," *Cambridge History of Classical Literature I*. Cambridge: 316–38.

Konstan, D. 1999. "What We Must Believe in Greek Tragedy," *Ramus* 28.75–87.

Korpel, M. C. A. 1990. *A Rift in the Clouds: Ugaritic and Hebrew Descriptions of the Divine*. Münster.

Koster, W. J. W., ed. 1969. *Scholia in Aristophanem*, vol. 2, ed. M. Jones and N. G. Wilson. Groningen.

Kovacs, D. 1980. *The Andromache of Euripides*. Chico, CA.

———. 1987a. *The Heroic Muse* [AJP Monograph 3]. Baltimore.

———. 1987b. "Treading the Circle Warily: Literary Criticism and the Text of Euripides," *TAPA* 117: 257–70.

———. 1993. "Zeus in Euripides' *Medea*," *AJP* 114: 45–70.

———. 1994a. *Euripidea*. Leiden.

———. 1994b. *Euripides: Cyclops, Alcestis, Medea* (Loeb Classical Library Euripides, vol. 1). Cambridge, MA.

———. 1995. *Euripides: Children of Heracles, Hippolytus, Andromache, Hecuba* (Loeb Classical Library Euripides, vol. 2). Cambridge, MA.

———. 1997. "Gods and Men in Euripides' Trojan Trilogy," *Colby Quarterly* 33: 162–76.

———. 1999. *Trojan Women, Iphigenia among the Taurians, Ion* (Loeb Classical Library Euripides, vol. 4). Cambridge, MA.

———. 2000. "One Ship or Two: The End of the Iphigenia in Tauris," *EMC* 44, N. S. 19: 19–23.

———. 2002a. "Rationalism, Naive and Malign, in Euripides' *Orestes*," in *Vertis in Usum: Studies in Honor of Edward Courtney*, ed. J. F. Miller, C. Damon, and K. S. Myers, 277–86. Munich.

———. 2002b. *Bacchae, Iphigenia at Aulis, Rhesus*. (Loeb Classical Library Euripides, vol. 6). Cambridge, MA.

———. 2003. "Toward a Reconstruction of *Iphigenia Aulidensis*," *JHS* 123: 77–103.

———. 2009. "The Role of Apollo in *Oedipus Tyrannus*," in *The Play of Texts and Fragments, Essays in Honour of Martin Cropp*, ed. J. R. C. Cousland and J. R. Hume, 357–68.

Kowalzig, B. 2006. "The Aetiology of Empire? Hero-Cult and Athenian Tragedy," in *Greek Tragedy III: Essays in Honour of Kevin Lee* =*BICS* Suppl. 87: 79–98.

Kranz, W. 1933. *Stasimon*. Berlin.

Kraus, W. 1984. *Aus Allem Eines: Studien zur Antiken Geistesgeschichte*. Heidelberg.

Kullmann, W. 1992. *Homerische Motive*. Stuttgart.

Kyriakou, P. A. 2006. *A Commentary on Euripides' Iphigenia in Tauris*. Berlin.

Lachenaud, G. 2003. *L'arc en ciel et l'archer: Récits et philosophie de l'histoire chez Hérodote*. Limoges.

Laks, A. 1983. *Diogène d'Apollonie*. Lille.

Larsen, J. 1995. *Greek Heroine Cults*. Madison.

Lawrence, S. E. 1997. "Audience Uncertainty and Euripides' Medea," *Hermes* 125: 49–55.

———. 1998. "The God That Is Truly God and the Universe of Euripides' 'Heracles,'" *Mnemosyne* 51: 129–46.

———. 2013. *Moral Awareness in Greek Tragedy*. Oxford.

Lee, K. H. 1976. *Euripides: Troades*. London.

———. 1997. *Euripides: Ion*. Warminster.

Lefkowitz, M. R. 1979. "The Euripides Vita," *GRBS* 20: 187–210.

———. 1981. *The Lives of the Greek Poets*, Ed. 2. London/Baltimore.

———. 1984. "Aristophanes and Other Historians of the Fifth-Century Theater," *Hermes* 112: 143–53.

———. 1987. "Was Euripides an Atheist?" *SIFC* [Ser. 3] 5: 149–66.

———. 2002. "Apollo in the *Orestes*," *Studi Italiani di Filologia Classica* 20.1–2: 46–54.

———. 2003a. *Greek Gods, Human Lives*. New Haven.

———. 2003b: "'Impiety' and 'Atheism' in Euripides' Dramas," in *Euripides*, ed. J. Mossman, 102–21. Oxford Readings in Classical Studies. Oxford. (=*CQ* 39 [1989] 70–82).

———. 2007. *Women in Greek Myth*. Baltimore.

———. 2012. *The Lives of the Greek Poets*, Ed. 2. London/Baltimore.

Leurini, A. 1992. *Ionis Chii testimonia et fragmenta*. Amsterdam.

Liapis, V. 2014. "Cooking Up Rhesus: Literary Imitation and Its Consumers," in *Greek Theater in the Fourth Century B.C.*, ed. E. Csapo, H. R. Goette, J. R. Green, and P. Wilson, 275–94. Berlin.

Lightfoot, J. L. 2003. *Lucian: On the Syrian Goddess*. Oxford.

Lloyd, A. B. 1976. *Herodotus Book II*. Leiden.

Lloyd, M. 1994. *Euripides: Andromache*. Warminster.

Lloyd-Jones, H. 1975. *Females of the Species: Semonides on Women*. London.

———. 1983 [1971]. *The Justice of Zeus*, Ed. 2. Berkeley.

———. 1990a. *The Academic Papers of Sir Hugh Lloyd-Jones: Greek Epic, Lyric, and Tragedy*. Oxford.

———. 1990b. *The Academic Papers of Sir Hugh Lloyd-Jones: Greek Comedy, Hellenistic Literature, Greek Religion, and Miscellanea*. Oxford.

———. 2005. *The Further Academic Papers of Sir Hugh Lloyd-Jones*. Oxford.

Lloyd Jones, H., and N. G. Wilson. 1990. *Sophoclea*. Oxford.

———. 1997. *Sophocles: Second Thoughts*, Hypomnemata 100. Göttingen.

Loraux, N. 1987. *Tragic Ways of Killing a Woman*. Cambridge, MA.

Macdowell, D. M. 1962. *The Law in Classical Athens*, London/Ithaca.

March, J. 1989. "Euripides *Bakchai*: A Reconsideration in the Light of Vase-Paintings," *BICS* 36: 33–65.

Marinatos, N. 1981. *Thucydides and Religion*. Königstein.

Marr, J. L. 1998. *Plutarch's Lives: Themistocles*. Warminster.

Mastronarde, D. J. 1990. "Actors on High: The Skene Roof, the Crane, and the Gods in Attic Drama," *Classical Archaeology* 9: 247–94.

———. 1994. *Euripides: Phoenissae*. Cambridge.

———. 2002. *Euripides: Medea*. Cambridge.

———. 2005. "The Gods," in *A Companion to Greek Tragedy*, ed. J. Gregory, 321–32. Malden, MA.

———. 2010. *The Art of Euripides*. Cambridge.

Matthiessen, K. 1968. "Zur Theonoeszene in der euripideischen 'Helena,'" *Hermes* 96: 685–704.

———. 2002. *Die Tragödien des Euripides*, Zetemata 114. Munich.

———. 2004. *Euripides und sein Jahrhundert*, Zetemata 119. Munich.

———. 2010. Euripides, *Hekabe*. Texte und Kommentare 34. Berlin.

McClure, L. 1999. "'The Worst Husband': Discourses of Praise and Blame in Euripides' *Medea*," *CP* 94: 373–94.

Mellink, M. 1943. *Hyakinthos*. Utrecht.

Mendelsohn, D. 2002. *Gender and the City in Euripides' Political Plays*. Oxford.

Merkelbach, R., and M. L. West. 1967. *Fragmenta Hesiodea*. Oxford.

Michelini, A. 1987. *Euripides and the Tragic Tradition*. Madison.

Mikalson, J. D. 1991. *Honor Thy Gods*. Chapel Hill.

———. 2003. *Herodotus and Religion in the Persian Wars*. Chapel Hill.

Morwood, J. 2007. *Euripides: Suppliant Women*. Oxford.

Mossman, J. 1995. *Wild Justice*. Oxford.

Most, G. W. 1984. *The Measures of Praise*, Hypomnemata 83. Göttingen.

Muir, J. V. 2001. *Alcidamas: The Works and Fragments*. Bristol.

Mussies, G. 1999. "Hyacinthus," in *Dictionary of Deities and Demons in the Bible*, ed. K. van der Toorn, B. Becking, and P. W. van der Horst, 434–7. Leiden.

Mylonopoulos, J. 2013. "Gory Details: The Iconography of Sacrifice in Greek Art," in *Sacrifices humains / Human Sacrifice*, ed. P. Bonnechere and R. Gagné, 61–85. Liège.

Nagy, G. 2013. *The Ancient Greek Hero in 24 Hours*. Cambridge, MA.

Neitzel, H. 1988. "Apollons Orakelspruch im 'Ion' des Euripides," *Hermes* 116:

Nervegna, S. 2014. "Performing Classics: The Tragic Canon in the Fourth Century and Beyond," in *Greek Theater in the Fourth Century B.C.*, ed. E. Csapo, H. R. Goette, J. R. Green, and P. Wilson, 157–87. Berlin.

Nestle, W. 1901. *Euripides, der Dichter der griechischen Aufklärung*. Stuttgart.

Norden, E. 1956. *Agnostos Theos*. Darmstadt.

Norwood, G. 1920. *Greek Tragedy*. Boston.

Nussbaum, M. C. 2001. *The Fragility of Goodness*, Ed. 2. Cambridge.

O'Connor-Visser, E. A. M. E. 1987. *Aspects of Human Sacrifice in the Tragedies of Euripides*. Amsterdam.

Ogden. D. 2013. *Drakōn: Dragon Myth and Serpent Cult in the Greek and Roman Worlds*. Oxford.

Onians, R. B. 1954. *The Origins of Indo-European Thought*. Cambridge.

Pack, R. 1965. *The Greek and Latin Literary Texts from Greco-Roman Egypt*, Ed. 2. Ann Arbor.

Page, D. L. 1934. *Actors' Interpolations in Greek Tragedy*. Oxford.

———. 1955. *Sappho and Alcaeus*. Oxford.

Papadopoulou, T. 2005. *Heracles and Euripidean Tragedy*. Cambridge.

———. 2008. *Euripides: Phoenician Women*. London.

Papastamati-von Moock, C. 2014. "The Theater of Dionysus Eleuthereus in Athens: New Data and Observations on its 'Lycurgan' Phase," in *Greek Theater in the Fourth Century B.C.*, ed. E. Csapo, H. R. Goette, J. R. Green, and P. Wilson, 275–94. Berlin.

Parker, L. P. E. 2007. *Euripides: Alcestis*. Oxford.

Parker, R. 1983. *Miasma: Pollution and Purification in Early Greek Religion*, Oxford.

———. 1985. "Greek States and Greek Oracles," in *Crux: Essays Presented to G. E. M. de Ste Croix*, P. Cartledge, and F. D. Harvey, ed., 298–326. Exeter.

———. 1987. "Myths of Early Athens," in *Interpretations of Greek Mythology*, ed. J. Bremmer, 187–214. London.

———. 1996. *Athenian Religion: A History*. Oxford.

———. 1997. "Gods Cruel and Kind: Tragic and Civic Theology," in *Greek Tragedy and the Historian*, ed. C. Pelling, 143–60. Oxford.

———. 1998. "Pleasing Thighs: Reciprocity in Greek Religion," in *Reciprocity in Ancient Greece*, ed. C. Gill, N. Postelthwaite, and R. Seaford, 105–25. Oxford.

———. 2002. "The Trial of Socrates: And a Religious Crisis?" in *The Trial and Execution of Socrates*, ed. T. C. Brickhouse and N. D. Smith, 145–61. New York.

———. 2005. *Polytheism and Society at Athens*. Oxford.

———. 2013. "Substitution in Greek Sacrifice," in *Sacrifices humains / Human Sacrifice*, ed. P. Bonnechere and R. Gagné, 145–52. Liège.

Pearson, A. C. 1963. *The Fragments of Sophocles*. Amsterdam.

Pickard-Cambridge, A. 1968. *The Dramatic Festivals of Athens*, Ed. 2. Oxford.

Platnauer, M. 1938. *Euripides: Iphigenia in Tauris*. Oxford.

Porter, J. R. 1994. *Studies in Euripides' Orestes*. Leiden.

Prag, A. J. N. W. 1985. *The Oresteia*. Chicago.

Pritchett, W. K. 1971–1974. *The Greek State at War*. Berkeley.

Pulleyn, S. 1997. *Prayer in Greek Religion*. Oxford.

Rees, B. R. 1961. "Euripides, *Medea* 1415–19," *AJP* 82: 176–81.

Richardson, N. 1974. *The Homeric Hymn to Demeter*. Oxford.

———. 1993. *The Iliad: A Commentary,* vol. 6: books 21–24. Cambridge.

Riedweg, C. 1990a. "*TrGF* 2. 624: A Euripidean Fragment," *CQ* 40: 124–36.

———. 1990b. "The Atheistic Fragment from Euripides' *Bellerophontes*," *ICS* 15 (1990) 39–53.

Ritchie, W. 1964. *The Authenticity of the Rhesus of Euripides*. Cambridge.

Robert, C. 1915. *Oidipus*. Berlin.

Roberts, D. H. 1987. "Parting Words: Final Lines in Sophocles and Euripides," *CQ* 27: 51–64.

———. 1988. "Sophoclean Endings: Another Story," *Arethusa* 21: 177–96.

Roller, L. 1999. *In Search of God the Mother: The Cult of Anatolian Cybele*. Berkeley.

Rose, H. J. 1953. *A Handbook of Greek Mythology*. New York.

Rösler, W. 1970. *Reflexe vorsokratischen Denkens bei Aischylos*. Beiträge zur klassischen Philologie 37. Meisenheim am Glan.

Rutherford, I. 2011. "The *Catalogue of Women* within the Greek Epic Tradition," in *Relative Chronology in Early Greek Epic Poetry*, ed. Ø. Anderson and D. T. T. Haug, 152–67. Cambridge.

Scheer, E. 1958. *Lycophronis Alexandra*. Berlin.

Schlesier, R. 1985: "Héracles et la critique des dieux chez Euripide," *Ann. Scuol. Normale di Pisa* (Cl. litt./filos.) 15: 7–40.

Schorn, S. 2004. *Satyros aus Kallatis*. Basel.

Schwartz, E. 1887. *Scholia in Euripidem*. Berlin.

Schwarze, J. 1971. *Die Beurteilung des Perikles durch die attische Komödie und ihre historiographische Bedeutung, Zetemata* 51. Munich.

Scodel, R. 1979. "*Admētou logos* and the *Alcestis*," *HSCP* 83: 51–62.

———. 1980. *The Trojan Trilogy of Euripides* (Hypomnemata 60). Göttingen.

———. 1984. "Tantalus and Anaxagoras," *HSCP* 88: 13–24.

Scullion, S. 1999–2000. "Tradition and Invention in Euripidean Aitiology," *Illinois Classical Studies* 24–25: 217–33.

———. 2003. "Euripides and Macedon, or the Silence of the Frogs," *CQ* 53: 389–400.

Seaford, R. 1984. *Euripides: Cyclops*. Oxford.

———. 1996. *Euripides: Bacchae*. Warminster.

Segal, C. 1996. "Catharsis, Audience, and Closure," in *Tragedy and the Tragic*, ed. M. Silk, 149–72. Oxford.

Seidensticker, B. 1996. "Tragic Dialectic in Euripidean Tragedy," in *Tragedy and the Tragic*, ed. M. Silk, 377–96. Oxford.

Shapiro, H. A. 1994. *Myth into Art*. London.

Sharples, R. W. 1998. *Theophrastus of Eresus*, vol. 3.1. Leiden.

Shipley, D. R. 1997. *A Commentary on Plutarch's Life of Agesilaus*. Oxford.

Small, J. P. 2005. "Pictures of Tragedy," in *A Companion to Greek Tragedy*, ed. J. Gregory, 103–18. Oxford.

Smith, P. M. 1980. *On the Hymn to Zeus in Aeschylus' Agamemnon*, American Classical Studies 5. Chico, CA.

Smith, W. 1967. "Expressive Form in Euripides' *Suppliants*," *HSCP* 71: 151–70.

Sommerstein, A. H. 1989. *Aeschylus: Eumenides*. Cambridge.

———. 2008. *Aeschylus, Fragments*. Cambridge, MA.

Sonnino, M. 2010. *Euripidis Erechthei quae extant*. Florence.

Sourvinou-Inwood, C. 2003. *Tragedy and Athenian Religion*. Lanham, MD.

Spira, A. 1960. *Untersuchungen zum Deus ex Machina bei Sophokles und Euripides* (diss. Frankfurt). Kallmünz.

Steidle, W. 1968. *Studien zum Antiken Drama*, Studia et Testimonia Antiqua 4. Munich.

Stengel, P. 1924. "Zu den griechischen Sakralatertümern," *Hermes* 59: 307–21.

Stevens, P. T. 1971. *Euripides: Andromache*. Oxford.

Stieber, M. 2011. *Euripides and the Language of Craft*. Leiden.

Strassler, R., ed. 1996. *The Landmark Thucydides*. New York.

Swift, L. A. 2010. *The Hidden Chorus*. Oxford.

Taplin, O. 2007. *Pots and Plays*. Los Angeles.

Tersini, N. 1987. "Themes in the Sculpture of the Temple of Zeus at Olympia," *CA* 6.1: 139–59.

Turner, F. 1981. *The Greek Heritage in Victorian Britain*. New Haven.

Van Groningen, B. A. 1977. *Euphorion*. Amsterdam.

Vellacott, P. 1975. *Ironic Drama: A Study of Euripides' Method and Meaning*. Cambridge.

Verrall, A. W. 1895. *Euripides the Rationalist*. Cambridge.

———. 1905. *Four Plays of Euripides*. Cambridge.

Versnel, H. S. 2011. *Coping with the Gods*. Leiden.

Walton, J. M. 2009. *Euripides Our Contemporary*. Berkeley.

Wassermann, F. M. 1940. "Divine Violence and Providence in Euripides' *Ion*," *TAPA* 71: 587–604.

Wehrli, F. 1967–1979. *Die Schule des Aristoteles*, Ed. 2. Basel.

West, M. L. 1959 [1895]. *Euripides Herakles*, Ed. 2. Darmstadt.

———. 1981. "Tragica V," *BICS* 28: 61–78.

———. 1985. *The Hesiodic Catalogue of Women*. Oxford.

———. 1987. *Euripides: Orestes*. Warminster.

———. 1992. *Ancient Greek Music*. Oxford.

———. 2003. *Greek Epic Fragments*. Cambridge, MA.

Wilamowitz. U. v. 1875. *Analecta Euripidea*. Berlin.

Wildberg, C. 1999–2000. "Piety as Service, Epiphany as Reciprocity: Two Observations on the Religious Meaning of the Gods in Euripides," *ICS* 24–25: 235–56.

———. 2002. *Hyperesie und Epiphanie* (*Hypomnemata* 109). Munich.

———. 2008. "Socrates and Euripides," in *A Companion to Socrates*, ed. S. Ahbel-Rappe and R. Kamtekar, 21–35. Malden/Oxford.

Wilkins, J. 1993. *Euripides: Heraclidae*. Oxford.

Willetts, R. F. 1959. "*Ion*," in *The Complete Greek Tragedies*, ed. D. Grene and R. Lattimore: IV 1–79.

———. 1973. "Action and Character in the *Ion* of Euripides," *JHS* 93: 201–9.

Williams, F. 1978. *Callimachus: Hymn to Apollo*. Oxford.

Willink, C. 1983. "Prodikos, 'Meteorosophists' and the 'Tantalos' Paradigm," *CQ* 33: 25–33.

———. 1986. *Euripides: Orestes*. Oxford.

Winiarczyk, M. 1984. "Wer galt im Altertum als Atheist?" *Philologus* 128: 157.

———. 2011. *Die Hellenistischen Utopien*. Berlin.

Worthington, I. 1990. "The Ending of Euripides' 'Medea,'" *Hermes* 118: 502–5.

Wright, Matthew. 2005. *Euripides' Escape Tragedies: A Study of Helen, Andromeda and Iphigenia among the Taurians*. Oxford.

Wycherly, R. E. 1978. *The Stones of Athens*. Princeton.

Yunis, H. 1988: *A New Creed: Fundamental Religious Beliefs in the Athenian Polis and Euripidean Drama*, Hypomnemata 91. Göttingen.

Zeitlin, F. 1980. "The Closet of Masks: Role-Playing and Myth-Making in the *Orestes* of Euripides," *Ramus* 9: 51–77.

———. 1996. *Playing the Other: Gender and Society in Classical Greek Literature*. Chicago.

Zuntz, G. 1955. *The Political Plays of Euripides*. Manchester.

SUBJECT INDEX

INDEX LOCORUM

Homeric Hymn 7 to Dionysus
55–7 . . . 139

Hyperides
Fr,171 Jensen . . . 246n61

Ibycus
PMG 291 . . . 241n26

Ion of Chios
392*FGrHist* F9 . . . 211n37

Lucian
Deor. Conc. 7 . . . 234n11

Lycophron
Alexandra
1466 . . . 227n2

Lysimachus
382*FGrHist*F2 . . . *226n63*

Machon
407–10 Gow . . . 209n19

Menander
Sicyonius. . . 231n31
*Monostich.*588. . . 210n30

Ovid
Metamorphoses
3.308–9 . . . 140

Panyassis
fr.1 . . . 215n10

Pausanias
1.28.7 . . . 96

1.33.1 . . . 225n49
1.35.3–4 . . . 220n4
1.43.4 . . . 234n18
2.32.1–4 . . . 234n11
9.11.2 . . . 54, 215n10

Phaenias
Fr.25 Wehrli=1012
*FrGrHist*19. . . 188

Philochorus
328*FGrHist* 217 . . . 41
328*FGrHist* 221. . . 208n16

Pindar
Nemean Odes . . . 233n58
3.23 . . . 223n33
7.40–2 . . . 237n44
7.46 . . . 237n46
Pythian Odes
4.11 . . . 239n4
4.11–6 . . . 238n3
4.240 . . . 246n62

Plato
Apology
17a . . . 29
18b . . . 37, 40
18b–c . . . 27
19b . . . 27
19c . . . 27
24b . . . 28
24c . . . 74
26d . . . 33
31d . . . 74
Euthyphro
3b . . . 74

Stesichorus
fr. 90.1 Finglass=PMGF
192–3 . . . 227n72
fr. 218 Finglass=*PMGF* 222a
fr. 32 . . . 117, 247n76
fr. 283 Finglass=PMGF
230 . . . 215n10

Stesimbrotus
107*FGrHist* F 9 . . . 249n92

Stobaeus
Anthol. 3.5.36.1–5 . . . 32

Strabo
8. 6.19 . . . 226n69

Strattis
Frs. 1, 63 K-A, *PCG* VII 624, 652

Suda
Epsilon 3695 . . . 42, 46
Omega 188 . . . 59
Pi 2365 . . . 43
Sigma 829 . . . 211n37

Teleclides
fr. 41 K-A, *PCG* VII,
683 . . . 30, 208n14
fr. 42 K-A, *PCG* VII, 684 . . . 30

Thucydides
2.56.4 . . . 135

3.50 . . . 206n10
3.82 . . . 113
4.47 . . . 221n13
4.116 . . . 113
5.3.2–4 . . . 206n10
5.47.8.13 . . . 80

Timon of Phlius
Supp. Hell.
fr. 779 . . . 212n43
fr. 798 . . . 211n38
fr. 819 . . . 212n41

Virgil
Aeneid
1.27 . . . 206n13
1.407–9 . . . 74
2.567–76 . . . 231n32
4.471–3 . . . 231n32

Xenophanes
21 A 25–6 DK . . . 53
21 A 32.23–4 . . . 215n3
21 B 11 . . . 53
21 B 11, I 132 . . . 93
21 B 15–6 . . . 215n3

Xenophon
Anabasis
2.2.9 . . . 221n12
Hellenica
2.1.18–9 . . . 249n91

CPSIA information can be obtained
at www.ICGtesting.com
Printed in the USA
BVHW081932070819
555351BV00002B/14/P